Bernard Keane has been C[...] [...] [...] [...] politics
editor in Canberra since 20[...] and
economics. He was educated [...] here
he studied history and faile[...] was
there at the same time. Bef[...] licy
adviser and speechwriter in transport and [...]. He
is the author of the ebook *War on the Internet* and an incessant
torrent of analysis, reportage and commentary on politics and
public policy for *Crikey*.

For more than two decades, Helen Razer has been broadcasting
and writing her way into disagreements of various scales. For
much of the 1990s she presented the breakfast program on ABC
radio's youth network with her non-biological brother, Mikey
Robins. She makes occasional returns to professional broadcast
but is now better known as a somewhat peevish columnist.
She has been employed as a contributor by *The Age* and *The
Australian*, and is now a columnist on dissent with *Crikey* and
a gardening correspondent for *The Saturday Paper*. Helen has
produced four previous books of humorous nonfiction, had
a rest and returned to collaborate with her friend Bernard
Keane to write her only serious work to date. Her frequently
published thoughts on the impotence of current public debate
are extended in *A Short History of Stupid*.

A SHORT HISTORY OF STUPID

The decline of reason and why public debate makes us want to scream

BERNARD KEANE & HELEN RAZER

ALLEN&UNWIN
SYDNEY • MELBOURNE • AUCKLAND • LONDON

Allen & Unwin
83 Alexander Street
Crows Nest NSW 2065
Australia
Phone: (61 2) 8425 0100
Email: info@allenandunwin.com
Web: www.allenandunwin.com

Cataloguing-in-Publication details are available
from the National Library of Australia
www.trove.nla.gov.au

ISBN 978 1 76011 054 3

Set in 12/16pt Bembo by Post Pre-press Group, Australia
Printed and bound in Australia by Griffin Press

10 9 8 7 6 5 4 3 2 1

Contents

Introduction—We don't know what we are doing

There is no such thing as a Stupid question. Whoever said this never worked in a shop, read a celebrity interview by a Murdoch journalist or had a conversation of any length with an actual adult human. Stupid questions are asked with all the restraint a snowboarder might show in front of a bong. Which is to say, none at all and please don't bogart my mull.

Naive or tedious or genuinely curious questions are not the problem. Why is the sky blue? What is particle theory? When is a polite time to tell my idiot right-wing uncle to get fucked? Questions that seek an answer are, in fact, in short supply.

If ignorant questions were commonly asked of people who know things, then we wouldn't be writing this book. We would be living in an intellectual utopia that provided material comfort to all, a solution to climate change and a convenient alternative to dental floss. Instead, we exist in an era of blundering know-it-alls who have just one question, and they ask it of themselves: Quick, what do I say so that no one finds out I am Stupid?

We've all but given up on facts, as any prominent discussion on climate change can attest. Facts do not matter. They have been eclipsed by opinion. And this is bad enough in itself. But it is not just that we feel entitled to our opinion, as nearly everybody does. We are *obliged to* have an opinion. Like a smart car or a nice job, an opinion—even and especially one untroubled by recourse to facts—has become a motif for strength and success.

An opinion is empowering. An opinion is a sign of high self-esteem. An opinion is the most hotly traded currency in all social networks, a requirement for dinner guests and the thing that now fuels traditional media.

Facts, in fact, have become a sort of optional extra. Even news providers have become candid about the departure of facts from their content. Facts are now presented as a curio at the end of broadcasts in a special 'fact checking' segment. This is not an encouraging moment showing journalism's dedication to its trade but a frank admission that everything previously said was not a fact but an opinion.

There was a time where we were not uncomfortable answering 'I don't know' if asked for our opinion on the Middle East, superfoods or early childhood development. Now, we would rather say 'one state solution' or 'acai berries are great for the libido' or 'little Harrison is showing signs of great executive function in the painting he made with his own shit' than nothing. Because we're all experts.

Although. Perhaps you, like us, suspect that you are not an expert. Perhaps you don't know what to do in Palestine. Perhaps you don't want to pay forty dollars a kilo for dried fruit. Perhaps you think your child needs to stop playing with his own waste. Perhaps you see all this opinionated bluster as the worst kind of Stupid.

What you know is that you do not know. What you see is that you cannot see. What you refuse, unlike the chipper and the mindful and the smug, is to believe the myth of total enlightenment. The false pleasure of easy illumination is something you can no longer allow.

In other words, you're in a bit of a muddle. Of course, most everybody is. But many of them believe that they have found a way to the light and, worse still, some of them don't even notice the darkness.

It's perfectly fine to find yourself in the dark. It is okay to feel benighted by the bedlam moon that everyday lunatics mistake for the light of reason. So, in our look at present-day Stupid and how we got here, let's agree that we don't know everything.

Let's agree that the sun of rational thought is yet to fully rise. Let's try to bask in its first rays as we break the illusory two-watt globe of false enlightenment. In other words, let us dare to 'shine a light' on our most forlorn attempts to shine a light. And then, perhaps, we can stop these ceaseless and clumsy enlightenment metaphors. What is this, a book on the history of poor Western thought or a lighting catalogue?

What you may happen to expect from a crabby book that tests your patience and consistently asks you to ignore its bad mood is the reward of hope; of hope for a world without Stupid. For this, we offer an advance apology as sincere as crabby authors can produce. It's best you lose hope right now.

Oh, come on. Surely you never expected hope, change and the deceit of the promise of wisdom? If you did, you'd be 'setting your intention' for the day in your lululemon Pilates pants and drinking from the well of homeopathic opinion.

But you are not at all that type of Stupid. You do not believe that you can attract good fortune or make a better world with the power of positive thinking. You do not believe this any more than you believe you can find a cure for all this viral Stupid in a single modest book.

Better to use imagery a bit less flowery to set our intention for this very cranky book. How about a proverb of statecraft? 'The enemy of my enemy is my friend.' The enemy is Stupid. And the 'friends', of course, are all of us. We, authors and readers, are united against Stupid in a mutual, if strategically divergent, battle for truth. Well, truth or something like it. Even if truth turns out to be impossible, we can at least look at the nature and history of its impersonators. We'll interrogate conspiracy theorists, denialists, conspicuously compassionate capitalists and other fakes.

We may not be particularly nice about quite a lot of people while we are doing this.

Niceness is no more a salve for the complex world's complex ills than are the designations of left and right. Speaking of which, your authors have made some kind of attempt to divest themselves of ideology. And this isn't easy. Ideology is, by its classic Marxist definition, the thing that cannot be consciously known. 'They do not know what they are doing but they are doing it,' Marx wrote in an attempt to explain those beliefs that unconsciously produce ideas that claim to be pure, such as 'poor people are lazy' or 'all right-wing people smell like Gruyere'. These are ideology or, if you like, unconscious opinion. These ideas came from somewhere. These are not pure ideas.

Of course, we can't hope for purity. But what we can do is offer a vulgar account of the way things like ideology and belief are formed.

We will draw on a partial history of ideas, both Stupid and great, as they have been written down, televised and discussed in the West. We do this not only to encourage your broad reading and to legitimise our claim that The World is Fukt; we do this also in a gesture of kind desperation. In an era of despair such as ours (and every other era), it is soothing to be reminded that there are people who have written down complex accounts of the world; people who despaired and said things like, 'They do not know what they are doing but they are doing it.' This habit we have of doing something without knowing why is pretty much what we mean when we say Stupid.

There is so much despair. We don't know we are despairing, but we are doing it anyway.

Homeopathy and past lives and plastic shamans and the promise anyone can get rich if only they work hard enough are all marks of a despairing culture. Never before in history have we so eagerly ordered so many brands of crap-in-a-cone, and we can't even blame religion anymore for its persuasive flavour. On that note, please be warned: we have not touched on God as much as some atheists might prefer in this book because (a) He gets so much press anyhow, and (b) He's just one more sad song in history's great hit parade of Stupid. In this book, we don't just wish to cruelly taunt a belief in one myth; we want to cruelly taunt belief in many.

We should also say, in case it is not already stonkingly obvious, that we are talking about Western Stupid. The kind of Stupid that was sparked in Greek antiquity, doused in Christian tears and dried off by the European Enlightenment before it was burned to the ground by the machines of the twentieth century. This account is of a Stupid that lives in the liberal democracies of the West, so it is necessarily an account of the despair that many people dismiss as 'first world problems'.

While it is absolutely true that we who have licence to read books and are not obliged to walk miles for clean water should stop a good deal of our whining, it is absolutely untrue that we do not feel despair. Not to come over all emo, but there is a crisis in the stuff of ourselves. We can try to solve it with the ideology that says 'poor people just like being that way' or with affirmations recited in lululemon pants. Or we can try to look at the way in which the crisis unfolded. We can try to be less Stupid about many things, including the stuff of the self.

'Know thyself' was written in the forecourt of the Temple at Delphi. Socrates fancied the slogan, too. Thomas Hobbes, like Augustine long before him, was keen on the idea that to 'read' the self was essential if one was to make any sense of anything at all. We think, for all his faults, he had a point. Search for yourself all your life; even and especially if it hurts. Know thy Stupid self. And be liberated from Stupid. Obviously, we are paraphrasing.

To cut a long story very short, the idea of self-knowledge holds that one can know nothing unless one knows what one knows. Or, to put it less infuriatingly: without a good grasp on one's own critical processes, one cannot think critically.

To know the self, then, is to take the first step towards knowledge. And to know what we are doing, even if we do it anyway. Ours is a time—we're hardly the first to say this; the author of *The Secret* knows it, too—in which the self is in crisis. We despair for our own disappearance. Despair becomes a pathology that is sometimes diagnosed as mental illness and treated with drugs; that sometimes turns into a fondness for conspiracy theories and is treated by the irrational belief that refusing vaccination for your children will improve the health of the world; that sometimes leads us into the company of mystics or cults or the sedation of shopping or booze or non-stop public declarations of 'outrage'. We'll talk about all these things in the book. We cannot promise that we will not poke fun.

But we will also talk with some degree of seriousness about the self that finds itself in crisis. The self no longer serves a useful social function. The self, for all the talk about its esteem and actualisation and help, that is actually surplus to the needs of a vast and ultra-rational world, one that has necessarily become one-size-fits-most. And so, as the thing we call the self—our conscious and rational minds—makes way for thousands of externally produced 'truths', it shrivels. It is no longer capable of easily producing its own reason.

It should become plain quite quickly that your authors do not really agree on a single truth. And you should probably be warned: if you're looking for a single truth about what you should do to make your life or the lives of the many better, we got zip. Our answer, over and over again, will be: think. On this, we both agree with the broad aims of the Enlightenment. We think that all individuals must dare, as Immanuel Kant said, to use their reason. This is the tricky thing about critical thinking: you have to do it yourself. It's not something you can get manufactured offshore.

Of course, when it comes to formulating reason on certain matters, it's okay to outsource and to ask (non-Stupid) questions. In fact, in many cases it would be foolish not to do so. On matters like climate change, car maintenance or physical health, recourse to experts is the reasonable and the only thing. Even the more impure sciences that seek to understand market economies and social habits have something to tell us. We don't need to come up with all the answers ourselves. Actually, we can't. Informed cynicism is just impossible in a world that works on as many systems as ours. No individual can sit in the centre of absolute knowledge and know everything. Knowing what we do not know is the primary weapon in the war on Stupid.

That many people do feel as though they have absolute knowledge or a single way of explaining the world is a central preoccupation of this book. What we urge, in short, is owning up to the inevitability of our ignorance so that we can reclaim the things that we know. The way out of Stupid will not be illuminated with a series of answers. The way out of Stupid inheres in the very exertion of understanding its darkness.

We don't know what we are doing. But, with this book, we refuse to continue to do it. And so, with the means we have, we will attempt to recount the history of Stupid.

1

'I'm worth it': L'Oréal and the fade-resistant rise of liberal individualism

I have longed to slap Heather Locklear for many years. This is due in no small part to her portrayal of Amanda Woodward, a hard-as-acrylic-nails Lady Ad Executive on 1990s prime-time youth soap *Melrose Place*, a program which, at the time of its broadcast, could not be lawfully avoided. Amanda Woodward was made of spite and capital and could very well have been the product of a motel union between Alexis Carrington of *Dynasty* and General Pinochet of Didn't You Kill All Those People in a Stadium fame. I disliked her very much.

It is not essential that you have seen the naked horror of Amanda, although, I can recommend the spectacle as a future sick pleasure. All you need to understand is that she was a lady to whom the idea of personal wealth was indivisible from personal value. If you are younger than me, think of Julie from *The O.C.* If you are older than me, think, of course, of *Dynasty*'s Alexis. If you are better read than me, just imagine Madame Bovary.

But I, in the meantime, am delighted by this opportunity to use the work of Heather as a means to describe a particular kind of Stupid. With Heather/Amanda as our guide we will chart the birth, youth and disappointing midlife of the idea of the 'individual' from its Enlightenment origins to the present day. From Locke to Locklear, if you will. Yes. You're right to groan. That was fucking awful. But not as awful as the prelude to the sort of orchestral nausea one feels when thinking rigorously about the idea of the 'individual'.

The Individual. Yes. It's a difficult idea. But I don't want you to get too panicky because we're not coming over all What Even Is Me here. We are still going to exist by the end of this chapter and so will Amanda, Alexis and Julie. But what we might do is strip the idea of the individual down a bit. It's off with the power suits, and back to the Enlightenment, to a time where 'self' as we know it was being slowly born.

To stare at the idea of the individual and examine what seems so natural for evidence of life might seem a kind of madness. It can be. There are those sufferers of personality or mental disorders who report feeling a loss or a fragmentation of the self and I imagine this must be horrifying. Even the mere thought of the existence of the self is enough to bring me out in hives. I can only imagine that Aristotle with his Soul or Descartes with his Cogito or Sartre with his Being were all absolutely covered in sores by the end of their formulations.

Fortunately, not everyone is a wuss like me. Staring at the self to see if it eventually stares back continues to be a key task for many great thinkers and scientists of the mind; if you really want your head screwed on the topic of Do I Exist?, head immediately to the work of Thomas Metzinger, who combined philosophy and neurology in his 2009 theoretical horror show, *The Ego Tunnel: The science of the mind and the myth of the self.* This work shreds all shreds of scientific evidence for self, consciousness and ego. Personally, I couldn't finish it as I found it at least as twice as frightening as Amanda.

Look, the point that I am making is that I completely understand that thinking Do I Even Exist? is as gratifying and relaxing as a trip to the periodontist. You want bleeding gums? Read Martin Heidegger's *Being and Time*. And get back to me with your notes. I couldn't finish that fucker any more than I could watch Amanda call Sydney a two-dollar hooker while having dental implants hammered into my mouth. Heidegger lost me at 'hermeneutic circle' and I still feel dizzy.

We're not going to think about the self as a philosophical concept. God, no. We're going to think about the modern individual as a social construction.

It is no fun to talk about the essence of the self and it certainly isn't necessary here. But what is necessary is to examine the idea of the self's expensively dressed first cousin: the individual.

So. Just to be very clear and in the ardent hope that you will stay with me throughout the Enlightenment and join me for the season premiere of *Melrose Place* and hang around for the after-party where we will tell rude jokes to each other about liberal democracy for being *such* a stupid whore, I. Am. Not. Asking. You. To. Consider. The. Possibility. That. You. Do. Not. Exist. Because, unlike Amanda, I'm not a total bitch.

Let's dust off this idea of individuality and inspect it for cracks. It's an idea with a very successful and dominant history. It's an idea that continues to inform the way we organise our nations, our morals and our shopping carts. It is possible that there are bits of the idea of the individual which are useful or even natural. It is also possible that there are bits of it that need urgent renovation if we are to move into a different era of thinking and a different, possibly better, organising principle for our nations and economies. And our prime-time soaps.

Bernard and I have agreed that we will both look, in our different ways, at how the individual has appreciated in value these past centuries. We both believe that viewing the individual entirely as a natural fact rather than something that happened contributes to Stupid. We both think that it's worth your time to consider the possibility that there are aspects of the individual, even and especially those associated with the idea of liberty, that may not be as natural and fair as you might suppose.

As such, Bernard has taken a rigorous approach and employs some impressive historiographical method to describe the rise of the individual and its present-day function within liberal economies. I went to Amazon and bought the boxed set of *Melrose Place*.

Before we go back to the publication of John Locke's *Two Treatises of Government* some three centuries before *Melrose Place* (by the way, I reread the First Treatise for this chapter and my advice is: don't; it is super boring, like the first season before Heather joined the cast), we should look at a few key developments in the history of the individual. And I am going to start with the beginning of the modern period.

Oh. Shit. But that means I have to go back a few hundred years further even than Locke to talk about the idea of rights that took flight in the Enlightenment.

Look. We have to go back to Magna Carta. Don't grizzle.

As it is, I'm leaving a lot of stuff about the individual and his worth out. I'll spare us Aristotle and his ideas of the individual man of the polis. I'll spare us the Christian philosophers. I'll just say that for a very long time in Europe, people identified themselves chiefly as members of a community or a city or a guild or a social class such as serf or baron. They were not individuals. They did not have rights. Rights are a new thing. And they are essential to the idea of the Amanda individual.

For the longest time in Western societies, there was no real idea of rights; there were only responsibilities. Of course, just to hammer the point home into your head like a cruel dentist, this did not mean that there was not an idea of the self or of the soul. It *does* mean that people went about with no idea of a 'right' other than those ordained by God, such as to rule or to serve.

Some historians might argue that the artisans of the European communes began to develop an idea of individual rights as they derived it from their labour and its product. But I'm not going into that now because we haven't got all day. So. Magna Carta time.

What we find in Magna Carta is the first written expression of individual rights. Now, it's important to remember that these rights were limited to the handful of self-interested nobles with the balls and the goods to confront King John in 1215. The charter, which sought to limit the power of the monarch, conferred rights only on those rich enough to ask for them. It is not exactly a statement of universal liberty; it exists to uphold the rights of feudal barons. (Aptly, an early copy was sold to a private equity businessman in 2007 for US$21.3 million.)

At the time of writing, Magna Carta remains on display at the US National Archives next to the US Declaration of Independence, the document that made Amanda Woodward possible and to which we shall soon return.

So let's agree that Magna Carta is the first legal expression of individual rights and say that the Renaissance gives us the first cultural expression of the individual.

The Renaissance in Italy is seen by some as the birthplace of the individual. The individual would eventually become the building block of modernity that would find its most doleful expression in 'I'm worth it'.

We need a few words on the emerging individual of the European Renaissance of the fourteenth to seventeenth centuries before we get to John Locke, Heather/Amanda, and the contemporary idea of the liberated self and how she functions to keep us paralysed in high-heeled Stupid.

Right: the Renaissance and the birth of the individual.

The formative work on this idea is by the nineteenth-century Swiss scholar Jacob Burckhardt. Burckhardt's 1867 work *The Civilization of the Renaissance in Italy* is a radical break from previous historical method in its use of art and culture instead of just plain old stories of conflict. Obviously, someone like Karl Marx had no time for a guy who thought the history of all existing society is the history of pretty paintings. Apparently, though, there's a bit of a soap opera that joins Marx to Burckhardt. They had a good mutual friend in Bettina Brentano; a Prussian writer, champion of Romanticism and muse to famous German poets. It is likely that the men met in Brentano's salon and we can only imagine that Marx kept yelling, It's the Economy, Stupid as Burckhardt countered with oil paintings of hot young individuals.

There is an argument to be made that Burckhardt is the *sine qua non* of cultural studies; that without him, we would not be so accustomed to looking for evidence of the way the world works through the art and culture it produces. We wouldn't, for example, be inclined to tolerate my proposition that through the work of Heather Locklear, we can see evidence of what the individual has become. But thanks to Burckhardt, we are able to address the slogan 'I'm worth it' for what it tells us about ourselves and our era.

Of course, the method of Burckhardt was, in my view, mildly Stupid and itself was claimed by Stupid in time; in recent years, people have begun to see art and culture as not just *evidence* of the way a society works but, in fact, as the *reason* a society works in a particular way. For example, one can read daily that the lack of 'real' women on catwalks or the over-representation of white people in Hollywood cinema or the consumerism of Christmas are the starting point for particular social practices and not, in fact, a reflection of them. These are all now seen as not only proofs of the crime of injustice but the perpetrator itself. But we'll get back to this arse-backward idea of social engineering through culture in the chapter on postmodern Stupid. For the moment, we are going to finish this stuff about the Renaissance as it was first described by Burckhardt.

This might seem like a terrible digression; more ridiculous than the plot points in *Dynasty*. But in order to get an understanding of the evolving individual and how she is understood, it is best to look at her both as Burckhardt sees her in the culture and as Marx sees her in material reality.

I'm going to let Burckhardt do much of the heavy lifting on his own account. In a much-quoted passage from his book, he says of the emerging Renaissance individual:

> [B]oth sides of human consciousness—the side turned to the world and that turned inward—lay, as it were, beneath a common veil, dreaming or half awake. The veil was woven of faith, childlike prejudices, and illusion; seen through it, world and history appeared in strange hues; man recognized himself only as a member of a race, a nation, a party, a corporation, a

family, or in some other general category. It was in Italy that this veil first melted into thin air, and awakened an objective perception and treatment of the state and all things of this world in general; but by its side, and with full power, there also arose the subjective; man becomes a self-aware individual and recognises himself as such.

This is a nice account of an individual that didn't really exist before and came to life in this period. I just happen to think that the art didn't create it so much as it documented it.

Burckhardt doesn't agree. He sees art as being as transformative as a document of property laws. The Renaissance, he says, gave the world the possibility of great personalities such as Michelangelo, Leonardo, Raphael and Titian. The idea of individual personality became possible, says Burckhardt, to those familiar with the charm of these artists. Great men not only represented realistic individual subjects in their work—before, there had only been supernatural icons—but themselves hinted at the possibility that an individual could make his mark on history.

As mentioned, Marx had a very different view of things as they unfolded in Renaissance Europe, and if he did ever meet Burckhardt, they would have almost certainly come to blows. The historical materialist—that is, the person who sees the material requirements of life as the chief force that organises and changes societies—would have an economic explanation for this change in perception. He would have said that the art was an effect of the economic conditions that produced it just as much as the emerging intellectual idea of the individual was a result of the slow rise of the bourgeoisie. 'The ideas of the ruling class are in every epoch the ruling ideas, i.e. the class which is the ruling material force of society, is at the same time its ruling intellectual force,' said Marx in *The German Ideology*.

To be both candid and unfashionable, I'm going to say that I mostly agree with Marx. The ruling ideas of the Renaissance age can be seen, and were not formed, in the pictures.

It is a very *individual* idea to believe in the redeeming power of art and the artist. We can see art as beautiful, of course, and we can probably agree to defend it and to see it as an expression of its time. But to see it as something that truly functions to change us may be a little naive. When the great Peter Cook was asked about the opening of his London stand-up comedy club in the 1960s, he said that it would be based on 'those wonderful Berlin cabarets . . . which did so much to stop the rise of Hitler and prevent the outbreak of the Second World War'. I'm not going argue that the cabaret of Weimar was not good stuff. But I will say that I think powerful ideas, like that of the individual, evolve around social organisation more than they do ladies in tights.

You can read about the prevailing conditions of the Renaissance one weekend and come to your own conclusions about whether it was powerful art or powerful market forces that changed the world into a place full of individuals. Or you can say it was both. Whatever you decide, you can agree that powerful ideas such as that of the individual and his attendant rights aren't simply beautiful things that just happen. They are ideas that form. They are not 'natural'. (Hey, nothing is.)

Let's think about the individual and how we see her as someone with 'rights'. Now, we suppose this to be everyone. 'Human rights' is a universal concept. But go back in time to the birth of rights and see that Magna Carta protects only the rights of the nobles, while its companion, the Declaration of

Independence, protects only the rights of white men. These 'rights' are the birth certificates of the modern individual. The pictures of the Renaissance are its baby photos.

We must remember Peter Cook's wonderful crack about the power of art that did so much to stop Hitler. Art did no more to stop or dissuade Hitler than it did to start or encourage him. The terrible 'approved' art of Nazi Germany is fascism's baby photo.

I take the opportunity to bang on about the role of art and cultural artefacts because I think it's worth making the point that none of this stuff can really shape history. Not like a document of property laws can. The most it can hope to do, at the time of its creation, is endorse or, less often, decry the conditions that produced it. We might see art and ideas as nothing but commentary on economics. When we see Amanda/Heather, the fade-resistant blonde, declare 'I'm worth it', to the casual Marxist she is declaring her value in economic terms. And her value was determined centuries ago by this chapter's Leading Man, John Locke. And we really must meet Locke before we get to the L'Oréal commercial in which Heather once starred and of which he would have approved.

Locke was to Thomas Jefferson as Aaron Spelling was to Heather Locklear. He provided all the ideas necessary for both the American Revolution and 1990s power-dressing.

Locke, a seventeenth-century scholar and physician, was, by many accounts, a discreet man whose radical ideas, first published anonymously, could not be guessed. Most unlike Heather, he was, as described by the Bishop of Oxford in correspondence, a 'master of taciturnity'. Quiet he may have been, but one hundred years after publication, his was a battle cry that won America and can still be clearly heard today. Locke is in us as surely as there is air in Heather's hair. Or, indeed, in the hair of Beyoncé, another star of the L'Oréal campaign. It was Locke who wrote down the idea of universal liberty. It was Locke who clearly articulated the idea of our natural rights.

The idea of natural rights now feels so, well, *natural*. But, like Heather's hair, natural rights have a history and a little help. Nothing comes to us *ex nihilo* and there were precedents for Locke's ideas of natural rights such as those we have already reviewed and in the work of other thinkers. Locke would never have written as he did without Hobbes; Thomas Hobbes was to John Locke as *Beverly Hills 90210* was to *Melrose*. (There could be a good argument made that Immanuel Kant was *Models Inc.*, actually. But even I'm not quite ridiculous enough to try that.)

So there is a lot to say about Hobbes but you can read it in *Leviathan*. The short version is that Hobbes is widely regarded as the stern great-uncle of liberal democracy while Locke emerges as its sensitive dad. Hobbes devised social contract theory which relied on solving the mystery of human morality. To do this, he came up with the 'state of nature' to describe humans as they would behave in an imaginary, pre-civil society. What he came up with was, pretty much, *Melrose Place* during a season finale. We're naturally inclined to a state of war.

Obviously, there are problems with imagining Humans As They Really Are; Aristotle had abandoned this chore millennia before when he said that man was, by nature, social. Hobbes didn't think so and urged for the organisation of the just state by villains like those on *The O.C.* or *Melrose*.

Locke also used the state of nature to describe human behaviour. He saw it more as the early relationship of Marissa and Ryan in *The O.C.*: faithful and governed by an innate sense of right and wrong. While Hobbes held that peace needed to be imposed by a central force—that would be Julie, in *The O.C.*—Locke thought it was the natural state. But he also thought that progress and prosperity was the extension of our natural state and, to achieve this, we really needed to make more stuff.

Property is really central to Locke just as it is to Amanda, the owner of the Melrose Place apartment block. Actually, Locke was pretty shameless about the esteem in which he held property; the well-known phrase in the US Declaration of Independence 'Life, Liberty and the pursuit of Happiness' was originally 'life, liberty, and estate' in Locke's Second Treatise. He would use the term 'happiness' in his *Essay Concerning Human Understanding*. But, make no mistake, Locke saw the preservation and the accumulation of property as a moral imperative. (So did Thomas Jefferson, although he wasn't so obvious about it.)

Locke describes property ownership as a moral imperative that comes from no less an authority than God. God, in whom Locke was at pains to believe, wants us to own stuff. Read Locke and you'll find the antecedent of the disgraced clergy of the Praise the Lord (PTL) ministry. In 2003, Tammy Faye of PTL released a self-help book for Christians called *I Will Survive . . . And You Will, Too!* Unfortunately, the prophecy was wrong and she died just a few years later, but not before I interviewed her for Melbourne newspaper *The Age*. I asked Tammy, who had by then divorced PTL big cheese Jim Bakker—a man disgraced by extramarital indiscretion and later convicted of fraud related to the construction of a Christian theme park—if she didn't think that her wealth, reportedly expressed in the form of solid gold bathroom taps on the PTL private jet, was not a little un-Christian. She answered me, 'No, I don't. The Bible says that the worker is worthy. I don't think there's anything wrong with being able to live in a nice home and drive in a nice car.'

Tammy went on to quote a verse of the New Testament that hazily justified the accumulation of sweet, sweet cash. But the Bible never did so well in its holy rationale for wealth and property ownership as Locke. In chapter five of the Second Treatise, we begin to see how America was made both so godly and so rich:

> God gave the world to men in common; but since he gave it them for their benefit, and the greatest conveniences of life they were capable to draw from it, it cannot be supposed he meant it should always remain common and uncultivated. He gave it to the use of the industrious and rational . . .

It is not just our right but our holy *responsibility* to better ourselves and, in so doing, better the world. To be frank, Locke makes Greed is Good sound like a greeting card. The guy developed a rationale for ownership that would be offensive were it not so compellingly written.

When we think of the 'inalienable' 'truths' and 'natural' 'rights' expressed in the Declaration of Independence, we see them as the foundation of all that is good. We see them as pure and self-evident not, as Marx would have it, the self-interested ideas of a dominant class. But it's there in Locke and it's there in the nation he inspired: we are gods who need to own property. And this idea of the individual has stayed with us if not unchallenged, then certainly undefeated for centuries. Growth, production and the mastery of natural resources are what individuals were put here on earth to accomplish.

You can't read Locke and you can't look at the liberal democracies for which he provided an instructional manual and ignore this idea of property that will be owned and worked by the most moral men. The Treatise is no Magna Carta in that it never explicitly passed into law, but it is still an influential charter of rights that extends to a *limited* number of individuals. It offers the sense of morality required by a new middle class for its growth; growth that depends on a hierarchy.

Locke ostensibly confers these rights on *all* humans. You are a god. You are an 'individual'. Now, go ahead and prosper. Those of you who don't are clearly less godly. In other words, if you fuck up and don't accumulate property, it's not because you were denied it; it's just because you are less of a human. It's your fault you haven't claimed your rights.

Some critiques of the Treatise argue that Locke's theory of liberty survives without God and some insist that God is central. Either way, Locke introduced to us the idea of an individual whose highest achievement was the accumulation of property and while Locke may not fall apart without God, he certainly falls apart without property.

Liberal democracy, of course, falls apart without property. It is Locke's suggestion that property is consonant with morality that stays with us—even though God doesn't—and informs the very idea of our individuality today. And what I want to urge is that to continue to assume that morals can be made into property is, if not actually Stupid in itself, a real barrier to life beyond Stupid.

If we cannot get past the view of ourselves as mini-gods who express their morality by the accumulation of wealth, then, I suggest, we are not thinking clearly.

•

By the year 2000, my memory of Locklear had begun to dim. Fade-resistant dye brought it back to vivid colour. Appointed to say 'I'm worth it' by cosmetics giant L'Oréal, the California gal hit screens with a campaign based on self-esteem.

I remember being shocked to hear the boast 'I'm worth it' when it aired for the first time in Australia. I was more recently shocked to find that this catchphrase, conceived by a young copywriter, had been airing since the 1970s.

L'Oréal's historians proudly recount the circumstances under which this Lockean catchphrase was coined. One of Locke's latter-day makers, a then twenty-three-year-old woman by the name of Ilon Specht, captured 'a new spirit of feminism'. 'A social revolution' prompted the I'm Worth It slogan in the time of Female Enlightenment.

I'm hardly the first to express my disappointment with a feminism that had but one critique of liberal democracy. To wit: women weren't terribly involved in it. That's not the problem with liberal democracy. The problem is that it sees morality as the same as ownership. You are worth it.

You're worth it. This is a pure expression of liberal democracy. But this *was* a pure expression of popular feminism, too. It is unreasonable to suppose that women had not come to believe that it was only *natural* to want to accumulate goods, wealth and property just as much as Locke's male mini-makers had. You are a mini-goddess. Your loftiest moral goal is to accumulate wealth. Your liberty inheres in mastery over capital. Your moral value is gauged by your net worth. Ergo, you're worth it.

In a detailed-but-uncritical piece on L'Oréal, Malcolm Gladwell sought out the I'm Worth It girl for the *New Yorker* in March 1999. Called 'True Colors', the piece reads like character notes for Peggy in Mathew Weiner's *Mad Men*. It's the inclination of advertising creatives to see themselves as the vanguard of social change; and to be fair, in Locke's world, where property is moral heft, they probably are. Specht is no exception as she recalls the lack of freedom she experienced in her industry. She was particularly cranky, she tells Gladwell, on the day she was assigned the L'Oréal job and could see but not directly experience the liberty of America. In a fit of anger, she wrote the ad with the tagline first brought to my attention by Heather Locklear. Suddenly, she made her own declaration of independence:

> I use the most expensive hair colour in the world. Preference, by L'Oréal. It's not that I care about money. It's that I care about my hair. It's not just the colour. I expect great colour. What's worth more to me is the way my hair feels. Smooth and silky but with body. It feels good against my neck. Actually, I don't mind spending more for L'Oréal. Because I'm . . .

And Gladwell reports that Specht, who is reciting the copy from memory some twenty-five years after she wrote it, pauses to beat her own chest.

> . . . worth it.

Locke's work was, in time, gratefully and greedily received by a people hungry for a moral justification for wealth, and with L'Oréal, we see the same rationale used for consumption. This new, mutant and female Enlightenment justified its freedom to spend just as the founding fathers justified their freedom to own.

In later decades, when the undisguised avarice of Locke-Lear had become unfashionable, there was a slight shift in selling hair dye. Thomas Jefferson concealed it. L'Oréal, with newer spokesmodels, would too. The persistent stain of liberal democracy keeps refiguring itself subtly and we go from unabashed I'm Worth It to the kinder promise from Beyoncé that You're Worth It.

These days, people like to dress things up in the drag of compassion. In the seventeenth century, John Locke donned the robes of a priest to sell his idea of the individual to whom greed is a genuine moral good. The individual writes others out of its charter of rights and we accept, thanks to Locke and a lot of hair dye and several seasons of *Melrose Place*, that this is natural. It's as natural as Preference by L'Oréal. It is as useful to a new way of looking at ourselves as changing the colour of our hair.

I am not saying here that property ownership is intrinsically bad. I am saying that we should question the idea that it is intrinsically good or intrinsic, in any way, to our character.

The very idea of our character is not built on art or ads; it is built on bricks and mortar. If we don't take the time to at least examine its foundations, then we are at high risk of maintaining the Stupid. Think about the idea of the individual and how we see her morality so bound up with what she owns. Think about a way out of the 'individual rights' that are expressed only in ownership and are made no more moral by virtue of the fact that they have been extended from nobles to career girls. Think about how the idea of the individual implies exclusion. Because you're worth it.

HR

2

Suffer the little children: Enlightenment and denialism

Measles—Called 'Gift from a Goddess' in Sanskrit, measles can help to mature the immune system, may help prevent auto-immune illnesses such as cancer,* asthma and allergies in later life.

—Someone on the internet, later repeated by the 'Australian Vaccination Network'

The WHO's newest measles summary in the Weekly Epidemiological Record reports more than 26,000 cases of measles in 36 European countries from January–October 2011 . . . These outbreaks have caused nine deaths, including six in France, and 7288 hospitalizations.

—World Health Organization

Something odd happened among Australian voters after the 2013 federal election, in which the conservative Coalition

---

* Yes, you're right—cancer isn't an autoimmune illness.

defeated the Australian Labor Party: progressive and conservative voters swapped economic mindsets, as if they'd opened up their skulls and handed each other their brains. A week after the election, according to a poll conducted by Essential Research, 68 per cent of voters who backed the Coalition believed economic conditions in Australia would get better in the subsequent twelve months. By contrast, just 16 per cent of Labor voters thought they would. They were more likely to believe conditions would get worse: 59 per cent of Labor voters thought the Australian economy would deteriorate.

But barely eight months earlier, when Labor was still in government, it was the reverse: 50 per cent of Labor voters thought the economy would improve in the subsequent twelve months while only 21 per cent of Coalition voters thought it would. Instead, 51 per cent of them thought it would get worse; just 21 per cent of Labor voters agreed.

The Australian economy hadn't changed much in the interim. It continued to be a low-inflation, low-interest rate, low-unemployment economy with a much-envied triple-A sovereign credit rating. By the standards of most of the last thirty years in Australia, the economy looked good. What had happened? With their side in power, conservative voters dramatically changed their view of the economy, seeing sunshine and prosperity when, merely months earlier, all had looked dismal. With their side out of power, Labor voters went from bullish to bearish in a heartbeat. It was like a body-swap comedy as imagined by economists.

Partisanship even affected how voters saw their own personal finances: if your side of politics is out of power, you're more worried about your financial situation; if your side is in, your affairs take on a much rosier hue. It's one thing to view the economy—a nebulous entity that frequently produces mixed signals—through a political filter but, weirdly, voters even do so about something they have first-hand knowledge of: their own money.

This has been demonstrated in other countries as well as Australia, particularly the United States, where independent voters can provide a third viewpoint for pollsters on economic and financial matters in addition to Republican and Democrat voters.

This is a specific kind of Stupid: denialism, a refusal to change one's viewpoint even in the face of indisputable data.* Denialism isn't scepticism, not even, per Descartes, radical scepticism; scepticism implies a willingness to accept evidence if it meets a certain standard. Denialism is a refusal to accept *any* evidence, no matter how good or epistemologically sound—unless it says what you want it to say.

Australia went through a fascinating period of economic denialism from 2010–13, with conservative voters and business figures refusing point blank to acknowledge the strong performance of the Australian economy because it was a progressive government presiding over it. Conservative voters thought the economy was in trouble, and even disagreed with economic data that showed how well the economy was doing; business leaders insisted the productivity of Australian workers had gone

---

* Climate change denialists routinely reject the word as somehow offensively anti-Semitic because it invokes images of the Holocaust. As British psychologist Paul Hoggett has noted, this misses the point that the most critical 'Holocaust denial' was not the behaviour of right-wing anti-Semites (and Iranian presidents) decades after the event trying to cobble together evidence that gas chambers never existed, but the denialism of the German people at the time that the Holocaust was being implemented by their own government.

into reverse under Labor, whereas official data showed strong growth in labour productivity; conservative politicians warned of a wages explosion even as data revealed slowing wages growth for the country's workers.

It's less clear whether the same flip-flop occurred when the Australian government last changed, in 2007, but the Australian economy was much stronger that year than in 2013, and the Coalition still lost office. When conservative prime minister John Howard channelled Harold Macmillan and told Australians—with perfect accuracy—that they'd never had it so good, his comment instantly became a potent weapon for his opponents, as if Howard had uttered some unspeakable heresy. He lost not merely government but his own seat in Parliament, only the second Australian leader ever to do so.

But, interestingly, this kind of denialism doesn't necessarily flow through to consumer behaviour. The same polling shows conservative voters made consumption choices at similar or often higher levels than progressive voters in 2012. That is, despite professing to view the economy and their own financial circumstances more dimly, conservative voters reported making major purchases, such as new cars, new homes and overseas holidays, at rates higher than progressive voters, who viewed the economy and their own circumstances more positively. So, thankfully, economic denialism seems to have little real-world impact. It's more accurately seen as an footnote of human nature revealed by our obsession with opinion polling, but without any consequences—unless you're a professional pollster.

But that's just your starter for this particular form of Stupid. There are other forms of denialism, and they have a lot more impact than voters seeing the economy through brown-tinted glasses because the party they support is out of power.

Climate change denialism

While refusal to accept anthropogenic climate change shifts a little over time and reacts to temporary things like extremes in weather, broadly it's been the same across Anglophone countries for some years: a small minority outright reject that there's any global warming, a sizeable minority refuse to accept any human contribution to warming, and about half or a little more of people accept what the world's climate scientists have been saying for a generation about human-caused global warming.

In Australia, the numbers haven't shifted much for some time—in late 2013, just over half of Australians believed in human-caused climate change while 36 per cent believed it was entirely natural. In 2012, a Yale/George Mason University poll found around 54 per cent of Americans believed global warming was caused by humans and 30 per cent thought it was natural; in 2013, a poll by UK specialist outlet Carbon Brief found 56 per cent of Britons believed humans were responsible and 33 per cent said it was natural. In Canada, the numbers were a little different—58 per cent and 20 per cent, according to an Angus Reid public opinion poll, with another 13 per cent rejecting it entirely.

So, overall, in English-speaking countries there's a solid chunk of people, between a fifth and a third of the population depending on where you are, who acknowledge climate is changing but refuse to see that humans have played any role in that change, in addition to a small number who refuse outright to accept what even some aggressive climate denialists now admit: that it's warmer than it used to be.

And we know who these people are. Data from Australian polling shows that there is a perfect correlation between age and a propensity to believe global warming is natural, rather than human-induced. The key age is around fifty-five; after that, people are more likely to dismiss anthropogenic climate change than accept it. Climate change denialists are not merely likely to be baby boomers, but are more likely to be male than female, and tend to be politically conservative. UK data suggests British denialists are older, conservative and male. Data from the US shows they're usually old, male, conservative and white. If greenhouse emissions also caused erectile dysfunction and prostrate problems, climate change would have been stopped dead decades ago.

These are, not coincidentally, the very people most challenged by social and economic change. Older white males grew up in a world that gave them social, economic and political pre-eminence, a world in which they could legitimately expect to have their own needs perceived as a priority by society, even if they were blue-collar males. They now live in a world that accords them less and less priority, whether it's politically, economically or sexually, a world in which they're expected to compete like everyone else. Climate change denialism is thus partly an angry reaction to a changing world—not one with a warming climate so much as a more inclusive society, a more diverse political class, a more competitive economy.

It also means that institutions traditionally controlled by older, conservative males, such as corporations, political parties and mainstream media outlets, are more likely to be climate change denialists than the rest of Anglophone societies—which is one of the reasons why in the West we've done so little about climate change despite so much evidence of the damage it will cause. Large corporations have channelled vast amounts of funding into anti-climate change science campaigns. In the US, Republican politicians have been strongly hostile to climate action; in Australia, the conservative Coalition threw out a leader committed to climate action and replaced him with a denialist who claimed climate change science was 'absolute crap' and who, once elected prime minister, set about dismantling a successful carbon pricing scheme established by the previous government.

The strong correlation between political conservatism and climate change denialism is likely the result of several factors: conservative political parties have stronger links with business, and particularly big business, many sections of which have a strong interest in preventing action to address climate change; and government intervention of the kind required to address climate change, even if via a market-based mechanism, is inconsistent with the small-government rhetoric of modern conservatives. But it also appears to derive from the conviction that climate change is a *political* rather than *scientific* issue. Framing it thus requires conservatives to oppose the existence of climate change and any action to prevent it because to acknowledge its existence is, they believe, to hand a win to their enemy: progressives. That kind of Stupid lies behind the death threats and savage abuse directed at climate scientists, who are perceived as political opponents by denialists, not researchers dispassionately explaining the evidence before them. That's despite the fact that climate action is fundamentally a prudential policy, that preventing uncertainty associated with dramatic environmental and economic change is an intrinsically conservative position and that a conservative icon like Margaret Thatcher (a scientist, perhaps coincidentally) advocated climate action more than two decades ago.

Unlike economic denialists, this form of Stupid has real-world consequences. To the extent that climate change denialists in Western countries are able to slow or (in the case of Australia) reverse action to halt the rise in greenhouse emissions, they inflict a range of costs on developing nations over the long term in relation to higher mortality and health impacts, and economic costs that poorer, less resilient and economically marginal nations will have greater trouble managing than Western countries.

But those same impacts will also be inflicted on denialists' own communities. Due to climate change, more older Australians will die in heatwaves, the impact of tropical diseases will be greater, the costs of extreme weather will increase and the economic impacts of rising temperatures on the agriculture and tourism industries, for example, will be borne by the consumers, businesses and taxpayers of the future. To the extent that eventually Western economies will have to decarbonise in face of catastrophic climate change, climate inaction also imposes greater costs associated with delay on future generations.

Climate change denialists are therefore engaged in intergenerational economic warfare on their own societies. They won't witness the worst aspects of climate change—luckily for them they'll die before they occur. But their children and grandchildren will be affected by them. The refusal of older people, and particularly old white males, to accept the need for climate action shifts costs that they themselves are causing onto their descendants, all of whom will pay higher prices, higher taxes and higher insurance premiums and enjoy poorer health, lower economic growth and fewer jobs because of climate change. Denialists are a form of economic parasite preying on their own offspring, running up a bill they'll die before having to pay. And every year of delay increases the costs that future generations will have to bear.

Still, there's another form of denialism that has a much more immediate and direct human impact than climate change denialism.

Vaccination denialism

In Australia, the US and the UK, vaccination rates for children for preventable diseases like measles are strong, at over 90 per cent. For measles vaccination, this represents a recovery from the massive damage done by Andrew Wakefield and his debunked claims of a link between measles vaccination and autism. But Wakefield still caused a vaccination gap in the UK, as a consequence of which large numbers of children over ten in Britain remain unvaccinated, thus providing a pool for the disease. In 2012, there were over 2000 measles cases in the UK, with twenty children hospitalised. Far from being a benign coming-of-age condition, as claimed by anti-vaxers, measles alone kills 150,000 people a year around the world.

And there continue to be pockets of anti-vaccination fervour. The number of children on the Australian Childhood Immunisation Register with a 'conscientious objection' has gone up nearly tenfold, to nearly 40,000, since 1999. This sentiment can be found among both well-educated, affluent urban parents and alternative lifestyle communities in regional areas.

The persistence of anti-vaccination sentiment in affluent communities is particularly strange, but seems to reflect middle-class parents who want to differentiate themselves, to demonstrate that they're not part of any 'herd', the immunity of which is so important for keeping preventable diseases contained. And if climate change denialism is associated with the right, vaccine denialism is associated not merely with too-posh-to-jab bourgeois denialists, but with the left, often linked to conspiracy theories about Big Pharma (in league, frequently, with the male-dominated medical profession) pushing 'chemicals' on 'our kids'.

In reality, 'our kids' are the victims of this form of Stupid, and not in the long term when they become consumers and taxpayers, but now: unvaccinated children (and there are a small number who for medical reasons can't be vaccinated) get sick and die from preventable diseases. Moreover, they can infect partially vaccinated children, thereby exposing to disease and death the children of parents who have acted responsibly in protecting their children, and babies too young to have begun vaccination.

Vaccination denialism is thus an insidiously evil type of Stupid: Stupid with a body count. It kills and harms kids, often injuring them permanently, and not just the children of denialists, which is horrendous enough, but even those of parents who have tried to protect their kids.

Like climate change denialists, vaccination denialists also tend to rhetorical excess; both have more rabid members who issue death threats to, and demand the jailing of, scientists who disagree with them (i.e. believe normal science). But vaccination denialists go further even than the most rabid opponent of the 'warmist conspiracy'. In Australia, they have called doctors 'full penetration' rapists, called vaccination programs genocide and (inevitably) invoked Nazi Germany. 'There will come a time,' a prominent Australian anti-vaxer wrote online in 2008,

> I pray to God that it will happen in my lifetime—when those who have pushed vaccines upon innocent, helpless babies—doctors, pharmaceutical companies, government officials—will be proven to have lied and cheated these instruments of death into our children's bloodstream. When that occurs, the outcry

will be heard around the world and there will not be enough
hiding places on the globe for these murderers to hide . . .

Worst of all, they have harassed grieving parents who have
lost children to preventable diseases, seeking to discourage
them from publicly blaming diseases like pertussis (whooping
cough). Australia also has the honour of having produced Ann
Bressington, a now former (thankfully) South Australian MP,
who managed the intellectual feat of combining climate change
and vaccination denialism with being an anti-fluoridationist, a
chemtrail believer and a self-proclaimed opponent of 'Agenda
21' and other tinfoil-wrapped causes (bringing to mind the
immortal question to Shirley MacLaine: 'Is there anything you
don't believe in?'). She has publicly claimed vaccination is in
fact a tool of global population reduction—yes, this woman not
merely votes, she actually *got elected*.

As with economic denialism and climate change denialism,
vaccine denialists are impervious to facts. Andrew Wakefield
has been discredited, struck off, had his papers withdrawn,
demonstrated to have engaged in fraud, demonstrated to have
acted unethically towards his (handpicked) child patients,
demonstrated to have planned to make money from the autism
scare he unleashed, and couldn't even get lawsuits up in the
litigation havens of the UK or Texas. However, his work is still
cited approvingly by anti-vax types and Hollywood Z-listers
Jenny McCarthy and Rob Schneider.* McCarthy eloquently
expressed the level of scientific understanding of anti-vaxers
with her memorable statement: 'Think of autism like a fart, and
vaccines are the finger you pull to make it happen.'

---

*   Whose work as actors is more likely to induce fatal reactions than vaccines—
boom tish!

There may be a small number of genuine sceptics in the ranks of economic, or climate change, or vaccination denialists, or poorly informed people who may change their mind in response to clear data, but the majority simply deny in the face of all contrary evidence—cherrypicking what data they can to support their own case, substituting anecdotal evidence for data, applying judgement inconsistently (how many climate change denying businessmen don't insure their businesses against risks far smaller than the chance of climate scientists being collectively wrong?) and dismissing—as Wakefield's supporters do—contrary data as the product of a conspiracy.

Meantime, the toll of misery, suffering and death caused by this Stupid mounts. Take pertussis, a debilitating and sometimes fatal illness that is particularly dangerous for newborns, as babies can't be fully immunised until they're six months old. Peer-reviewed studies have compared both international and domestic US rates of infection based on differing rates of vaccination and show a very strong correlation between lower rates of vaccination or higher rates of 'conscientious objection', and higher pertussis infection rates—even among children who have been partially vaccinated.

•

The persistence of denialism often prompts the lament that key authority figures in a debate aren't 'communicating effectively'. Doctors should be better at explaining the benefits of immunisation, we're told; or politicians have lost the power to explain themselves to voters, to discuss complex economic ideas, to communicate anything that doesn't simply confirm voters' pre-existing beliefs; scientists, more used to fussing around with their beakers and Bunsen burners than talking to actual people, don't effectively communicate climate science—and anyway, scientific method, with its caveats and hypotheses and refusal to embrace absolute certainty, is tailor-made for cherrypicking.

There's some truth to such complaints, and there are always ways to package truth more effectively. For example, explaining that climate change and carbon pricing dramatically improves the economically dismal case for nuclear power is likely to garner support from conservative older males. But the complaint doesn't address the core of denialism—no matter how well-explained facts are, no matter how compelling the presentation, they'll be rejected because denialists are being guided by their own emotional needs, rather than reason.

Denialism is an expression of 'motivated reasoning'—an inability or unwillingness to separate emotion from reasoning, meaning we reason to reach a preferred conclusion, rather than to find the truth regardless of what we'd personally like. We use our core of personal beliefs, personal preferences and individual experience, rather than an objective framework, to guide our reasoning. Voters opposed to the party in power don't want to admit the economy is doing well, given that would reflect positively on a government they loathe, so they claim the economy is underperforming even while they behave as though it is fine. Anti-vaxers prefer anecdotal evidence of the effects of immunisation and dismiss as the efforts of a conspiracy the reams of data available on its safety and benefits. Climate change denialists see climate change as a left versus right issue and thus regard it as a political argument that they and their political tribe must win, regardless of the facts, or a Vast Left-Wing Conspiracy they must unmask, not an issue of scientific fact or prudent judgement.

'Motivated reasoning' isn't just about why people tie themselves in knots trying to refuse evidence and logic; it also embodies the tension between reason and sentiment, a tension that has long, and significant, historical antecedents in Western intellectual history. The conflict between what we *want* to believe, and what reason and evidence tell us is true, has been at the centre of European thought for centuries, and denialism often repeats exactly the same arguments that have been used against reason throughout history.

To trace this tension, we need to go back to the role of organised religion in Western society, and for that we have to start with a methodological note of sorts.

There's plenty that is Stupid in religion. And not just silly Stupid, reflecting that the primary purpose of religion is to give self-obsessed humans the illusion that their lives might have some higher meaning rather than being a mere accident of physics in an otherwise indifferent cosmos. As we'll see later in this book, religion is a delivery mechanism for dangerous forms of Stupid—Stupid that kills and hurts and victimises huge numbers of people. But religion is also a powerful driver of non-Stupid things—of philanthropy, of aid to those in need, of education, of solace and comfort. In this sense, religion is probably better understood as an amplifier of and vehicle for other human characteristics, rather than being innately Stupid or non-Stupid.

But in the modern, secularised West, we have little understanding of just how central to European society Christianity has been for most of the last thousand years. We also have a skewed conception of Christianity as anti-, or at least resolutely non-, intellectual, seguing easily from the Inquisition and the persecution of Galileo through to the modern Republican Party of Intelligent Design and Legitimate Rape. But Christianity (meaning both the Catholic Church and later Christian movements like Protestantism) in the high Middle Ages and the early modern period was the key engine of Western thought. Moreover, because of its central role in Western society, not merely was that society suffused with religion to a much greater degree than we can now comprehend, but Christianity was suffused with social and secular concerns in a way that would be equally incomprehensible to people of the twenty-first century.

Indeed, it is hard to distinguish between Christianity and Western society in intellectual terms up until the seventeenth century. Thus, intellectual developments within Christianity were in effect intellectual developments in the whole of Western thought. That's why we're now, however improbably, detouring back to the Reformation to explore why Jenny McCarthy wants people to stop pulling fingers.

Printing and the split between head and heart

In the fifteenth and sixteenth centuries, the theological monopoly of the Catholic Church came under unprecedented pressure from two different directions—humanism and Reformism. Both are important movements in the Western intellectual tradition. Both challenged the basic position of the Church, that *it* was the only body able to interpret the divine will, that its priests were a necessary medium to connect ordinary people with the Christian deity and that its teachings were the only path to salvation.

We'll deal with some of the other consequences of this challenge in later chapters, but for now we'll stick to the intellectual impacts. The Church's 'no salvation without us' business model—and 'business model' isn't sarcasm, this was an institution of enormous economic as well as political power—couldn't withstand the arrival of a disruptive technology: printing. The early modern Church was the music industry of its day, albeit with less cocaine and better composers, hapless in the face of a new technology that empowered the people formerly known as its worshippers. It wasn't merely that people could now—assuming they were literate—read a wide range of material on religious and political matters. Rather, both humanism and Reformism posited a much greater role for individuals in religion and, it would become clear, beyond religion as well.

Humanism emphasised the use of reason and evidence—in particular, critical textual analysis, the historical importance of which has long since been forgotten. Humanism celebrated source documents and subjected them to searching scrutiny, trying to extract as much information from them as possible. Classical and early Christian texts were pored over, as were the books of the Bible itself; it was no longer sufficient to accept either the official position of the Church on what a particular text said, or even the commentaries of philosophers and Church fathers. If possible, the original texts on an issue must be accessed and analysed to determine not just their authenticity, but the historical circumstances in which they were written and the message they were intended to convey when they were written.

Humanist scholarship was boosted by an historical accident: western Europe was at this point rediscovering, or seeing for the first time, a number of key classical books—many after the fall of Constantinople in 1453 to the Ottomans, which sent Orthodox scholars fleeing westwards with them.

This sort of focus on books had been seen before in Europe, particularly during the eighth- and twelfth-century renaissances (yes, there were several renaissances; it wasn't all buboes and flagellants between Christopher Plummer's death in *Fall of the Roman Empire* and Michelangelo), but this time it was fuelled by printing. Printing had a stupendous scholarly impact on Europe, even through simple things like standardisation of texts and a massive expansion in readerships, let alone more complex long-term impacts. Some of those, such as the epochal reorientation of humankind towards the visual, are discussed by Marshall McLuhan in *The Gutenberg Galaxy*: McLuhan described printing as causing a 'split between head and heart' in Europe.

Consider how important standardisation was: medieval copies of even the most crucial patristic and philosophical texts were riddled with errors made by the photocopiers and printing presses of the Middle Ages—tired monks beset by cramped hands, poor light and minds numbed with drudgery. Printing enabled different versions of key texts to be shared and compared so that errors could be identified and eliminated. And the widespread dissemination of printed texts dramatically expanded the number of readers scrutinising them, the result being many more standardised, authoritative philosophical and theological works and many more scholars to examine the same text, whether in Edinburgh or Vienna.

Most of all, the Bible itself, previously chained up like a wild beast in the local church, became increasingly available to anyone who could read—a truly radical development. Martin Luther, for example, could plausibly claim to have never read a Bible before he arrived at a monastery.

Printing thus provided a massive spur to new religious thinking—the spread of early Protestantism can be tracked in England along trade routes that carried books to literate communities, such as weaving towns, where books would be distributed and (even more importantly) discussed by people by themselves, without guidance from institutional churches.

But while Reformism encouraged a much more personal faith than that offered by the Catholic Church, which continued until the twentieth century to perform its central ritual in a tongue virtually no one spoke, it wasn't much more encouraging of reasoning than Catholicism. Key Reformers like Luther and John Calvin saw reason as having only a limited, and subordinate, role in religion; both emphasised, albeit with different weighting, the crucial nature of grace. Humanism might have helped create the conditions for the Reformation, but they were very different intellectually. Humanism was bibliocentric, focused heavily on the written word and its derivation; Protestantism was Bibliocentric, focused on the Bible; 'the Word' in Protestantism was that of God, and oral, not written—a distinction that will continually reappear in this discussion.

Moreover, Reformed churches quickly learned the lesson the Catholics had long ago learned: that letting people go their own way on religion fragmented and undermined organised worship. Institutionalised Reformism thus copied the Catholic Church in repression. Calvin executed the intellectual Michael Servetus, who had outraged not just the Catholics with his biblical interpretation, but the Lutherans and the Calvinists as well, a trifecta that saw him burned alive in Geneva. And the flames in which he perished were just a warm-up. Elizabethan England was tough on Catholicism and tough on the causes of Catholicism, with what would later be called a zero-tolerance policy for Romish priests: they were assumed to be spies and were tortured and executed virtually on sight.

Or there was the Thirty Years' War, an epic of sectarian bloodshed between different rulers (the idea of wars between states, rather than monarchs, was still developing), the numbing brutality of which Bertolt Brecht sought to re-create by making us sit through *Mother Courage*. That conflict was eventually settled on the basis that people would have to accept the religion of whoever was ruling them at the time, and if they didn't like it, they'd have to move somewhere else. Somewhere else, as it turned out, often meant the afterlife—if, for example, you were a Huguenot in France in 1572, or one of the tens of thousands of women killed after being accused of witchcraft (the witch crazes peaked at the end of the sixteenth century).

For others, elsewhere meant another continent. Many Protestants were so disgusted both at the persecution they endured at the hands of their rulers and at having to live in the same country with people who didn't share their religious views, that they left Europe altogether, sailing west until they reached North America, where they set up their own colonies. There, fulfilling the fears of endless division of the early Reformers, some split off to form yet more colonies over ever narrower doctrinal differences. We'll come back to them.

Back in Europe, the Holy Spirit was out of the bottle, too. Handing individuals a personal link to their god drove a proliferation of faiths that even savage crackdowns couldn't halt. The availability of the Bible, and other texts, fuelled this proliferation—thus we first start to see censorship in the Reformation context; among the first books banned was the Bible itself, by Henry VIII.

The humanist impulse contributed to this ever-fracturing process of religious evolution. The remarkable seventeenth-century Dutch Jewish philosopher Spinoza (strictly speaking he was a lens grinder who did philosophy in his spare time) contrasted religion as developed by churches, almost entirely without the Gospels, with a close study of the Gospels themselves. Spinoza, in the humanist tradition, argued that the Gospels should be treated as literary texts composed by many authors, rather than divine revelation (and anyway, Spinoza argued, God was an infinite substance who was everywhere, not a single being). Treating the Bible as holy writ meant, for Spinoza, worshipping paper and ink. Close study of the Bible, he said, would reveal the simple, uncluttered message of religion, which was limited to loving the deity and loving one's neighbour as oneself.

For Spinoza, it followed from this that no one had any business dictating a person's interior faith, a view fundamentally at odds not merely with the Catholic Church, but with much of Reformism: both gave themselves the right to dictate faith and remove from society (well, remove from life, in practice) anyone who disagreed with them. Spinoza wasn't the first to urge toleration, but he provided an intellectual basis for it that, along with his reasoning that democracy was the most effective form of government and his argument that there was no point trying to regulate free speech, were to prove profoundly influential in the eighteenth century.

So, okay, what does all this have to do with Jenny McCarthy's autistic flatulence, apart from Martin Luther's famous claim he could chase Satan away with a fart? It sets the scene for *the* critical clash between reason and sentiment, in the Enlightenment.

To understand this better, we have to understand there were, like multiple renaissances, multiple Enlightenments, and not just those in individual countries (your Scottish Enlightenment, your French, your German and so on—please say them in the appropriate accents); the term 'family of Enlightenments' has been used by historian J.G.A. Pocock, while Jonathan Israel has, crucially, divided it into 'radical' and 'moderate' Enlightenments, which is the more important distinction for our purposes.

The moderate Enlightenment is the one we all know—Voltaire, salons, wigs, epigram-ready table talk and so on—which was primarily reform-minded and anti-clerical in nature, rather than genuinely politically radical. There was even Enlightened Despotism, an early example of ambush marketing by some eighteenth-century monarchs who wanted to distinguish their particular brand of kinder, gentler tyranny from run-of-the-mill absolutism.

But the radical Enlightenment fully embraced the application of reason, no matter where it ended up, and its adherents didn't stop at wanting to turf out the Church. They eventually argued for fundamental social and political reforms, such as democracy, women's suffrage and anti-colonialism.

Both these Enlightenments were, crucially, elite phenomena—a characteristic their critics wouldn't forget. Those being freed from the grip of the Catholic Church and absolutism were mainly middle- and upper-class, educated Christian men. Voltaire famously told dinner guests to stop discussing atheism in front of the servants unless they wanted to be murdered in their beds, because religion was all that kept the lower orders in line.

And despite the famous role of women in hosting salons, barely a quarter of women could read in eighteenth-century France. 'Enlightenment is man's emergence from his self-incurred immaturity,' is how Immanuel Kant commenced his 1784 pamphlet 'An answer to the question: What is enlightenment?' and he wasn't merely following personal pronoun convention. Kant was, per Monty Python, a real pissant when it came to women: they were, the philosopher considered, 'timid, and not fit for serious employment'. Rousseau, who sits apart from the French Enlightenment but who was a hugely influential figure, was deeply misogynistic and convinced that women had to be kept controlled and domesticated. And Voltaire and the encyclopaedist Denis Diderot, like Luther, shared Europe's rich history of anti-Semitism and poured out bile about Jews that could have been used by the Nazis.

But Diderot stood apart from Voltaire and particularly Rousseau in extending Spinozism to fundamentally more radical ideas than Voltaire, who was a friend and faithful correspondent of despots enlightened or otherwise. In an intellectually aggressive phase at the end of his life, Diderot called for wars of liberation of oppressed peoples against monarchs, aristocrats and clerics, attacked colonialism and supported the education and liberation of women. And Voltaire and Rousseau were infuriated by their inability to defeat the radical *philosophes* and Spinozists through argument.

Rousseau's objection to Diderot and the more politically radical *philosophes* was one that is at the core of the tension between reason and sentiment: he criticised *reason itself*. Reason, for Rousseau, was a corruption caused by civilisation, the faculty that had led humankind (or more accurately, for Rousseau, *man*kind) away from the simplicity of the natural state in which it had been happy, into an age of misery. Rousseau's attack on reason, drawing on two centuries of 'noble savage' stereotyping induced by Europe's contact with the New World, was a key moment in anti-intellectualism. Reason wasn't merely useless but *corrupting*; it had all gone wrong once humans—sorry, men—began using their brains logically; until then, they had existed in a state not of Hobbesian brutality, but of simplicity and instinctive bliss. McLuhan's 'split between head and heart' caused by printing had now been articulated clearly.

This Edenic soft primitivism of Rousseau, by the way, is echoed in the thinking of many denialists: the anti-science views of climate change denialists (former prime minister John Howard declared in 2013 that his 'instincts' told him climate change wasn't real) and the bizarre argument of anti-vaxers that a disease like measles is a benign coming-of-age process visited upon lucky children by Nature (portrayed as a maternal, nurturing female deity) with which the *unnatural*—and male—forces of science and medicine shouldn't interfere. Rousseau couldn't think of any arguments to counter those of Diderot and other radical *philosophes*, but he knew they were wrong *in his heart*, he said.

Rousseau had a fan in a political figure who emerged in the French Revolution: Robespierre. The Jacobins condemned not merely moderate Enlightenment *philosophes* but the whole Enlightenment project, and particularly radical Enlightenment ideas of free speech and a free press. Those *philosophes* still alive by the time of the Terror were hunted down and executed or, like Thomas Paine, forced into hiding. And the greatest Jacobin charge against the radical Enlightenment was, echoing Rousseau, its elevation of cold rationality over emotion and the sentimental simplicity of common folk.

Orality and literacy

Robespierre was a devastating orator, and his rise to power was partly built on his rhetorical gifts. And the conflict between reason and sentiment was also partly one between literacy and orality, which echoes the bibliocentric–Bibliocentric distinction between humanism and Reformism. This is a key theme of McLuhan's in *The Gutenberg Galaxy*, the supplanting of oral/aural culture by the homogenising, specialising, hierarchical culture of the printed word.

This literacy–reason/orality–sentiment tension can also be observed in the American history of religion. While the French Revolution was underway, across the Atlantic, the American colonies—by now liberated and federated with the help of pre-Revolutionary France, the genocide of native Americans and some signally inept British statesmanship—had begun developing their own anti-intellectual tradition.

Fifty years ago, in *Anti-intellectualism in American Life* (1963), Richard Hofstadter argued that it was the American evangelical tradition as it emerged in the eighteenth century that created an actively anti-intellectual form of religious expression in the United States. The American churches established by the Puritan refugees we saw earlier in this chapter were, if not overtly humanistic, still scholarly in nature—Harvard was established less than twenty years after the arrival of the *Mayflower*, at Cambridge, a town named after the university (famously, the more Puritan of the English universities).

But with the American Revolution and the growth of the new republic, the established colonial churches found themselves fighting a losing battle against uncontrolled, populist frontier evangelicism. This time, the disruptive technology was the human voice, not books: Americans were voracious readers and would soon create a massive newspaper market, but books themselves could be few and far between in many American communities, particularly on the ever-moving frontier (although novels were frequently serialised in magazines and, occasionally, newspapers). Preaching—particularly of the fire-and-brimstone variety—was central to the second Great Awakenings that swept the new nation from the middle of the eighteenth century.

Preaching had always been a key part of the Protestant tradition. English Protestant Reformers demanded, and got, a graduate clergy in the sixteenth century, and the university curricula of the time remained focused on the profoundly *oral* medieval scholastic tradition of the trivium and quadrivium, aimed at delivering a graduate skilled in oratory and verbal argument. Sixteenth- and seventeenth-century Puritans expected sermons lasting three hours at a minimum when they attended service, and sometimes complained when that was all they got; ministers who failed to occupy the pulpit for such heroic lengths were mocked as 'dumb dogs'. The preaching of the Great Awakenings and of Methodist preachers also saw Herculean feats, not in duration but in volume: preachers such as colonial-era Methodist George Whitefield could, Benjamin Franklin reported, address unaided 20,000 people at open-air gatherings.

This literacy–reason/orality–sentiment distinction keeps reappearing. The spoken word delivered by a gifted orator to a group is personally engaging, an unrepeatable performance that delivers a communal emotional experience, one that engages both aural and visual senses. The written word is visual only, more detached and analytical, less emotional, homogenising, capable of constant repetition, consumed alone.

Hofstadter suggests that in the febrile environment of nineteenth-century American religion, Darwinism and then industrialisation and urbanisation (in which the South conspicuously trailed the rest of the United States, and still does) elicited a backlash against modernity and provided the historical antecedents for twentieth-century Christian fundamentalism. Where Rousseau had accused intellectuals of being unwilling to lift a finger to save the lives of their fellow citizens, early-twentieth-century American fundamentalists declared college graduates were going straight to hell. A similar mindset was to be found in the Ku Klux Klan, whose 'Imperial Grand Wizard' in the 1920s contrasted emotion and instinct with what was 'coldly intellectual'—the former 'have been bred into us for thousands of years' (presumably 6000 years maximum), 'far longer than reason has had a place in the human brain.' Rousseau could not have expressed it better.

The Scopes Trial in the 1920s encapsulated the pure form of American anti-intellectualism, as articulated by the unusual figure of William Jennings Bryan. Bryan, aka 'The Great Commoner', had been a three-time Democrat candidate for president in a remarkable populist political career (in his first run for president in 1896, he was, and remains, the youngest-ever major party candidate, at just thirty-six). Bryan's political success had been powered by—here we are again—his prodigious oratorical gifts: he routinely spent several hours a day delivering long speeches, and his 'cross of gold' speech against the gold standard that secured him the Democratic nomination in 1896 remains the, um, gold standard of US political oratory.

Bryan, who had personally campaigned against evolution both for religious reasons and because he believed it promoted conflict and had helped cause World War I, argued in the Scopes Trial that evolution should not be taught in Tennessee public schools not merely because it was 'condemned' in the Bible, but because few Tennesseans believed in it. Teaching evolution amounted to the undemocratic imposition of the rationalist views of a small number on 'the views entertained by the masses'. In other words, Bryan wanted science by ballot box. Bryan won the case (the result was later overturned), but was humiliated by his opposite, Clarence Darrow, on the stand and died soon after, thereby becoming an unlikely symbol of Southern fundamentalism.

A different, if only partial, resolution of the reason–emotion tension had been proposed by late-nineteenth-century New England philosopher and psychiatrist William James (brother of Henry). We'll return to James later in another context, but in the late 1870s, in his essay 'The Sentiment of Rationality', he made the point that rationality can incorporate characteristics of sentiment, such as aestheticism. As per Ockham's Razor, we prefer simplicity—or, as James put it, 'parsimony'—over complexity and lack of clarity in explanations, and a coherent and satisfactory explanation provides intellectual comfort in a way something less satisfactorily rigorous does not. James, perhaps unfortunately, never taught in Tennessee, and remained a Harvard man all his life.

The United States isn't the only country to be labelled anti-intellectual (either from the left or the right: critics like Allan Bloom have charged American universities with fostering irrationality). In fact, the lament, that '_____ is the most anti-intellectual country in the world' is routinely applied to their own country by Australians, New Zealanders and the British as well as Americans, although Vichy France, Nazi Germany, Fascist Italy and Franco's Spain all displayed a strain of anti-intellectualism.*

---

*   Anti-intellectualism is also regularly treated as a new phenomenon—as Hofstadter noted, intellectuals seem to have a 'lamentably thin sense of history'.

In the US and Australia, the reason–emotion tension has been channelled into a standard conservative attack on progressives, with a powerful, out-of-touch liberal 'elite' alleged to be somehow controlling governments in opposition to the needs of ordinary people. In this myth, which echoes the Jacobin hostility to the *philosophes*, the average voter invariably possesses 'common sense' (although that doesn't get celebrated so much when they throw out conservative governments or re-elect progressive ones) while elites are always 'intellectual', 'sneering' and 'technocratic'—a term that encapsulates the entire charge of cold, unfeeling rationality. The elevation of personal experience—which we discuss later—to the apex of sound argument in public discourse is another form of privileging sentiment over reason: facts and logic are no match for the real emotional experiences of people; to *know* is one thing, but to *feel* is better.

In a culture where rationality is contrasted negatively with the instinctive pragmatism of 'ordinary folk', in which 'intellectual elites' are characterised as a kind of public enemy, denialism, whether it's the killer kind peddled by the anti-vax crowd, or climate change denialism peddled by old white men, or ordinary refusal to acknowledge how the economy is performing, is enabled. If our institutions have changed since the early modern period, we've retained much of the Stupidgenic environment that the humanists and the *philosophes* faced.

In such an environment, data and logic, carefully compiled and written down, become suspect, the tools of manipulators, or simply irrelevant and elitist, compared to the emotional life of ordinary people. How can it make kids healthier to put diseases in them? And 'I heard of someone whose little girl got sick after being immunised.' 'It was hotter in summer when I was a kid.' 'How can the economy be doing well when I know someone who lost his job?' Instinct and anecdote, in a manner that would have delighted Rousseau and Robespierre, remain more credible than written evidence. Denialism remains as easy to embrace as it has ever been throughout history, driven by our urge to reason our way to what we want to believe, not what might be true regardless.

BK

3

Look who's talking: Why uttering our 'identity' makes us Stupid babies

Once, I lived under rule where criticism of Oprah Winfrey was a serious offence. Of course, one can only take so many Inspiring Stories of Personal Triumph and this domestic regime did not last. But, while it did, I learned to laugh, cry and sing along with the protagonists of Harpo Productions' real-life drama. Cancer patients who had beaten the odds and found new health through positive thinking. Rape survivors who had beaten the odds and found new positivity through healthy thinking. Fat mothers who had beaten the odds and positively thought their way to a new dress size through healthy eating.

There were so many stories with such a similar rhythm, their details were easily forgotten. But it didn't matter. The important thing was they always ended well; even when they ended badly, they were structured to reveal a 'teachable moment'. And even if you forgot what that teachable moment was, none of them mattered so much as the founding myth of *Oprah*, which, of course, was Oprah herself. A survivor of weight loss, rape, sexism and racial discrimination, she was there as the victorious end to a wonderful story.

Eventually, I found myself hating Oprah. I hated all her 'moments' and wanted them to be a bit less fucking teachable. My own life was lived in stasis and produced moments no more teachable than 'it was probably wrong for you to move in with someone who likes Oprah'. Even under expert editing, my life would fail to produce an Uplifting Moral. At most, it was a Cautionary Tale.

Of course, stories can be useful in communicating a point. I'm telling one now to underscore the usefulness of stories in communicating a point. This is my Brave and Personal Journey Towards Not Giving a Fuck About Stories. Because stories, I found, had begun to grow my Stupid.

Since Oprah finessed real life for daytime TV and managed to make it seem instructive, stories have become commonplace. There has always been storytelling by politicians, of course. The former factory-hand who worked his way up from nothing thanks to the power of the union. The former factory-hand who worked his way up from nothing thanks to the power of free enterprise. But in the past few decades, the stories have become more elaborate and heartbreaking. Now, with their everyday details, these biographies serve as mission statements in themselves. Australian Prime Minister Julia Gillard wooed the female vote with a powerful personal story of sexism in the workplace. Australian Prime Minister Tony Abbott wooed the female vote with a powerful personal story of non-sexism in the raising of his daughters.

In newspaper features, the writer has emerged as a central figure. About a decade ago, I began receiving the curious instruction for pieces on social issues to 'put more of yourself on the page'. Obviously, this is a habit I cannot kick, but there is really no professional reason that I should in a world that runs on the quick-fix personal drug of Upworthy, which believes This One Guy Will Change Your Life.

It is absolutely true, of course, that a story can move us to a different way of thinking. When I was a kid, *The Autobiography of Malcolm X* had an extreme and enduring effect on my world view. My ideas about race evolved into good sense at speed and I am not so much of a snob as to suppose that Oprah, at one time or another, has not had a similar influence on some of her viewers. But when personal stories become, as they have lately done, the premier method of communicating an idea, I wonder if they don't lose their power. I have begun to suspect that the only idea they can now communicate is actually a pretty shitty one. And that is: Anything is Possible Through the Power of the Human Spirit.

In fact, Malcolm X was communicating the opposite of that idea. His message was that Possibilities are Limited by the Idiocy of the Human Spirit. His life, which ended with an assassin pointing a sawn-off shotgun to his chest, pretty much underscored this point. In his life, as in his narrated account of it, the message was: history has taken a terrible turn. In Upworthy, Oprah, politics and even in the serious news, the message is now Watch This One Guy Change History.

This has become the single, hopeful, depressing cry of Stupid: personal stories matter. The ubiquity of the personal story has led to its impotence. When we have come to believe that the only way to convey a big idea is through a small story, all stories have the same Stupid moral. And that is not only that every big idea can be reduced to a single narrative, but that the individual will triumph. Even if the individual doesn't actually triumph over reality, his individual story will triumph simply by virtue of being (properly) told. A story is edited until it becomes a 'teachable moment'. Even without the consent of the person about whom the story is being told.

In 2012, fifteen-year-old education advocate and student Malala Yousafzai was shot three times on her way to school in Pakistan. Her assailants were Taliban and so this extraordinary young woman was quickly pressed by propagandists into the service of justifying US military interests. This might sound like a paranoid view until you follow the less 'teachable' moments of Yousafzai's real story.

Hailed by President Obama for her bravery, she was welcomed to the White House. The Western world had expected her to become an ally of the US. In the 'teachable' version of this story, she would thank Obama for his continued liberation of her country. Instead, she asked him to stop the drone strikes for which history will eventually remember his administration. The US-ordered drone strikes, she later told the press, sometimes killed children on their way to school.

In refusing her time as a 'teachable moment', Yousafzai reminded the world that the deaths of more than 200 children by US drone have been recorded in Yemen and Pakistan. There's no doubt that her bravery in the face of Taliban soldiers is inspiring. But Yousafzai is also a hero for her refusal to function as a personal story. This moment was so unteachable, it filled me with optimism. Here was someone not only strong enough to stare down thugs, but curiously intelligent enough to see beyond her personal story into a much wider political reality. The personal, for Yousafzai, was political. So political that she saw no reason to talk about the personal.

When I was a young idiot, I learned the phrase 'the personal is political' and I found it very handy. It meant that *my* perspective was universal and, heck, I'd always suspected as much. For a young woman angry About Things, this maxim gave all my blurry feelings instant focus, even and especially lovesick ones. For example, if I fancied the president of the student council and he did not return my interest, I could say that this personal thing for a (political) dude was 'political'. The student council president's lack of interest in me was not, in fact, a personal inaction without meaning but a loaded political act. Every caress I did not enjoy was an act of political calculation as cold as that which drove him to make a preference deal with the Labor Right. His failure to attend my one-woman show on bisexuality in the union bar was not a good decision. (NB: It *was* a good decision. If you have little in your life for which to be currently grateful, be grateful you never saw me perform the experimental poem 'Sexual Seahorse'.) It was a bad decision that constituted a rejection of my glorious and unapologetic femininity and he didn't love me because of the patriarchy.

Patriarchy!

The patriarchy was also sometimes responsible for my uneven grades. It was responsible for me feeling less beautiful than Caitlin, the expensively educated cheesecloth-wearing WHORE of the student council president. And it was responsible for some other stuff, such as my parents not loaning me money, my flatmate Andrew refusing to share his pot and the hairdresser that leased the property beneath ours who blamed my bad housekeeping for the rats that ate through the power cord of his curling wand.

Patriarchy!

When you're young or selfish or both, this idea that the personal is political or that the intimate is always attached to the public realm feels quite natural. And you don't have to be a tedious young feminist socialist with terrible study habits and a raging libido to think this. You can be anyone—even a rugby-loving engineer whose idea of a good time is Ayn Rand and an ounce of blow—and still have ideas about You and the World.

We have likely all felt, at one time or another, that the 'world' is against us or that the 'world' has certain characteristics that we exemplify. Consciously left-wing and consciously right-wing people are more likely to view the world as a system and this produces in them, respectively, feelings of oppression and feelings of freedom. The world and its systems gave us these things. But even people who think less often of the political economy are still likely to give agency to the world at times for their feelings and their fortunes.

'You are only saying that because I'm pretty' or 'He was promoted because he is British' or 'You hate me because I can't play sport' are all statements made possible by the agreement that there are systems in the world to which one is subject.

The political can and often does have a personal manifestation. Prejudice and profit on the basis of good looks, nationality or sporting ability are real events. And no prick in their right mind (surely?) would argue against the free expression of a person with an account of how they are disadvantaged by any of these systems.

Except, you know, I might. I will. I am. But not as bravely as Yousafzai.

The fact is, of course, there are systems in the world to which we are subject. I mean, only a Stupid would say that there is no system that offers cultural, physical and financial advantage to people with lighter skin. Only a Stupid could fail to see how bias is one way in which this system maintains itself. Only a Stupid would bother to say that there is no observable pattern of racism in the world.

There are two ways a Stupid might dispute the fact of worldwide racism. First, and most Stupid, they would say—as some people to whom I am related do—that black people are lazy or just no damn good. This is essentialism of the most depressing order and I recommend you do not argue with such a sluggish level of Stupid. When I hear someone utter 'born that way' or 'not trying hard enough', I almost feel that the intellectual poverty to which they doom themselves is its own kind of punishment. Honestly, this is a Stupid so stupid that Bernard and I haven't been arsed to give it much attention.

Second, a faintly more sophisticated kind of Stupid might try to dispute the evidence of racism by recourse to personal anecdote. That is, they will tell you about that time a person from a different ethnic group to them was rude. Or even themselves 'racist'.

One will hear these arguments about sexism, too. Now, any look at widely available national or international data will show that the experience of men and women is different. Women in liberal democracies, for example, tend to experience poverty more often than men, especially in old age. Men in liberal democracies tend to hurt or kill themselves and others significantly more than women.

Again, the 'born that way' argument can be used here—and this one holds more social legitimacy as an account of gender difference than it does of racial difference. Even advocates for gender equality will sometimes argue that men and women are 'just different'. I have no fucking idea why anyone does this; even if biological sex difference is true and not, as I suspect, an alibi for neat social organisation—and there is no evidence to suggest that there is any biological sex difference to account for social difference—I do not see the point of this argument. I do not see the point of the evolutionary biology upchucked in service of this argument. Say you *do* find out that women lack ambition *genetically*? Say you do find some way to observe a non-socialised female brain and give me objective peer-reviewed evidence that women are Just Different and less biologically inclined to social dominion? Are you talking about dominion in Palaeolithic societies and, if so, can these be creditably compared to our modern, highly socialised corporate systems? Are you really trying to tell me that because a woman is less likely to kill a wildebeest with her teeth than a man that she is also less likely to adhere to business guidelines? You stupid Stupid. Even if your proof—which you have not yet found—is founded in science, your argument is complete pants founded in caveman fantasy. Give it a rest and turn your mind to useful science.

We also see the Personal Is Political anti-reason applied to argue against the case of sexism. 'I know women who are violent' and 'I know women who are rich' is used to counter the social evidence that men tend to be more violent and women tend to have less wealth.

I mean, that's nice, you know. It's great that you know Powerful Role Models who are Exploding Stereotypes and that there are women of your acquaintance accumulating large amounts of wealth by torturing kittens. It is just so fantastic and inspiring that you have met black people who are also wealthy and mean. I am immediately convinced that all data at the Australian Bureau of Statistics is actually not derived from a census but from lies, lies, lies, because you know a couple of nasty, violent black women. Seriously. This is great evidence and I think we should base all social policy on it from this moment. Please. Tell me you share your keen observation on a blog?

Ugh.

Anyhow, this sort of thinking is clearly Stupid. But, really, my early feminist thinking was just as Stupid. Using personal experience as proof of a system is just effing wrong at a fundamental level, even if that personal experience does tally closely with verifiable social fact. Of course, as a means to an honourable end, the description of individual hardship *might* work quite well in some cases. It is an accepted liberal practice that works—I presume effectively but I do not know—in liberal contexts such as the United Nations; here, speakers will often use a personal experience to make a political point. Telling a story about a particular life is an entertaining way to engage an audience in a broader social problem and, so we must suppose, a good means to a social solution. And if this does work, as I must believe it sometimes does, to encourage policy changes, then jolly good, Oprah. If the matter at hand is clean water and the means of purification is someone singing about the children being the future, I say bring back Whitney.

Whitney and water, by the bye, gives us good pause to visit the difference between consequentialist and deontologist ethics. It's a *partial* sidebar but it's a terribly useful distinction that I can guarantee you'll enjoy learning more about if you're not already familiar with it. For your quick reference, the most famous consequentialist is Peter Singer, and he would hold that the ends justify the means. Which is to say, even if you do need to endure Whitney Houston's second-worst recording (the first is the theme from *The Bodyguard*, obviously), it is okay so long as it produces a good result at the UN, like clean water. The most famous deontologist is Immanuel Kant, and he would hold that only good means can produce a truly good end. Which is to say, our motives must be pure. And obviously, if you have been recently listening to 'Greatest Love of All', you are already corrupt and in violation of your duty to universal law, the first article of which is: Do unto others as you would have them do unto you—i.e. don't play people bad Whitney. (I have not read *Grounding for the Metaphysics of Morals* for many years, but I believe that Kant says an action can only be truly moral if one has just been listening to 'I Wanna Dance with Somebody'.)

It is difficult not to be a consequentialist when it comes to clean water. Even if you have very sound objections to the use of emotion in achieving an end—and Kant does—it is really difficult to say that pictures of dehydrated children shown at the UN are bad if it achieves clean water. But I have begun to suspect that these moments of 'identifying' have become too numerous to really work on a broad scale any longer. You hear the story of a Child who is Our Future often enough, and you just stop fucking listening. Peter Singer stopped listening; you can read his thinking on this in a really good 2014 piece in the *Washington Post*. He writes:

> . . . the unknown and unknowable children who will be infected with malaria without bed nets just don't grab our emotions like the kid with leukemia we can watch on TV.

We will talk more about this problem of feeding our compassion in chapter eleven. But what we also need to look at in addition to the Stupid effects of emotion is the Stupid produced by our need to 'identify'.

It is possible that all we are doing in recognising other identities is getting stuck in the personal idea of 'us'. And Singer's unknowable children don't stand a chance unless they are seen to have identity. As Singer has it, to move us out of Stupid when it comes to malaria—a horrible disease that the World Health Organization, UNICEF and other bodies all agree is preventable—we need solutions. Not identity.

But identity continues to inform a lot of thinking. Of course, it informs the sort previously described which allows the personal experience of a world without racism to mean a world without racism. Of all the logical fallacies, recourse to anecdote is possibly my least favourite, even when it is enacted by people with whose broad political aims I agree. Unfortunately. Let's have a look at feminism, whose broad political aims I embrace but whose prominent methods, which I once enacted myself, I despise.

'The personal is political' is the mission statement of what was once, and disparagingly, known as 'identity politics'. The first recorded use of this phrase is found as the title of a 1969 essay by US feminist thinker Carol Hanisch. Honestly, as far as manifestos for a self-critical activism go, this short piece is surpassingly good. A lot of it is pretty Kantian in that it describes the ethics of the 'therapy' or 'consciousness-raising' women's groups of that time as being essential to better social outcomes. Hanisch certainly doesn't imply that all lived experience is evidence of politics. She wouldn't have been very patient with my assumption that the student council president's preference for Caitlin in her flouncy skirt was political. And she is at pains to point out that the therapeutic aspect of consciousness-raising is not for personal benefit but a sort of collective attempt at psychoanalysis.

'There are no personal solutions at this time. There is only collective action for a collective solution,' says Hanisch. What she advocates is not so much an opportunity to vent, or a game of Who's the Most Oppressed, but an ongoing process of ridding the unconscious mind of prejudice so it is better placed to find solutions. This is an un-Stupid idea. But, like a lot of good things from the un-Stupid era of the sixties, it was dulled by an interest in the self. A lot of thinkers from the sixties and seventies were using these therapeutic techniques with great caution. Even the Marxist Herbert Marcuse had a joke about the personal as political in an interview with *The Listener* magazine in 1978. 'Not every problem someone has with his girlfriend is necessarily due to the capitalist mode of production,' said Marcuse. This is pretty funny for a Marxist.

People often blame feminism for the prevalence of identity politics in conversation. The thing is, identity is used by a great many people of all political hues to describe the world. It is just used very obviously in feminism and I think this is worth examining, because here is a very clear case of the elevation of the personal story defeating the political aim.

This game of one-downmanship that proceeds along the lines of 'well, I'm a disabled Lesbian of Colour with a state school education and an emotionally unstable beagle' is, to be honest, quite easily heard in feminism. In fact, of late, that is much of what feminism has become; it's an activism still led by women of quite considerable privilege but decorated with the baubles of identity. I am quite conscious that this account of feminism is shocking and you may be horribly offended by the suggestion that the well-to-do women who continue to domi-nate this essentially Western way of thinking are engaging in tokenism when they 'welcome' 'allies' with 'diverse' 'identities'.

But this is my view of a movement—any movement—that is enamoured of the 'identities' of its participants. When identity itself becomes an object for trade and a source of reason, you get a lot of Stupid. As long as you have a multiply oppressed ally in your action group, or you at least say that you are supportive of 'identity', you are pretty much good to go.

And this is putatively good because Everyday People Have a Voice; because you have proximity to Personal Stories. But what happens when your 'allies' have a primary value as Personal Stories? Are they not then cheapened and edited as they would be on daytime television? Stories and descriptions of the identities with them cannot tell us everything. They can tell us only a little. And the more they are told—and need to be told within the fast and formulaic form of Upworthy or TED talks—the less that they say.

The failure to see the forest for a sentimental attachment to its trees is a widespread problem. This thinking has long been common in individuals who, for example, may refuse to acknowledge racism because they have no experience of it. This basic, deluded empiricism does not pass for reason either at the personal level or the political level. But now it functions both in people's atomised understanding of the world and in the mass reason of formerly very reasonable movements like feminism.

Look. If you don't think the basic tenets of feminism are reasonable—that the masculine matter of violence and the feminine matter of poverty need social redress—then you are a Stupid who can't read evidence. But you are also a Stupid if you think that a reasonable idea like feminism can be advanced through accounts of your 'lived experience', whether these occur as emotional stories on *Oprah* or as plots on a map of identity.

Identity is not a good guide to the world and not a way of thinking that allows clear reason. It is a way of elevating, and even celebrating, one's social coordinates. I mean, you may be a gender-queer low-vision something something, but what does this tell me other than that you are someone who can describe your identity within a world? Does it tell me about the world, which one or both of us have agreed we want to change?

How does plotting our place on a map of the world do anything but affirm the map? Shouldn't we be ripping up the map? We might both feel better in the short term for having explained ourselves, but perhaps we overestimate the power of mutual understanding. Perhaps all understanding can provide is a nice moment. 'I understand that your life is different from mine.' We have mutual understanding. To put this in the crudest terms, a master and his indentured servant could have mutual understanding, too. They might describe the condition of their lives to each other in emotional TED-talk detail. What happens then? Perhaps the servant feels like he has got something off his chest and the master feels a bit less guilty for having listened. Storytelling and understanding is perhaps most powerful in shutting us up for a bit.

Personally, I have had a gutful of this kind of navigation. It is taking me to Stupid Street, where they spend all day telling personal stories, each one with the same moral: stories can tell us everything.

Yousafzai knew that her personal story had diminished value. So she told someone else's. I don't like to think of individuals as 'inspiring', but when someone rips the map up like that, it's difficult not to use such an Upworthy term.

HR

4

'Nudge them all—God will know his own': Soft, hard and extreme paternalism

. . . it would be possible to create a national smart card system . . . Using data from the card system, a sliding scale of taxes could be introduced . . . The more alcohol you purchase, in any form, at any time within the statement period, the higher tax you pay . . . On a night out, drinks would become progressively more expensive. Loading up on alcohol before you go out wouldn't help, as the system would take into account the takeaway purchases you'd made earlier.

—Dan O'Keeffe, *The Conversation*, March 2013

For a country with a reputation as a bunch of boozers, Australia now has a strange attitude to alcohol. Official data shows that our per capita consumption has fallen by a third since 1975, and is now below, and often well below, that of most European countries. In 2013, levels of daily drinking were at their lowest since at least 1991, including a big drop since 2010; the number of Australians who don't drink at all has risen by more than half between 1991 and 2013 and is now at the highest levels ever recorded. Binge drinking by young people has fallen dramatically, and binge drinking by women is down too.

You'd think, on the strength of those outcomes, public health types would be well pleased. Not at all. Indeed, quite the opposite: Australia is in the midst of an anti-alcohol crusade that constantly warns of an 'epidemic' of alcohol abuse with massive 'social costs' that needs to be curbed by more regulation, more surveillance of consumers and price rises. Some of the highlights of this War on Alcohol include:

- The Australian Medical Association proposed raising the legal drinking age to twenty-five because neuroscience suggested that was when brain development halted.
- In 2008, the federal government pledged to end the 'epidemic' of binge drinking among young people, despite evidence that the incidence of binge drinking had been falling for a long time.
- A public health body called for alcohol consumption to be banned on school grounds because drinking at fetes or barbecues 'undermines the alcohol education programs for young people in schools'.
- Public health bodies now regularly warn about 'pre-loading', a sinister term they have developed to describe drinking alcohol at home prior to going out, which 'is causing alcohol-related crime, violence, hospitalisation, assault and death' and must be curbed by alcohol price rises.
- A government department proposed to force employers to discourage alcohol consumption on the basis that 'in some work settings, workers who do not normally drink in their

own leisure time may find it expected of them by their colleagues or workplace'.

However, the term 'War on Alcohol' may well be too narrow: other perceived sins are targeted as well. Various Australian academics, politicians and campaigners have also called for bans on and censorship of social media, bans on online apps, bans on supermarkets selling pain relief, bans on advertising of junk food, bans on soft drink and high-sugar products, bans on clothing that 'sexualises children', drug tests for everyone in the country using opioid pain relief, licensing of smokers and, as we saw at the start of this chapter, licensing and surveillance of drinkers to track their alcohol consumption.

This last idea has particular appeal to public health lobbyists because of its extendability: once in place, a universal monitoring system could be used to track and deter whatever is the subject of the most recent moral panic: the consumption of junk food and soft drinks, sugar, television, pharmaceuticals, video games, ringtones, pornography, hoodies and whatever music form or artist enjoyed by our feckless youth is currently considered unacceptably corrupting (we'll return to that).

Based on the proposals routinely floated by public health lobbyists, you might think Australia faced a major health crisis requiring urgent action. In fact, according to the World Health Organization, non-indigenous Australians are the equal fourth longest-lived people in the world (indigenous health outcomes are a very different matter). That's despite spending far less of its GDP on health than many other developed countries, despite its apparently shocking alcohol consumption, despite Australia's 'obesegenic society'.

Public health groups look to bridge this reality gap between the rude good health of non-indigenous Australians and their hysterical claims about alcohol consumption and diet by emphasising what Australians think about everyone else's lifestyle choices. Polling from public health bodies now regularly shows Australians reporting they themselves are drinking less, but they are more and more worried about how much everyone else is drinking—unsurprising, given they are constantly bombarded with claims about 'epidemics' of alcohol and obesity.

Paternalism in theory and practice

What drives these health-motivated interventions in Australia is the same thing that has driven many other forms of state-sponsored intervention in people's lives—paternalism: the conviction that you know what is best for others, and that that knowledge gives you the right to regulate and control others' behaviour to make their lives better, whether they want you to or not. It is one of history's most pervasive and damaging forms of Stupid.

There are numerous kinds of paternalism—most usefully, for our purposes, are those described as soft and hard paternalism. The soft–hard difference comes in two kinds. One relates to how far a paternalist will go to interfere with someone else. If I decide to play Russian roulette with a semi-automatic pistol, not realising it works differently from a revolver, a soft paternalist would intervene to stop me and make sure I was fully informed about the basics of firearms before letting me proceed; a hard paternalist would seize the weapon, or have me committed to a psych ward, because I have no right to take my own life.

But the more common soft–hard paternalism distinction is between *methods*: soft paternalism seeks to influence or 'nudge' its target's decision-making, but stops short of outright prohibition, which is reserved for hard paternalists, who simply prefer to ban things they don't like. Soft paternalism sometimes gets the oxymoron 'libertarian paternalism', the sort of term likely to infuriate both nanny-state types and rugged individualists.

The case against paternalism has been mounted by a succession of philosophers, starting with Locke (Spinoza as well, although less directly), followed by the likes of Kant, who argued that paternalism is innately hostile to the concept of human equality, and particularly John Stuart Mill, who formulated the classic argument against paternalism:

> . . . [T]he only purpose for which power can be rightfully exercised over any member of a civilized community, against his will, is to prevent harm to others. His own good, either physical or moral, is not a sufficient warrant. He cannot rightfully be compelled to do or forbear because it will be better for him to do so, because it will make him happier, because in the opinion of others, to do so would be wise, or even right . . . The only part of the conduct of anyone, for which he is amenable to society, is that which concerns others. In the part which merely concerns himself, his independence is of right, absolute, over himself. Over his own body-mind, the individual is sovereign.

Mill's most acute point was that individuals are inevitably the best judges of their own interests; there is no other party with more or even the same knowledge about what is best for that individual. Moreover, no other party, and particularly no government, shares the exact value system and priorities of an individual, however closely affiliated to them they may be. In Mill's famous examples, intervention in others' decisions about themselves was only justified in rare cases: a person could be prevented from selling themselves into slavery, as he would 'defeat his own case for liberty', or a pedestrian should be warned of an unsafe bridge—even if that necessitated force to ensure they were aware of it—but once they were aware of the danger, left to make their own decision about whether to cross or not.

Some arguments in favour of paternalism do stand up better than others. In particular, the argument that we are, in effect, multiple selves, and can make decisions that may be costly to our future selves, is a solid one, particularly if one's current self is making decisions based on insufficient information—information that would be available to a future self—or one is temporarily cognitively impaired. And as we see repeatedly elsewhere in this book, humans are pretty poor at making rational, evidence-based decisions. This reinforces the 'multiple selves' argument: over time, as a group of our multiple selves—like those episodes of *Doctor Who* in which different Doctors join forces—we might reach sensible decisions, but individual decisions are likely to be affected by a host of the sort of problems we identify in this book.

Against the multiple-selves argument, however, is the response that it is *exactly* our current decisions, for better and for worse, that make our future selves better; that we need the freedom to make poor decisions and mistakes in order to become wiser, and how we use our freedom is fundamental to how we develop as humans. A decision to undertake an activity that's risky either to our health or, perhaps, to our future income, like undertaking humanitarian work abroad, embracing political activism or climbing a mountain, may in fact significantly change and improve us as people even if these activities are, from a risk-averse point of view, ill-advised. Life, even the most anodyne life, must contain some risk, and how we manage and assess risk is one of the most important aspects of our characters and how we live.

That said, there are some forms of paternalism that all but the most hard-hearted libertarian would surely endorse. Permitting slavery, even voluntary slavery, is a straightforward case. So too depriving a drunk of their car keys. But the problem with those examples is that, once granted, they can logically be extended to other acts that might permanently reduce one's personal autonomy, such as preventing suicide or banning dangerous drugs—restrictions with which a great many people would have a problem.

Such shades-of-grey individual scenarios, however, are more games for philosophy students than practical guides. In the real world, paternalism is considerably wider, and Stupider, than people looking to have themselves enslaved or pedestrians wandering towards dodgy bridges. Australians live in a society riddled with paternalism. Like other Western countries, we have drug laws designed to minimise the personal harm from consuming some chemicals and plants, a form of Stupid that inflicts far more damage on society than that caused by their consumption. Drug laws restrain personal liberty, inflict a massive economic cost from law enforcement and criminal justice, and create a violent and destructive criminal culture. And it certainly doesn't stop at drugs: we have a range of limitations on gambling which are in effect competition restrictions maximising profits for approved operators. We retain a censorship system to stop adults from viewing materials deemed harmful to them. We have laws intended to prevent terminally ill people from receiving advice and assistance on euthanasia options. We have a costly consumption tax exemption for fresh food, designed to encourage low-income earners to eat more healthily.

Australia's paternalism, like that of other countries, is also remarkably inconsistent—we ban certain drugs but allow others that produce greater harms, for instance. And we're bizarrely *un*paternalistic about interfering in people's freedom posthumously: we allow people with certain illnesses to die and suffer because others are allowed to retain their healthy organs after death. Indeed, in Australia families can override the wishes of the dead who have indicated their desire to donate their organs—where's a little paternalism when organ donors need it?

As with other forms of Stupid, there are also hierarchies of paternalism, which—not coincidentally—closely resemble power structures within society. It is only a matter of years since Australian states had 'hard paternalism' based on sexual preference, while a variety of financially discriminatory practices against gay couples were only removed more recently. Our welfare policies are structured so that middle-income earners are given generous transfer payments by governments without even having to fill out forms to claim them, whereas low-income earners are subjected to schemes such as Work for the Dole and stringent reporting requirements, and Aboriginal Australians are subjected to income management.

We also have a gender-based hierarchy of paternalism: men are subjected to less intervention than women, who are forced to endure both hard and soft forms of paternalism in relation to their bodies. In particular, women are constantly pressured to moderate their behaviour and consumption of drugs because they have uteruses. Such paternalism infantilises women: in 2013, an Australian public health body ran a campaign to encourage men not to drink while their partners are pregnant, as if women are easily influenced into unhealthy behaviours by partners. And this gender-based paternalism hierarchy is at odds with the high correlation between having a penis and *poor* health outcomes, like dying younger and the likelihood of becoming a victim or perpetrator of violence or inflicting costs on society via the criminal justice system.

Paternalism is also, as the word suggests, particularly directed at young people. Despite falling levels of alcohol consumption, less violent crime and less binge drinking, the young men of Australia are the object of perennial lamentation about their out-of-control alcohol consumption (and consumption of *insert current object of media drug panic here*) fuelling an epidemic of violence, while young women are portrayed as binge drinkers constantly placing themselves at risk of sexual exploitation, or worse. This, of course, is an eternal cycle that each generation is doomed to repeat as the reckless, drug-abusing youth of today become the concerned parents of tomorrow, poised to criticise their offspring for the sins they committed to worse degree.

Discussions of paternalism are most commonly complicated by the fact that many ostensibly paternalistic actions by the state prevent an individual not merely from damaging themselves, but also from inflicting economic or social costs on others or the rest of the community, something which a state is entirely justified in preventing. Laws against drunk-driving, and police enforcement of them (for example, via random breath-testing) are now widely accepted, not merely because they reduce the numbers of drink-drivers who kill and injure themselves, but because they reduce the number of other motorists and pedestrians killed by drunks.

We also have laws requiring the wearing of seatbelts by vehicle occupants and helmets by bicycle riders. These are ostensibly aimed only at individuals, but in fact they reduce the broader costs of individuals' poor decision-making: if a driver decides to not wear a seatbelt or a cyclist prefers not to wear a helmet, the costs of a subsequent accident in terms of healthcare costs will be greater than if they had been better protected. Outside of a strict user-pays healthcare system, this means those additional costs will be borne by the rest of the community—so seatbelt and helmet laws are justified purely from an economic standpoint and on the basis that individuals don't have a right to inflict costs on the rest of their communities.

In a RonPaulistan libertarian utopia, the sort of place where men are men and bureaucrats are nervous, there could conceivably be a system in which you *may* elect not to wear a seatbelt, but in doing so agree to pay all healthcare costs beyond that which would have accrued if you had been wearing one. But such a system would be an administrative nightmare, and in any event what civilised society (well, outside the United States) would leave, say, a brain-injured non-seatbelt wearer who could not afford rehabilitation to rot? It's also hard to see how to apply such an arrangement when individual decisions contribute to a systemic cost, like higher crime and suicide levels across a whole society because of widespread gun ownership. Firearms have a form of network effect in which, no matter how safely and responsibly an individual weapon is used and stored, the greater the number of firearms in a community, the greater the number of firearm crimes and deaths.

Australia also has a compulsory superannuation system that forces all workers to save for their retirement. Unlike other forms of paternalism, there are significant medium- and long-term economic benefits from the large national savings pool generated by compulsory superannuation: Australia's one and a half trillion dollar-plus superannuation pool, for example, was an important factor in mitigating the effects of the global financial crisis on Australian financial institutions. Most particularly, compulsion (as opposed to the generous tax incentives that are also intended to encourage retirement saving) will provide a significant saving for future budgets as the population ages and there is less reliance on aged pensions than would otherwise be the case.

Another example is tobacco excise. The mere use of tobacco causes health problems, and unlike alcohol, which can be consumed in safe and indeed healthful doses, it has no offsetting health benefits for the range of illnesses it inflicts. Tobacco users therefore inflict greater costs on the healthcare system than they otherwise would. It is thus not paternalism to charge smokers a tax on tobacco sufficient to cover the significant extra costs they impose on the health system (as happens in Australia); nor is it paternalism to make smokers puff away from anyone who may breathe in second-hand smoke, especially children. But any additional tax beyond that level, or restrictions such as curbing advertising, retailing and packaging, are mere revenue-raising and a form of paternalism, imposed purely because society believes it can make a better decision about tobacco consumption than individuals.

The extent to which you can apply this argument, however, can be difficult, because calculating net social impacts of behaviour is complex. Opponents of compulsory bicycle helmets, for example, argue that requiring helmets reduces the incidence of cycling, and thereby reduces the overall health of the population, a cost that may be sufficient to offset the benefits of reduced head trauma. Such calculations of the social costs of an activity targeted by paternalists forms an increasing part of campaigns to regulate certain behaviours, because policymakers are more likely to accept the need to override individual decisions on the basis that economic welfare will thereby be improved than if paternalists simply argue that they don't like particular activities.

What never features in estimates of costs is the harm from interfering in people's rights—that is, the social costs of Stupid. Merely because the infringement of individual rights is a nebulous kind of wrong, one hard to pin down or adequately cost, doesn't mean there aren't real-world consequences. Soft paternalism in time can lead to hard paternalism, as has happened with tobacco, which is now heavily restricted and which could plausibly be banned once consumption rates drop into single digits; the demonisation of alcohol and junk food by public health lobbyists has the same goal of creating a climate for ever greater restrictions. And as the array of proposals put forward by public health lobbyists suggests, they view surveillance and infringement of privacy as a small price to pay for the perceived benefits of imposing their own priorities on people.

History's perennial paternalists

This connection between the tools of governmental control—surveillance and curbing of basic rights like privacy—and paternalism is no accident. The longer history of paternalism shows how fundamentally it is a tool of social and political control as much as an expression of communal interest in the individual targeted.

For example, religious persecution is mostly a form of paternalism. That's not to dismiss the role that other motivations, such as old-fashioned bigotry, play. But religious persecution in Western cultures has been persistently justified by the conviction that a heretic or non-believer was in danger not of poor health outcomes but of disastrous spiritual outcomes, as they faced eternal damnation because of their views. If you actually believe those sorts of superstitions, religious persecution is entirely logical. Forget John Stuart Mill's example in which a damaged bridge risks a pedestrian's life—one's physical existence is nothing compared to an eternity of hellfire, and anything in this world is justified in saving your soul in the next.

As with smoking or gambling or other modern sins, the role of external agencies is also important in religious paternalism—Satan, like tobacco companies or advertising agencies, was said to possess remarkable powers of manipulation and persuasion that further justified taking action to prevent his misleading weak human minds (noting that paternalists naturally possess superhuman powers of resistance to the wiles of Satan and marketing companies).*

Moreover, such people risk leading *others* to damnation as well as themselves; that is, there was believed to be a spiritual form of social cost in allowing heretics to communicate with others. It's hard to say what those social costs of heresy would be without the appropriate economic modelling, but they are probably $\$\infty$, given Hell is forever, which, even using Net Present Value, is an awfully long time.

---

* Similar logic is to be found in the warning of the head of the Australian Security Intelligence Organisation that the internet allowed 'unfettered ideas' to radicalise people in their 'lounge rooms', conjuring a nightmare scenario in which you might be relaxing watching television or enjoying some time with your family, when you'd suddenly be transformed into a jihadist ready to wage war on the unbeliever.

By such logic, torturing heretics is a mere nudge in the right direction; outright killing, a kind of spiritual public health measure, a religious quarantine. Killing an unrepentant heretic was unfortunate, as it would dispatch them to Hell, but better that than their taking others to Hell with them. See the logic?

Now, it's incorrect to suggest the Christians invented the killing-heretics-as-spiritual-sanitation form of Stupid; recorded history gives that honour to the Greeks, although one imagines the invention of religious persecution was contemporaneous with the invention of religion. But it was the Greeks from whose philosophical traditions the Christians took so much. Socrates was condemned to death by the Athenians for both impiety and 'corrupting the minds of Athenian youth'—the first recorded use of what would become a favoured paternalist justification, protecting the kids. On the other hand, Roman persecution of Christians appears to have been motivated mostly by reasons of state: Christianity was, unlike Judaism, a new, non-traditional superstition, and adherents of other superstitions like Jews and pagans strongly resented them, threatening the *pax Romana*.

But institutionalised persecution didn't receive a full-blown treatment until Christians were able to take over the Roman state apparatus and use it themselves. Even key Christian thinkers who still get good press centuries later, like St Augustine, were enthusiasts for the spiritual equivalent of hard paternalism. 'It is wonderful how he who entered the service of the gospel in the first instance under the compulsion of bodily punishment, afterwards labored more in the gospel than all they who were called by word only,' Augustine declared in the fifth century (and don't you love his *New York Times*–like euphemism for torture?).

But Augustine's 'Lord, persecute me, but not yet' approach was too timid for some, such as thirteenth-century cleric Arnaud Amalric. When faced with the vexing problem of sorting out Catholics from Cathars during a Crusade in 1209 (for those playing at home, the primary difference is believing Satan was an evil version of God), Amalric declared, 'Kill them all, God will know his own,' a mentality that suggests, had he been born several centuries later, he might have become one of those serial killers the media ends up inventing an exotic name for, or, at least, a senior Bush Administration official.

It was in response to the Cathars that the Inquisition was first established by the Catholic Church; it survived, in different countries and in various forms, into the nineteenth century as one of the premier organs of Stupid. The last victim of the Spanish Inquisition was a schoolteacher executed for teaching deism in 1826, by which time the United States had had four presidents who were deists. By the time of its abolition, the Spanish Inquisition could look back on a job well done—it had overseen the execution of at least three to five thousand people and the condemnation of hundreds of thousands more, a huge number of them Jews or Jewish converts. (Forced conversions of Jews and Muslims was common as Christian rule was re-established on the Iberian peninsula up to the end of the fifteenth century.)

But the Catholic Church's zero-tolerance approach to heterodoxy didn't always work, and heresies of one kind and another routinely cropped up around Europe. Even as Martin Luther was indulging himself by vandalising the door of a Wittenberg church, there persisted in England a sect called the Lollards (chiefly celebrated today as the first internet meme) with a sort of Central European subsidiary called the Hussites.*

By that stage, however, the Church had a new problem, and it ushered in a new era of paternalism. In an earlier chapter, we looked in detail at the role of printing in the schism between reason and emotion in the European mind after 1500. But printing was also rocket fuel for paternalism. The medieval Church didn't have a problem with books, beyond the dearth of them—it was difficult enough storing and distributing them and making correct copies of key sources for scholars. The arrival of printing fundamentally changed that, making the sheer number of books a problem, because books could spread ideas. While the Church and individual rulers had previously suppressed certain inconvenient sacred texts or ones judged inauthentic, the role of printing in the spread of Reform ideas prompted the beginnings of modern literary censorship. From the 1520s, national Catholic churches began issuing indices of banned books, and the Vatican itself issued its first *Index Librorum Prohibitorum* in the 1550s.

Such lists only had moral force; it was secular rulers who ultimately implemented censorship. In England, Henry VIII, whose outcomes-oriented take on religion meant the state church varied depending on whom he wanted to marry and how he was faring financially, decided to add a particular entry to the list of banned books in 1543: the Bible itself.

---

* Named after Jan Huss, who was executed by the Church after being given a promise of safe conduct to the Council of Constance—promises to a heretic didn't need to be kept, it was decided. That turned out to be probably the most expensive broken promise in history, resulting in fifteen years of war in Czech lands, the complete desolation of Bohemia and the Church forced to accepted the Hussites until the Reformation overtook events in the sixteenth century.

> Many arrogant and ignorant persons had taken upon them not only to preach, teach, and set forth the same by words, sermons, and disputations, but also by printed books, ballads, plays, rhymes, songs and other fancies, subtly to instruct the people, and especially the youth of the kingdom,* otherwise than the Scripture ought to be taught.

Thus, in one of the great moments of Stupid, to protect Christianity, Henry banned reading and discussing the Bible, despite funding and distributing an English Bible himself just two years previously.

Individual English translations of the Good Book had been banned before, but now reading any Bible was outright banned by the *Act for the Advancement of True Religion*—banned, that is, if you weren't part of the ruling elite, because this was another example of paternalism with a hierarchy. 'Noblemen and gentlemen' and 'noble and gentle women' were permitted to read the Bible. For the lower orders, the penalty was one month in prison for reading it, aloud or silent, in public or private. Similarly, anyone who publicly discussed the Bible could be locked up for a month.

How many people were prosecuted for having a quick squiz at Genesis or reading the Lord's Prayer is unknown; it was unlikely to have been very many; within four years Henry was dead, but his example of absurd, and hierarchical, paternalism would live on. Governments naturally banned more than religious books. Early modern governments understood the threat posed by the new technology of printing, and controlled it through printing licences and copyright regulation. The Stationers' Company became the official monopolist for printing in England, and as

---

* There are the kids again!

part of that deal supported the Tudors' censorship regime; in the 1750s, the Parlement of Paris condemned Denis Diderot's *Encyclopedié*, demanded it be submitted to theologians for approval and revoked its copyright protection, which meant the work, even though it was still published, was instantly pirated, leading to losses by its publishers. (We'll come back to the Stationers, who demonstrated one of the eternal truths of Stupid: that the copyright industry will always support censorship and suppression in media.)

We encountered Diderot earlier as, eventually, a radical *philosophe*. Diderot had been briefly jailed for his published views on religion as a young man. He was also one of the early—if not the earliest—observers to note what we now call the Streisand effect, pointing out that censorship 'encourages the ideas it opposes through the very violence of its prohibition'. A more sensible approach, he suggested, would be to allow bad ideas to be publicly aired and ridiculed—another idea that is still with us centuries later. Diderot's case was helped by the remarkable grabquote-laden blurb for the *Encyclopedié* issued by an angry Pope Clement XIII when it was added to the *Index Librorum Prohibitorum*:

> The said book is impious, scandalous, bold, and full of blasphemies and calumnies against the Christian religion. These volumes are so much more dangerous and reprehensible as they are written in French and in the most seductive style. The author of this book, who has the boldness to sign his name to it, should be arrested as soon as possible.

Putting to one side the idea of an encyclopaedia being written in a seductive style, if anything, the Streisand effect was a greater danger in early modern Europe than in the twentieth century. Prominent politicians, writers and officials kept up a high level of correspondence with each other, affording an alternative means of circulating ideas beyond books alone. Enlightenment readerships were smaller and often confined to a well-connected elite—but that meant they knew which books were being censored and banned, and often circulated copies among themselves, including across national boundaries, to see what the fuss was about. In particular, scholarly texts of no interest beyond academics risked being widely circulated if they became the subject of government censorship: Spinoza was a particular target of Enlightenment censors, and considered so dangerous that even works *criticising* his ideas were banned in parts of Germany—which of course merely led to their dissemination well beyond the academic elites who would have otherwise read them. Perhaps the Streisand effect should be renamed for the Dutch Jewish lens grinder/philosopher.

Moreover, the scholars and bureaucrats who implemented censorship policies were members of the same elites, often-times forced to balance implementation of official policies with personal, well-informed views. The *Encyclopedié*, for example, was greatly helped by the indulgence of Malesherbes, Louis XV's chief censor, who supported the project and many other officially banned books and often gave censored publishers advance notice of his own raids.

Nonetheless, the most effective ways for controversial authors to evade the personal consequences of censorship in early modern Europe was either to await the arrival of a friend-lier regime—John Locke published his major political works after returning to England in the wake of William of Orange's invasion, which drove out the Catholic James II—or to die: much of Diderot's non-*Encyclopedié* work and Spinoza's most significant treatise, which influenced generations of scholars and alarmed governments across Europe, were published after their deaths.

While Diderot was in prison for his views on religion, London was undergoing the first drug panic in history. Mid-eighteenth-century British governments, spurred by an outraged upper class (which voraciously consumed alcohol itself), launched an assault on gin consumption among poorer English people, which had risen dramatically off the back of trade protectionism, other forms of paternalism (heavy beer taxes) and inept regulation. The poor, British elites felt, drank too much and didn't work hard enough. Attempts to regulate and tax gin out of the reach of poorer people were, it was felt, justified not merely by moral righteousness but on economic grounds: consumption of gin caused poverty and idleness in an economy struggling to compete with its European rivals, as well as fuelling riots and crime and degrading Britain's military capacity.

As with twenty-first-century public health moralising—and, for that matter, Stupid generally—the evidentiary basis for the campaign against gin was flawed: consumption of gin dramatically increased up to the 1750s, but despite a rapidly growing population, London's crime rate per capita remained about the same. And just as even the smallest level of drinking by pregnant women is now seen as bordering on criminal behaviour, gin was said to damage the capacity of English women to produce the healthy children required by a growing imperial power competing against continental powers such as France. But even contemporaries questioned the demonising of gin, pointing out that social conditions in London and the rioting of a growing lower class had more to do with degrading poverty and wretched living conditions than alcohol.

Alcohol isn't the only paternalistic obsession that keeps coming around again and again despite the passage of centuries. The wave of Stupid engendered by the arrival of the new medium of the printed book was replicated repeatedly as new media emerged in the twentieth and twenty-first centuries. Catholic groups led the charge against the morality of movies in the United States in the 1920s (partly because a number of studios were headed by Jews) and the result was over thirty years of self-censorship by Hollywood. Of particular concern for movie censors was—wait for it—the impact of movies on children, whose 'sacred . . . clean, virgin . . . unmarked' minds might be corrupted by films, although early efforts to find any evidence for this foundered. There was also evidence, suppressed at the time, of a Mae West effect: boycotts by the Catholic Legion of Decency increased ticket sales for controversial films. But even in the 1920s, complaints about films were already well-established—the Women's Christian Temperance Union had lamented the effect of films on youth as early as 1906, and in 1914 blamed them for violence and delinquency.

The new technology of radio, too, was seen as damaging fragile young minds, discouraging healthy activities like reading, and driving children to delinquency through exposure to radio serials like *The Shadow*. Who knew what evil lurked in the hearts of men? Paternalists knew—despite, yet again, the dearth of evidence of any negative impacts. Then it was television's turn to desensitise children, encourage violence and undermine morality: by the 1970s an entire academic industry existed dedicated to charting the impacts of television on children, while morals campaigners like Mary Whitehouse in the UK demanded censorship of sex and violence on the box. Alas, the evidence for the negative impacts of television, like that for radio and movies, was hard to track down.*

Meantime, music had become the preferred target for hand-wringers. Indeed, music had long been the target of Stupid: the waltz had caused a remarkable scandal in the early nineteenth century, when it was regarded as indecent and fit only for prostitutes and adulteresses. First African American music in the 1950s (insert racist stereotyping *here*), then white versions thereof, then drug and anti-war songs in the 1960s, all caused alarm among concerned paternalists, until rap and hip-hop generated full-blown moral panics in the 1980s and 1990s. The American Academy of Pediatrics mused in 1996 that there were few studies of the impact of explicit lyrics in 'heavy metal' and 'gangsta rap', and no link proven between sexually explicit or violent lyrics and adverse behavioural effects. This was partly because, the study found, many teenagers had no idea what the lyrics of their favourite songs were—although sadly the opportunity for a doctoral thesis on the link between mondegreens and youth crime doesn't appear to have been taken up. Eighties hair metal band Judas Priest even found themselves in court in 1990 facing claims their alleged backmasked message of 'do it, do it, do it' in a song had driven two men to attempt suicide.

And by that stage, music was already losing its menace to video games, first in arcade form (remember them?) and later on home consoles, which became the new bogey, encouraging (yes) delinquency and, later, warping young minds with sex and violence.

---

* Older readers might remember the seventies factoid that 'the average American child will have watched 8000 murders on television by the age of twelve'.

Paternalism goes online

Printing, movies, radio, music and TV all prompted paternalist responses; in fact, about the only new communications technology that didn't induce Stupid was the fax. But the internet was like all of these rolled into one, unleashing a new drive for censorship from people concerned about the dire impacts of new forms of content delivery. And while modern Henry VIIIs have sought to censor, block or otherwise disrupt the internet outright because of its potential to foster political disruption, any number of paternalists have blamed the internet for social problems as well. Handily, however, the internet only became widely used in the 1990s, so we have plenty of data to measure the alleged impacts of the nefarious series of tubes on society.

Let's take suicide, for example, and especially youth suicide. The internet—presumably replacing the collected works of Judas Priest—is often held to be a key cause of suicide among young people. It used to be online 'death pacts' and 'suicide websites' that were driving people, and especially our vulnerable youth, to kill themselves. These days that's been replaced by cyberbullying, and more latterly the threat of 'trolls', phenomena held to regularly drive young people to take their lives. Indeed, a small 'cybersafety' industry has grown up in Australia that makes money from purporting to advise schools, governments and professional associations about online bullying, child cybersafety and moral panics like teen sexting.

Now, true, many young people have, indeed, tragically, taken their lives in response to bullying, online and off. But is the problem getting worse? What does the data tell us?

In Australia, the overall suicide rate has fallen in the last twenty years.* In 1996, the overall death rate from suicide was 13 per 100,000 people. In 2011, it was 11.2 per 100,000. The rate has fallen particularly for men, from 21 to below 17 per 100,000. The death rate among males under thirty has also fallen significantly, by between a quarter and a third, since 2002—despite media claims that suicide is a 'cultural epidemic' among young men; in 2012, the teenage male suicide rate reached an eight-year low and was at the second-lowest level since the 1990s.

True, the decline isn't consistent—there's been no fall in suicide rates among indigenous people since 2001; some states have fallen faster than others, and there has been a rise in recent years in the suicide rate of teenage girls, traditionally the demographic least likely to take their own lives. But whatever the specific causes of the overall fall in the number of people taking their lives, it has coincided with the spread of the internet.

Perhaps Australia is unusual. How about the United States? The overall suicide rate in the US is about where it was in 1996, and below where it was in 1991, at around 14 deaths for 100,000 people. Suicide among American ten- to twenty-four-year-olds peaked in 1994 and is well below that level now. Youth suicide has also fallen significantly in the UK since the 1990s, as it has for people over sixty. Overall, the suicide rate was 12.4 in 1995 in the UK compared to 11.8 in 2011.

But if there's little evidence for a connection between the internet and rising suicide rates, what about the supposedly degrading effects of pornography, which is suddenly far more

---

* The Australian Bureau of Statistics has expressed concern about the accuracy of suicide statistics, in particular those from before 2007, but the issue relates to underreporting. That is, the likely level of suicide was even higher in the 1990s and early 2000s compared to now.

available than in the analogue era, when it required a trip to the local newsagent or, if harder stuff was your fancy, actual sex shops? There are plenty ready to declare that today's 'epidemic*' of pornography, and men with a 'porn addiction', leads to rape, whether they're speaking from a feminist perspective, or a religious perspective. Others claim it is warping the minds of young men and causing problems in their relationships. Attacks on internet pornography often combine these themes and other tropes of paternalism, although it is rare to find as many crammed into one article as in a March 2014 piece, 'Campus rape culture linked to online porn', from Canada's *Western Catholic Reporter*, about 'the widespread availability of increasingly violent and degrading pornography called Gonzo porn on the Internet':

> Catholic therapist Peter Kleponis, who specializes in men's issues and porn-addiction recovery, said in an interview that he sees a 'big relationship' between pornography and the 'violent, sexual aggression we see among young men today . . .
>
> 'Now kids have access not only through computers, but through smart phones, tablets and various gaming systems such as Xboxes, PlayStations and Wiis . . .
>
> '. . . men are learning it's "okay to get a woman drunk and get a bunch of guys together to rape her" . . .
>
> Kleponis called porn 'the new drug of choice' . . . that 'it can easily come and take your life without your even knowing it . . . It's the new crack cocaine . . .' Except unlike crack, with porn there are no 'gateway drugs' gradually leading to it. First time exposure is generally to hard-core deviant porn.

---

* The reader will have noted that 'epidemic' is a recurring word in paternalist-speak

And some governments actually believe this: the UK govern-ment recently went so far as to ban online rape depictions as part of its (entirely useless) internet filtering scheme, which will at least have the fortunate consequence of preventing the online distribution of *Fifty Shades of Grey*.

But the data doesn't support claims about the impact of online pornography. Putting aside the issue of reporting rates, the sexual assault rate in Australia in 2012 was 80 per 100,000 people, roughly the same as the rate in 2000, of 85, and about the same as the rate of 79 in 1996. In the United States, sexual assaults on women declined by more than half between 1994 and 2010.*

Has pornography led to unhappier relationships? It's a hard claim to prove or disprove. For what it's worth, the Australian divorce rate has been declining since 1996 (and at a much faster rate than the decline in number of marriages); the US divorce rate has been declining since the 1990s and more broadly since the 1970s, has been declining since the early noughties in the UK and has been relatively stable in Canada for the last decade.

Whatever the impacts of the internet on Western societies, there is little evidence that it has prompted a rise in suicide, or that the 'porn epidemic'—and access to more graphic and exotic kinds of pornography—has had any impact on sexual assault levels or relationships; at the very least, those who would censor, filter, block or otherwise play nanny to the internet have to demonstrate how falls, or even bigger falls, in suicide and sexual assaults and divorces would have occurred but for the negative impact of the internet.

---

* Again, this is unlikely to be uniform—women from indigenous backgrounds, women with disabilities and women with abusive partners are more likely to suffer sexual abuse.

A key characteristic of this form of Stupid, whether it's focused on reading the Bible, gin, waltzing, silent movies or rap music, is profound historical ignorance. Any attempt to link one particular phenomenon to crime inevitably founders on the fact that Western societies are dramatically less violent now than historically. The Australian Bureau of Statistics concluded that homicide in twentieth-century Australia was significantly lower than in the nineteenth century (before, presumably, Aboriginal victims of white settlement are counted as well). Estimates of the US homicide rate show it has fallen by more than half since the mid-nineteenth century and is continuing to fall, notwithstanding government-engineered surges in homicide rates caused by paternalism (Prohibition and crack cocaine) in the twentieth century. Similarly, European data shows big falls in homicide rates compared to earlier centuries. But data, of course, is no match for anecdotes: *you* might be able to point to long-term declines in rates of violent crime, but *I* know some guy who got punched when he was out drinking one night, which demonstrates how the world is going to hell in a handcart and something must be done about gin/video games/heavy metal/waltzing/reading the Old Testament.

Comparing not merely drug laws but health-motivated 'soft paternalism' to religious persecution and censorship may seem a stretch to nanny-state types, but while differing in methods, all reflect the same logic: that the powerful have both the superior knowledge and the right to make decisions for the welfare of the less powerful, and to impose those decisions on them or use resources to seek to influence them in the desired direction.

This is why the same paternalist targets, themes and rhetoric repeat throughout history in a recurring cycle of Stupid. The impetus to paternalism is the vehicle for very old elite attitudes toward 'sin' behaviours—sex, drinking and other drugs, bad diets, popular entertainment and gambling. It is always is the lower classes and less powerful who are the target of paternalism while elites are left alone; threats are hyped to justify dramatic action; the need to protect children is always invoked; remarkable powers of manipulation are attributed to external agencies; serious impacts (now called 'social costs') are asserted without evidence; women and the young are targeted for special restriction. And in their rhetoric, modern-day public health advocates are hard to differentiate from the panicked middle classes of Hanoverian England; moralists who want to censor the internet are indistinguishable from the groups who railed at silent movies; anti-pornography campaigners hard to tell apart from the Athenians who executed Socrates.

Part of the impetus for paternalism now comes from progressives, who since the success of liberal economics in the 1980s and 1990s have embraced forms of paternalism as the primary tool of social engineering. Having, in effect, conceded the fight on basic economics in favour of liberal capitalism, sections of the left now look to achieve progressive goals not through economic reforms to restore the sort of communitarian government control lost with the economic reforms of the 1980s, but through changing the 'choice architecture' people face in consumption decisions. Rather than wages and price fixing, tariff barriers, high taxation and a fixed currency, we have price signals, regulation and 'nudge' policies that seek to amplify the impact of social norms on people in deciding how they spend their money and time.

This was vividly demonstrated in a much-cited 2013 *Lancet* paper, 'Profits and pandemics: Prevention of harmful effects of tobacco, alcohol, and ultra-processed food and drink industries', by some of Australia's most senior public health figures. The paper argued that large corporations were in effect deadly viruses themselves:

> The term industrial epidemic has been used to describe health harms associated with various goods including tobacco, alcohol, vinyl chloride, asbestos, cars, and the food and drink industries. In industrial epidemics, the vectors of spread are not biological agents, but transnational corporations. Unlike infectious disease epidemics, however, these corporate disease vectors implement sophisticated campaigns to undermine public health interventions.

This is an elegant example not merely of how paternalism refracts an economic tradition hostile to liberal capitalism, but of the now-common technique of pathologising what paternalism opposes. Thus, drinking at home becomes 'pre-loading'; pornography becomes a 'sexual addiction' and corporations become vast, world-straddling disease vectors that, like a good B-movie villain, fight back against the plucky heroes trying to save humanity.

This has the effect of reasserting the role of the state back into regulating the economic choices of low-income citizens that liberal capitalism withdrew it from, albeit via different, more subtle mechanisms. Low-income earners are perceived by paternalists to be less capable of making informed, competent decisions about their consumption than paternalist decision-makers in academia and government. In particular, they are seen as more prone to being manipulated by corporate interests—poorer Australians, apparently, are easily swayed into becoming addicted to nicotine, they're gulls for the clubs industry which wants them to throw away their money on poker machines, they're prone to drinking too much because of the alcohol industry's incessant advertising, they look at the 'crack cocaine' of online pornography too much and they eat too much bad food sold by multinational companies. Liberal capitalism has delivered greater wealth even for low-income earners compared to two and three decades ago, and lifespans continue to increase, but, like their ancestral nanny statists warning about the wiles of Satan, paternalists believe low-income earners are incapable of navigating liberal capitalism for themselves, that they are unable to resist the dark arts of the marketing industry and thus are in need of a forceful hand to guide them in how they spend their income.

But in arguing that we should construct 'choice architecture' to encourage people to be healthy, happy participants in capitalist society, maximising their productivity and capacity to consume and, in the case of women, bear the next generation of healthy workers and consumers, progressive social engineers turn out to closely resemble conservative policymakers. Much of the economic agenda of the right in Australia has been based on transforming low-income workers into aspirational, shareholding, private education-and-healthcare small business owners. They have been offered financial incentives to have their children schooled privately and to use private health care; 'mum and dad' investors were encouraged to acquire shares in major government privatisations; the taxation system was structured to encourage them to shift from being employees to 'independent contractors'; they were encouraged to shift from having mere employment-based superannuation into 'wealth management'. At the same time, the left wanted to encourage them, via regulation and 'nudging', to be healthy consumers who disdain the right sins (drugs, gambling, bad food), live long, economically productive lives, bear children the right way and then nurture them properly.

For both sides, inside every working-class person is a bourgeois just like them that needs to be set free. As a consequence of their joint efforts, the average human type will rise to the heights of a healthy small business owner, a nonagenarian self-funded retiree, or a McMansion resident with a vegie patch.

And above this ridge, new peaks of Stupidity will rise.

BK

5

The inflexible Safe Space: The injurious yoga class of the mind

Once, I had an epiphany in yoga class. It was not spiritual. It was not transcendent. It had nothing to do with the downward dog. In fact, it happened when I was upright in the foyer and it, like me at the time, was pretty straightforward: *Someone needs to tell this place it's Stupid.*

Someone did, as things turned out.

Yes. I am going to tell you a Powerful Personal Story of exactly the kind we insisted it was Stupid to tell in our third chapter on the negative Stupid of positive storytelling.

What was it I said? Something about how the Inspiring Journey of the TED talk and personal myth is now so necessary to the communication of a thought that all thoughts must become personal stories. Something about how the pleasure of crying and laughing along to a story is now accepted and *demanded* as the only effective means to receive an idea. Something about how the need to laugh, cry and identify with

This One Video That Will Change Everything You Know About Disabled Kids Forever actually crushes the possibility of difficult thought. Anything that does not fit the parameters of a Teachable Moment is considered surplus and has no value and now the Oprahfication of wisdom is so complete that big ideas are cut down to shareable stories that can say nothing more than 'the individual is so important'.

Things haven't changed since we read that chapter. It is still the case that our new custom of demanding a personal story—and this need is reflected in the now common use of the word 'narrative' to describe even political campaigns—is producing Stupid. The well-written form of *This American Life* might convince us of its depth and universality, but it is actually feeding our long-held hunger for the low light of false enlightenment. And so My Powerful Story—which actually happens to be about a seriously ill friend who Beat the Odds and Changed Things For the Better—is just another form of narrated chicanery.

Well. Yes. In one sense, it kind of is a bit shit of me. I will reveal some Personal Details about my own adolescence and some Inspiring Stories You Won't Believe about my friend at a yoga class. But I do so not only because they use the emotional shorthand of this Stupid storytelling age. I do so because our stories were, as it turned out, at odds with a world of teachable moments. And I do so to reveal the hypocrisy of the Safe Space that demands safe, edited and acceptable stories. Our stories were rejected. They were surplus and valueless in their lack of teachable moments.

I do not wish to claim these stories, or any stories, have intrinsic value. But I do want to show how a story, or an idea, that threatens the order of things is easily rejected. And I want to talk about how the safe story is also a sanitised one.

My friend Kylie has one of the most important-sounding diseases of which I've ever heard. As far as ailment names go, multifocal motor neuropathy, or MMN, is pretty serious. Not as serious as cancer, but pretty close—and even closer at the time of her diagnosis, which preceded by a year or two the wide availability of blood-based treatments on which MMN patients now depend.

Once, MMN was a near-guarantee of paralysis; its flares were treated with steroids and its progression was the business of fate, not of medicine. I saw how Kylie's motor nerves had begun to deteriorate when we went to *The Age* Christmas party together: my glamorous, pint-sized friend was unable to wear her heels.

'The foot-droop I can take,' she said. 'But going to a party in flats is too much.'

Kylie is now, as she long has been, a bright and stubborn journalist, and so her approach to the management of a potentially disabling illness was bright and stubborn. She was informed less by positive thinking and much, much more by evidence-based medicine. Kylie was moved by a need for outcomes and these she pursued with the bolshy expertise that serves good hacks who like good heels so well. That she did this while falling over, gripping on to hand rails and getting stuck while crossing our city's tram lines lent real grace to her scholarship.

A year or so after Kylie's diagnosis, she was given a treatment that restored her to strappy sandals within a month. It was one of those research miracles that makes you want to hug anyone in a white coat. But access to the treatment was quickly dropped in a bureaucratic toilet. The blood supply needed to produce the modifying drug had been cut off due to institutional Stupidity. She cried a bit and then she acted. Kylie became something of a lay immunologist; she campaigned in the media and lobbied government to open up the blood lines. And she didn't stop until the supply for her own and other immune diseases were flowing.

But Kylie's tenacity is hardly my point. Who am I, Deepak, and what is this, A Story of the Power of One? No. It's a story, more or less, about Kylie's bung foot and what happened to it at yoga class. (It's also a reminder that you should give blood. Seriously. People are depending on that stuff.) But before we get to the yoga class, I need to assure you that Kylie is a very reasonable person. I do this to provide some mooring for a story which takes place in an ocean of woo; in a batty yoga class where I, in fact, am the star nutty mariner. Call me Ishmael. I made the booking for the Bikram class. Yes. It was me.

There was a time I found shelter in 'holistic' (read: unscientific and flattering) 'healing' (read: rip-off bollocks with a whale-call soundtrack). There was a period I spent a lot of time in 'spaces' described as 'safe'. In fact, if you care to check my youthful oeuvre, you might even find me using the term 'Western medicine'. And you could, if you looked hard, find me publicly defending the right to a 'safe space' for women at Sydney University. I badgered the union for allocation of a Women's Room that, I can tell you with absolute and embarrassed certainty, was frequented by no more than a dozen women. All of whom were my friends. Three of whom I had sex with. In the 'safe space'.

Once, I sought 'safe spaces'.

Is it any wonder Bernard Keane used to anonymously troll me on a nasty blog calling me (although he denies this) 'The most intellectually empty cunt to emerge from Canberra since Margaret Reid'?

He had a point. I recently looked at an old book I had written which contained a dreadful chapter recommending cranberry juice for the treatment of bladder infection. Like many people who frequented the 'safe space' of alternative medicine, where queries about scientific method are forbidden because UNSAFE, I believed that fruit drink could save you from renal failure. This canard was so widespread that the US National Institute of Health reviewed all studies on the effectiveness of cranberry juice as a prophylactic to urinary tract infection in women and found that it tasted very nice with vodka. A 2012 meta-analysis found that cranberry products 'cannot currently be recommended for the prevention of UTIs'.

The safe space of my naturopath's suite, where faith and acceptance were privileged over science and deduction, was not only Stupid but unsafe.

Safe space. If it is not a safe space, then it should have a 'trigger warning'.

About ten years ago, I began seeing the term 'trigger warning' at the beginning of news stories. At first glance, this just looked like a new version of the old courtesy that gave you warning of carnage in case you were a 'sensitive viewer'. There is no problem with this old technique at all; in some cases, it is just plain evil not to offer your audience the chance to look away. Take, for example, the case of suicide. In Australia, the matter of suicide has been studied with some care and it has been found that the description of a suicide—its method, its perceived 'causes', its location—causes a spike in suicides in the weeks following its report. The thing called 'suicide contagion' is real and measurable and the public discussion of suicide should be appended, if not preceded by, a warning that this discussion might be troubling and here is the number you call if you'd like to get help.

That kind of 'trigger warning' is good sense. There are other cautionary notes we see in the electronic culture that also seem utilitarian. Pictures of war or detailed descriptions of pain should, if they need to be made at all, continue to have their extreme violence heralded. There are some stories so brutal that we can assume their public telling may not be in the best interests of some of the people subject to their unfolding. This is a simple practical measure. Your children might be watching the news with you when Chelsea Manning's video of atrocity in Iraq airs. You deserve the chance to change the channel or get them out of the room. Our most vulnerable citizens are surely entitled to the chance to avoid the extreme. But now some of our most powerful citizens are demanding a safe space as well.

In 2014, student politicians at the University of California passed a resolution to institute mandatory trigger warnings on class material. It was reported that a student who had previously been a victim of sexual assault felt threatened by the screening of a video that referenced this crime. The student felt that the stress triggered by this viewing not only compounded her distress but impeded her ability to learn.

In 2013, staff at Oberlin College, Ohio, were advised that potentially 'triggering' material should be removed from the syllabus. Again, it was held that depictions of injustice, especially those which could potentially remind students of the 'racism, classism, sexism, heterosexism, cissexism, ableism, and other issues of privilege and oppression' to which they may have previously been subject, was an impediment to learning.

These may be sincere attempts to protect the right of the socially maligned to learn. They could also turn out to be an inadvertent attack on the possibility of learning. And, perversely, learning, in particular, about social injustice. You can't understand conflict without having it described. To learn about the French Revolution without a potentially troubling account of the Terrors makes about as much good sense as learning French without access to its verbs.

Look. I am not an ultra-con nutbag who thinks everyone should just harden the fuck up. I don't think your kids should have unfiltered access to violent things they don't yet understand. I don't think victims of sexual abuse should just 'get over it' and accept the prurient coverage of rape as news media entertainment to which they are so often subject without warning. I am ardently opposed to irresponsible discussion of suicide and I am in the regular habit of reporting guideline violations. Free speech must be a right, but its broad exercise is a serious responsibility. I will fucking tell your boss or the press council if you fuck up because I believe one of the best traditions of top-down journalism is the responsible recognition of one's power. The mass-media worker should know by rote those things likely to trigger stress on a large scale. But the academic must never be subject to these sorts of constraints.

There's a time and a place for serious discussion of abuse and conflict. It is not on your television at 6 p.m. It is in your universities. Electronic media is indiscriminate in its reach and so must be discriminating in its framing of material. Anyone could be watching. An academic lecture, on the other hand, addresses a very particular audience who are there to develop their own powers of discrimination. In other words, university itself functions as a 'trigger warning'. The study of humanities in particular is an elaborate attempt to frame all the pain of the world. I couldn't get out of bed for a week when I first learned about the systematised rape deployed as a weapon in the Balkan wars. It was Very Triggering. But all stories about conflict are triggering and unsafe. You could call a first-year module in international relations Trigger Studies, I suppose. But the pain of learning about the world, I think, is inferred by all decent students.

I once expected trigger warnings and frequented safe spaces: places where the price of admission is to agree. Well, agreement and twenty-five dollars for fashionable yoga. Plus an extra dollar for losers who did not have their own yoga mats.

'This is a safe space,' said the young, belligerently calm white woman whose inner glow was offset with a bright artificial tan the colour of chicken tikka. 'Welcome. This is a safe space.' And we signed the form indemnifying the safe space in case it killed us.

I hadn't heard the term used since the early nineties. But here it was again in a new century. And it has subsequently re-emerged in contexts for which it was never intended. Yoga classes. Speaking events. I even saw it used in the window of a beauty salon once.

You know the place; one of Enya's bastards continues a wilful tradition of pan-pipes. There's a Buddha next to an oil-burner next to a display of take-home 'botanicals' as used in the 'Goddess Array' facial which promises to balance your oily T-zone and chakras as never before. There are almost some ornamental references to Bali, here. And Japan. Definitely India. There is a treatment named in the honour of Deepak. Probably. I don't know. I didn't go in.

I remember thinking I'd prefer a guarantee of hygiene and tepid wax temperature over one for safe spiritual space any day. I had my labia groomed elsewhere. But, I'd learned my lesson by then and have become perhaps only the second or third most intellectually empty cunt to emerge from Canberra since Margaret Reid. I went to a literary afternoon in 2013 where one of the writers said she felt confident reading out her awful work because organisers had assured her it was a safe space. In 2011, I was asked not to attend a homosexual arts festival on the grounds that it was a safe space. (To be fair, I had written an editorial asserting that a festival promoting homosexuals in the arts was about as desperately needed as a festival promoting white privately educated men in politics.) If art feels the need to call itself safe, it should not also be entitled to call itself art.

Art is not safe. Thinking thoughts of consequence is not safe. And neither, as it turned out, was the yoga class. We had an unsafe afternoon.

There is, of course, sometimes a civic need for safe spaces. I should make a point about what I recall as the etymology of the term because it didn't always mean 'an assembly of dills committed to say nothing even mildly provocative lest it disrupt the circle jerk'. These days, the term is used to advertise readings of awful feminist poetry and end-of-year performances for remedial circus arts graduates. Back in the eighties, a 'safe space' quite specifically meant refuge for kids turfed out of their family homes due to queer orientation or a women's refuge.

Leisure-progressives, including myself and my girlfriends at Sydney University, stole 'safe space' away from homeless people and used it as a way to describe 'a room full of people who will uncritically applaud reeking word turds'. Leisure-progressivism has the habit of co-opting a sense of terror; it needs to in order to justify itself. For the endurance of, say, a poem by Maya Angelou, fear of something worse than the poem itself is necessary. I mean: Maya. This woman was the go-to laureate for all sorts of progressivism-tinged major events from Clinton's inauguration to Oprah's last show. Goodness, the occasional verse she wrote for Oprah was especially awful. She may as well have just said 'Everyone gets a car! Everyone gets a car!' in that gravitas-enriched stateswoman voice. I know why the caged bird sings too, Maya. It was trying to drown out the sound of your vile retching, like:

> Men themselves have wondered
> What they see in me.
> They try so much
> But they can't touch
> My inner mystery.

> —Maya Angelou, 'Phenomenal Woman'

Hideous. Not quite so hideous, of course, as the inner mystery of the Sydney University Safe Space for Women. The mystery was that I abused my student privilege to found a personal on-campus fuckpad. But still. Maya was pretty bad. Yes, I know that Angelou worked in poetry's oral tradition and we can't expect the James Earl Jones of doggerel to look as good on the page as she did showered in the credulous ejaculate of liberal gratitude. But, bugger me, someone has to say it: Maya Angelou was a wonderful activist but a genuinely terrible poet and someone should have broken her pencils. Of course, I cannot say this because she is dead and THAT MIGHT BE TRIGGERING FOR YOU.

When she was alive, I used to dream of breaking into a State occasion she threatened to ruin with her rot, hacking the teleprompter and replacing her nonsense about 'summer puffs of wind' or whatever with the words from the Mentos ad. Her voice was wonderful but her poetry no nobler than:

It doesn't matter what comes, fresh goes better with life,
And Mentos is fresh and full of life.
Nothing gets to you, staying fresh staying cool,
With Mentos, fresh and full of life.
Fresh goes better, Mentos freshness, fresh goes better
With Mentos, fresh and full of life.

Are you triggered? Sorry. I should say that I acknowledge Angelou as a significant figure. I should also say that at one point in my life, I had actual need of a safe space. (As Maya certainly must have when enduring the Stupid of racism.) I was a Queer Teen and my mother wasn't exactly Celebrating My Difference. We argued quite violently about my Lifestyle Choice, which I denied with my lips but affirmed with my haircut, so she sent me to a homophobic psychologist. The homophobic psychologist assured me that her offices were a safe space and so I conceded that I had Feelings for Ladies—one in particular who had a motorcycle and remains the only lezzer of my acquaintance who had good taste in music. The homophobic psychologist rang my mother and, reportedly, said, 'I am so sorry about your daughter. She is a homosexual.'

If I had not been genetically burdened with an ego the size of a small moon, I may have become quite self-loathing at that point. My mother shrieked that I was sick. She raved about perversion and theorised that marijuana, a gentle father and Boy George were to blame. Being a smart-arse, I told her the delicious taste of vagina was to blame. Things didn't go well after that. I sought asylum from her disgust; chiefly at an ultra-leftie community radio station, but a few times at a place set aside for kids just like me.

Years later, as I was writing the editorial about the safe space of the gay arts festival, I remembered my need for an actual gay safe space; a *genuinely* safe space free from duplicitous psychologists and angry mothers who urged their children to hate themselves. I felt like queer itself had turned its back on the most urgently needed safe spaces. I know there are kids hearing the same selfish, unsafe shit from their parents, and what they need, more often than not, is a place to go. I ran away from home for a brief spell; I have had the merest experience of homelessness but many other kids endure it for longer. And they need a safe space to run to. But this is no longer a preoccupation of a movement itself absorbed with re-creating the conditions of the Sydney University Women's Safe Space.

A few years after I had written my first truly offensive editorial about the new, safe preoccupations of the queer movement, I had another piece published by an online newspaper. It was on a more general theme of These Social Justice People Are So Concerned With Making the Culture Nice and Safe They Don't Look Out For Material Danger. It wasn't especially good and I can't remember for whom I wrote it and how much I was paid. But I copied and kept one of the comments from a young queer man:

> Your argument reminded me of a queer student activist meeting where queer homelessness, youth poverty and housing shortages were raised. Neither the discussion, nor the plan decided upon, had anything to do with the material problem. Instead, the focus was entirely on 'the heteronormative language used by real estate agents', and the symbolic 'critique' we were going to use to 'combat' it. I sat there thinking, what the f*** does this have to do with anything? Why aren't we asking how many

queer youth are in financial difficulty, un/underemployed, struggling to find accommodation, or homeless? How does this compare to the rest of the population? How do we get resources to people who need them?

Instead, the focus was, 'White picket fence language is discriminating against gays, let's put up anti-heteronormative satirical posters around campus.' When my mate suggested we at least depict the goals we were trying to achieve/who we were trying to help, the reply was, 'We're not really into that, we're really into, just, like, critique.'

They decided in the end to stick a 'male' mannequin in a dress outside [real estate agent] Hocking Stuart.

He is much, much more promising as a human and a scholar than I ever was. I liked my space for activism safe at his age; almost certainly, I would have helped pick out the mannequin's frock. Which is peculiar, really, given that I had an experience of homelessness just a few years before I segued into the pointless, safe work of cultural critique. I would like to be able to say that my insistence on a safe space for women at Sydney University sprang from my own rather vicious experiences at home, but by then, I had forgotten the terrible feeling and I quickly became mired in, rather than awed by, the privilege of actual safety. Life at a university good enough to make my mother proud of me again did not turn me into a good student. I was a bad student and a sloppy thinker who sought only the safety of agreement and the solace of sex in a room I'd disbursed my youthful energies defending when I could have been reading books about economics, which could have turned into action a bit more decent than the care of the self.

I read Derrida instead. And he is certainly remarkable but dangerously safe for a selfish young mind. Postmodern critique provided even more padding to the ennui of the women's safe space. Oh, it's all just culture, I said and turned my spotty adolescent back on material danger for the safety of any literary criticism that wasn't Harold Bloom.

This is not to say there should not be literary criticism. This is not for a minute to suggest that we should not be 'critics after dinner', as Marx famously promised we could be after a day of working in the fields. The thing is, though, I had deluded myself into believing that my feeble 'deconstruction' of literature written for a tutor unlikely to do anything but encourage my onanism was Making a Difference to the Real Political World. I'm telling you: you're not going to change shit 'unpacking' a 'text'. Which is fine. I just happened to believe that I was changing the world from my academic safe space. I saw danger where there was none.

It took all of my youth to acknowledge that I had long preferred safety over rigour. And I still hadn't acknowledged the toxic nature of my love for 'safety' when Kylie and I arranged to meet for yoga.

I am not proud but I *am* obliged to tell you that this was a date for 'hot' yoga; a ninety-minute endurance test of copyright-protected bullshit enforced with a thermostat set to thirty-seven degrees by a wafer-thin bint whose $7000 student fee paid to the Bikram Academy of Yoga entitled her to talk in faux Hindi about the 'known' connection between the human immune response and chakras.

Look. I know. That two reasonable adults had spent money for the 'wisdom' of a dodgy franchise whose most notable contribution to the world was emissions from an over-worked heater is woeful. I had read on a HOLISTIC website that Kylie's multifocal motor neuropathy is a condition that responds well to heat. Because yes: I was once the kind of person who decried Big Pharma and urged a return to holistic approaches. You know that shit. It believes there was a Golden Time when humanity Followed Its Instincts and that 'herbs' provide a system of treatment better than that offered to us by evidence-based medicine. The success of so-called holistic 'medicine' does not inhere in its chemistry but in the way it is able to flatter its patrons much more than science (SO TRIGGERING) can. Generally, a GP has neither the time nor the professional inclination to hold your forearm warmly as an aromatherapy humidifier upchucks ylang ylang into air thick with the irresistible question, 'So how are YOU?' The attachment to 'wellness' I had developed came from vanity and the urge to be 'understood' and safe.

The desire to be understood and truly known is, I'd guess, fairly widespread. I'm also going to say it is fairly unwholesome. It is a nasty craving that has driven me to do some pretty silly stuff at times, including:

1. Asking my partner if he really understands me
2. Telling a therapist my mother has never understood me (which is true but boring)
3. Choosing a career that is entirely based on my need to be heard and understood by people I have never met.

I had heard from an associate—who has since been lost to the cheap meth of personal development seminars and whose every utterance is riddled with phrases like 'I have invented a possibility for myself' or 'I would like to enrol you in my possibility'—that the Bikram yoga instructors really *understood*. And the need to be safely understood drove me to yoga. Actually,

Kylie drove me to yoga. Which was a little unnerving as I wasn't entirely confident that her dodgy foot could work the brake. But she was, as I have told you, a practical lady and she had the car retrofitted.

The car accommodated her but the chicken tikka spray-tan lady didn't. Kylie told her, as per the request on the Indemnify the Safe Space form, that she had a bung foot. And she said, 'So don't be surprised if I can't do all the postures.'

'Don't be surprised if you can,' said Red Rooster.

'No,' said Kylie, 'I will definitely not be able to do tree pose. I can't stand on one foot because of the nerve damage.'

'We have had people get up from wheelchairs,' the instructor said. 'You need to believe. If you don't believe in the power of Bikram, you will never recover in your pain body.'

By this stage, I was a scarlet so vivid as to make Miss Safe Orange Space seem pale. I asked Kylie if she wanted to fuck off and she said no, she'd give it a go. She'd been trying a meditation class here and a cupping therapy there, she said, to see if it helped with the anxiety her condition had produced. Some of the stuff was soothing. The massage in particular took her mind off limbs that sometimes felt dead. But a lot of it was pretty irritating and she was, by now, habituated to hearing wankers tell her that her nerve damage was 'all in the mind'. Besides which, we had both heard that you could lose a kilogram or two in sweat and she was going out on a date that night.

There was no access lift; not that Kylie needed one, but I had asked when I'd made the booking just in case she was having a shitty day. We climbed up the stairs to the yoga room and I wondered briefly how the miraculous wheelchair recovery person had managed.

'This is a safe space.'

'This is a place where you'll be understood.'

Like understanding ever changed the fucking world or produced a good idea. The proletariat doesn't start a revolution by asking the bourgeoisie to understand it. Understanding is a placebo. Unless, of course, it is undertaken rigorously. Say, at university. Which is very difficult if you are worried about being 'triggered'.

We went to the class.

Kylie had been a jogger for years and was strong. She did downward dog perfectly; she did a very creditable warrior. I didn't as I am shit at yoga and was really in it for the heat-induced inch-loss. But the teacher didn't correct my crap asanas despite the fact they were the most ungainly in the room.

Instead, she picked out Kylie.

'Kylie, Kylie,' she said to Kylie. 'Feel your Hindi-Word-I-Didn't-Recognise-And-Am-Therefore-Unable-To-Reproduce-In-Text so you can achieve your Something-I-Am-Pretty-Sure-That-Nasty-Orange-Bitch-Made-Up.

'Do your Mystical Whatsit so you can get in touch with your Chumbawamba and release your Spicy Fruit Roll.'

And then it was time for the tree pose, which might very well Enhance the Root Chakra as claimed but, given that it demands that all one's weight be carried by a single foot, is pretty much impossible if that foot has sustained significant nerve injury.

'You need to believe, Kylie.'

We need to get the fuck out of here, Kylie.

The safe space has become a fixture of some contemporary social justice movements. In the safe space, all participants agree not to critique a certain set of principles. It's a bit like bringing peanut butter to kindergarten. It will result in your expulsion.

A few years ago, I was asked to do a funny piece at a feminist fundraiser. I wrote a short comic poem on the topic of penis and my new enthusiasm for it entitled 'She's Back on Solids'. But it turned out to be a fundraiser *and* a safe space.

I picked up a copy of the rules and they requested that anything likely to 'trigger' negative responses be signalled with a 'trigger warning'; that is, if one was planning to mention the topic of sexual abuse in particular, one should give ample time for those Viewers Who Might Find This Disturbing to leave the room. It also requested no 'Feminism 101' speak, which meant that all participants agreed that the basic principles of feminism be understood.

Now, I can see how it might be profitable to discussion to observe both of these rules. Essentially, one is creating the means for a more advanced exploration of a topic without menace or inconvenience. But I also saw, in what turned out to be an okay evening, how these rules begin to take on the appearance of natural justice and how one very quickly can become enamoured of their enforcement. At university, I adapted quickly to seeing a reflection of my own views; any crack in the looking glass was a transgression. It hardly needs saying that the experience of exchange without opposition is seductive. And habit-forming.

Creating a temporary zone for particular thought has its intellectual uses, but our tendency to take the temporary and make it permanent is one of our species' least laudable and most dependable traits. God, we are good at explaining our worst and most Stupid habits away as 'natural'. The formalised safe space sees any resistance as the work of a 'troll' and action outside narrow margins as 'hostility' and, as it has made its rules explicit, I guess it is entitled to do so. But it troubles me that these ground rules, intended to privilege the normally marginalised, reproduce the framework they seek to defy.

This is what happens in the naturopath's office. It happens in an increasingly niche electronic world where birds of a feather tend to tweet, 'like' and 'share' together. Once, I suppose, it happened in church, but there was not then the pretence of empowerment by participants; just the promise of heaven. In church, one consented to rules set by a Higher Authority or one was excommunicated. The authority of Understanding Each Other is far more duplicitous because it claims to be consensual. And one never knows when one has broken the rules until the naturopath has told you that your irises are blotchy or your book club strikes you off because you called literary fiction 'just another genre' or you are un-friended. You don't know when you've broken rules often unwritten and always devised with 'safety' in mind.

'Kylie. KYLIE,' said the ginger tan to the falling tree. It was quite clear that the orange lady was concerned far less for Kylie's safety than she was for the safety of The Space.

Kylie broke the rules by toppling over; the failure of her body was an affront to Bikram.

That Kylie was unafraid to topple is to her credit. The composed, yogic look on her face as she went down conveyed the stupidity of the safe space so invested in the protection of itself and not those within it. Being unafraid to make a misstep in one of these unsafe safe spaces takes a courage I couldn't muster for years. Perhaps now, having abandoned the need for intellectual safety, I can get off my arse and build some genuinely safe space for people persecuted by a force more awful even than 'triggering' poetry.

HR

6

National stupidity: How the War on Terror is killing and impoverishing us

They hate our freedoms.

—George W. Bush, 2001

Much, indeed most, of the Stupid we've encountered so far has been traceable through a long lineage in Western thought. The Stupid we're about to examine reflects many of the urges and causes of historical Stupid, but is of a considerably more recent development: primarily since 9/11, but with its roots in the national security state that has developed since the Second World War.

When it comes to modern examples of extreme Stupid, it doesn't get bigger, vaster, more historic, more epochal, than the Iraq War.

First, there was the cost.

The United States is estimated to have spent $1.7 trillion on the Iraq War so far, with much more expenditure to come in the decades ahead via healthcare and veterans' costs. The final total could be in the order of $4 trillion. The cost to the UK of its participation was a fractional, but still substantial, US$14 billion in 2010; the cost to Australian taxpayers of Australia's trivial support role in the 'Coalition of the Willing' had, by 2011, reached $2.4 billion. Nearly 4500 US troops died, along with 179 UK servicemen and women, with many thousands more injured and crippled. US Iraq veterans continue to have a frightening rate of suicide.

Then there were the results.

The most significant direct achievement of the war was the death of hundreds of thousands of Iraqis—estimates vary between 100,000 and 600,000. Whatever the number, so many Iraqis died during the ensuing allied occupation and civil war that, according to the World Bank, life expectancy in Iraq fell by two years between 2002 and 2007; in 2010 it had still not recovered to pre-war levels. Iraq itself has now fallen apart in another sectarian civil war, with the country now divided into a relatively effective Kurdish state, a nightmarishly brutal and aggressive Sunni terrorist state, and what's left of southern Iraq, likely to become a client state of Iran. Meantime, the West is once again ramping up its rhetoric and deploying its military to address what is deemed to be the 'apocalyptic' threat of the Islamic State.

Then there were the consequences.

Putting aside that the justification for the war—Saddam's weapons of mass destruction—didn't exist, the attack had other effects as well. In 2006, a US intelligence report concluded that 'the Iraq war has made the overall terrorism problem worse'. That conclusion was echoed by a UK government report that year into the 2005 London bombings and confirmed by the head of British intelligence service MI5 in 2010 in evidence to the Chilcot Inquiry in the UK. The then head of the Australian Federal Police had also reached that conclusion in 2004, and was attacked by the conservative Howard government when he expressed that view publicly, just as the Blair government had initially rejected any link between Iraq and the increasing risk of terrorism. And the Islamic State that has emerged from the Iraqi and Syrian civil wars is regarded as so dangerous that a new round of military intervention is underway.

This is a type of Stupid so vast that people seem unable to fully comprehend it: the governments of the United States, Britain, Australia and the other countries that participated in the attack on Iraq together spent trillions of dollars and caused the death of hundreds of thousands of people only to make their countries, by the admission of their own intelligence and law enforcement agencies, *less safe* from the threat of terrorism.

But when it comes to the War on Terror, everything is big. Big costs. Big body counts. Big infringements of liberty. Big Stupid. The post-9/11 era has been characterised, indeed *defined*, by Stupid. We are surrounded by it, but we've become inured to it, our ability to use perspective and logic dulled, our capacity for astonishment pushed ever higher, so that we find nothing noteworthy in things we would have found ludicrous or outrageous twenty years ago. It was Voltaire who first claimed that those who can make you believe absurdities can make you commit atrocities, but in his eagerness to coin the ultimate anti-clerical bon mot, he framed it too restrictively: those who claim to prevent atrocities also want you to believe absurdities.

This is just a short list of some of the recent moments of vintage Stupid provided by the War on Terror:

- In February 2013, the US Secretary of Defense announced a new medal for drone operators to honour their service in remote-controlled killing. In recent years, drones have killed, according to conservative estimates, several hundred civilians, including dozens of children, in Afghanistan, Pakistan and Yemen. After an outcry from veterans who had actually faced real combat, the Pentagon plan was abandoned.

- The Central Intelligence Agency's torture program produced no useful intelligence, a report by the US Senate Intelligence committee, which oversees the CIA and other intelligence agencies, found. Instead, the CIA took intelligence gained by the FBI using traditional methods and claimed it had obtained it via torture, lied to Congress and the US government about the benefits of torture, and kept secret some of its more barbaric methods. In order to try to stop the report, the CIA spied on the committee itself and then launched a public attack on its chair.

- One of the most vociferous Congressional critics of whistle-blower Edward Snowden and the journalists who have reported his revelations, Peter King—Republican chairman of the House Subcommittee on Counterterrorism—has for thirty years been a strong supporter of the IRA and refused to condemn its atrocities.

- In the United States, if you're within 100 kilometres of a border—which amounts to two-thirds of the US population—you can have your laptop or mobile device searched by law enforcement agencies without cause under a 'border exemption' from normal due process. You can also be prosecuted if you refuse to tell authorities your password.

- The UK government made *The Guardian* go through an elaborate piece of theatre in destroying hard disks containing information on NSA and GCHQ spying provided by Edward Snowden, despite all parties knowing the same information was held on offshore servers and was just a click away.

- In 2011, the US Transportation Security Administration said that it 'stood by' its airport security officers after they insisted on patting down a wheelchair-bound ninety-five-year-old woman with cancer and compelled her to remove her adult nappy while going through security at a Florida airport.

- It took two years for the conviction of British man Paul Chambers for joking on Twitter about blowing up a Yorkshire airport to be overturned by British courts.

- The White House counterterrorism adviser Lisa Monaco used a speech to the Harvard Kennedy School to warn parents that 'confrontational children' could in fact be terrorists.

- After the fall of Muammar Gaddafi, documents recovered from his security agency showed that the CIA and MI6 had repeatedly abducted Libyan dissidents in other countries and delivered them to Gaddafi to interrogate and torture. 'I congratulate you on the safe arrival of Abu Abd Allah Sadiq,' a senior MI6 official wrote to Gaddafi henchman Moussa Koussa about one of their victims. 'This was the least we could do for you and for Libya to demonstrate the remarkable relationship we have built over the years. I am so glad.'

- The US government's own files, and former Bush Administration officials, acknowledge that over 150 inmates of its Guantanamo Bay facility (for 'the worst of the worst' in lingua Dubya), including boys and old men, were entirely innocent; many were held for years anyway, including an Al Jazeera cameraman held for six years so he could be inter- rogated about that media company.

- In September 2013, several Iraqi torture victims were ordered by a US court to pay the legal costs of the company whose employees tortured them in Abu Ghraib during the Iraq War, after a court ruled the company could not be sued in the US for its actions in Iraq.
- Among the 'trigger words' that the NSA uses to filter internet communications for evidence of terrorism are 'import', 'Elvis', 'illuminati', 'dictionary' and, as if to prove that terrorists aren't real men, 'quiche'.
- Under the Obama Administration's 'Insider Threat Program', developed in response to Edward Snowden, the Pentagon advised its staff to consider reporting anyone seen reading satirical news site *The Onion* or progressive online news site *Salon* as potential security threats.*

These absurdities aren't merely disturbing, laughable or undignified, they come with a prodigious cost, even if we put aside as a one-off mistake the fact that the Iraq War has been a multi-trillion-dollar exercise in reducing Iraqi life expectancy.

So, forget everything you've been told about the War on Terror, and let's go back to basics, in order to de-Stupidise it.

---

* Speaking of *The Onion*, the West doesn't have a monopoly on absurdity: in 2011, al-Qaeda criticised Iranian president Mahmoud Ahmadinejad for peddling 9/11 conspiracy theories. 'Why would Iran ascribe to such a ridiculous belief that stands in the face of all logic and evidence?' al-Qaeda lamented, in a complaint that echoed an *Onion* parody video in which an al-Qaeda representative argues with a 9/11 truther.

A cost–benefit analysis of the War on Terror

Between 9/11 and 2011, the United States spent an additional US$700 billion on homeland security, separate from its military spending—spending on bigger budgets for security, law enforcement and intelligence agencies, spending on a new Department of Homeland Security, spending on irradiating airline customers with X-ray body scanners, spending on security furniture and scanners at every government building across the country, and people to staff them. It also incurred an estimated $400 billion in losses derived from additional security measures.

Was this $1.1 trillion cost justified? There have been no mass-casualty attacks in the US since 9/11, and few terrorist incidents of any kind (more of which later). Did this *additional* spending—remember, the US, like every other government in the world, was already spending a lot of money on security, law enforcement and intelligence before 9/11—stop attacks? It's impossible to tell, isn't it? To determine what *might have been* without that additional $1+ trillion in spending and extra costs?

Well, yes, it is indeed impossible to tell, but it turns out there is actually a way to determine if the spending was justified—a different question, but one with a much easier answer. Two academics, John Mueller and Mark G. Stewart, have tackled the question in their 2011 book, *Terror, Security and Money: Balancing the risks, benefits, and costs of homeland security*—the seminal text on understanding the mind-numbing stupidity of security spending. To grossly simplify their approach, they answer the question by working backwards—take how much additional money has been spent to prevent terrorist attacks, work out the cost of terrorist attacks, estimate the reduction in risk achieved by the extra spending and calculate how many terrorist attacks would need to have been thwarted to justify the extra spending. Yes, true, such an approach doesn't account for the devastating emotional toll of a mass-casualty attack, the trauma for survivors, for families and friends of those killed and the wide-scale shock for a whole society, but it can put additional spending into an economic perspective.

Based on Mueller and Stewart's conservative estimates, including very generous assumptions about how much additional spending has reduced the risk of terrorist attacks, the additional expenditure on homeland security by the US would have only been remotely economically justified if the additional spending *by itself*—apart from pre-existing security spending—had prevented more than one 9/11-level attack each and every year, or prevented 1700 smaller but economically significant attacks every year. And bear in mind, while the US was spending a lazy trillion on homeland security under the pretence of making itself safer, it was spending as much again on its Iraq occupation, which by common agreement made it less safe.

But even if you dispute Mueller and Stewart's numbers or assumptions, their analysis points to one of the central absurdities of national security spending: terrorism is a negligible cause of mortality and economic cost in Western countries.

This is where Stupid starts to mount up. For example, in the US, among the things that are more fatal to people than terrorism are not just obvious threats like gun violence or car accidents,* but threats as varied as malnutrition, falls, swimming accidents

---

* One researcher estimates nearly 1600 more Americans died on US roads after 9/11 than would have otherwise been the case, because they opted not to fly.

and work accidents, each of which kill more Americans annually than the death toll from 9/11, let alone the ongoing annual death toll from terrorism, which is negligible—in fact, so small it ranks below bathtub accidents and shootings by toddlers as a cause of death. In terms of demonstrated threat, terrorism is on par with exotic diseases, skydiving accidents and choking in restaurants.

Indeed, Americans need more protection from their own police forces than from terrorists. On average, American police shoot, taser or beat to death around 400 of their fellow citizens a year, often for the most spurious of reasons, with the mentally ill and African Americans featuring prominently as innocent victims. In 2014, a North Carolina police officer called by the parents of a mentally ill teenager shot him dead even after two other officers had restrained him, declaring, 'I don't have time for this.' Oklahoma police beat a man to death in front of his family after he had tried to intervene in a dispute between his wife and daughter. In 2013, Iowa police shot dead an unarmed teen whose father had called them because his son had taken his truck to buy cigarettes. Georgia police shot dead a diabetic man after his girlfriend rang 911 for medical assistance. Washington DC police shot dead an unarmed mentally ill female driver with a toddler in the back of her car. In 2012, Houston police shot dead a mentally ill double amputee in a wheelchair. These are only some of the more high-profile recent victims of America's hyper-aggressive and heavily armed police.

In Australia, there has only been one terrorism-related death since 2001, when a Christian fundamentalist killed an abortion clinic security guard, though authorities insist they have thwarted four mass-casualty attacks during that period. Approximately 100 Australians have also died because of terrorism overseas since 2001, mostly in Indonesia. Even accepting at face value the claims of security agencies about the planned mass-casualty attacks, the possible death tolls from such attacks would have been small compared to nearly 19,000 Australians who have died in road accidents in the same period. As it stands, about three times more Australians have died falling out of bed since 2001 than have died at the hands of terrorists. But in the decade after 9/11, Australia spent nearly $17 billion on additional security, increased funding for intelligence and law enforcement agencies, and our involvement in Afghanistan and Iraq, to which we committed as a dutiful ally of the US. That expenditure is in addition to other national security-related costs inflicted on Australian industry (the aviation industry in particular) that also run into the billions.

National security has sucked up huge amounts of money that, based on the policy objective of saving lives, obviously should have been spent elsewhere. Directing vast amounts of additional resources into national security beyond those that were *already* being directed to it before 9/11 means fewer resources to direct at the long list of preventable and treatable health threats we face. Those resources could be used for improving roads and road safety, or ensuring people have enough to eat, or providing better mental health services, or lifting economic growth potential through spending on infrastructure and education, or paying off government debt, the future interest on which will reduce our capacity for such expenditures. Or it could just be used to cut taxes: a US university study suggests a billion dollars in defence spending produces around 20 per cent fewer jobs than a billion dollars in tax cuts.

Hating our freedoms

But it gets more Stupid. If the War on Terror costs money, health, lives and opportunities, it also comes with a heavy cost to basic freedoms. Our response to an enemy that purportedly 'hates our freedoms' has been to curb those very freedoms through anti-terrorism laws. For some reason, Australia has some of the most voluminous anti-terrorism legislation in the West, far bigger than legislation passed by US Congress or in other Anglophone countries. And under Australian laws, basic legal principles have gone by the board: people not charged with any crime can be detained by secret court order, without legal representation; people not charged with any crime can be subjected to strict controls on their freedom of speech, freedom of movement and freedom of association; the crime of 'sedition' even made a sinister comeback; simply writing a book urging violence has seen an Islamic extremist in Australia jailed for over a decade—despite no harm coming from it, despite the book being cut-and-pasted rubbish.

Better yet, if you're lucky enough to have been targeted for 'rendition' by the US, you'll be sent to a third country and tortured, with an ASIO agent in attendance, while the Australian government denies knowing where you are.

Moreover, the legal framework of anti-terrorism in the United States has been used by governments as the justification for expanding their powers well beyond even the generous remit provided by policymakers in areas such as torture, extra-judicial killing (including of Americans) and, above all, mass surveillance. Since 9/11, the United States, with the assistance of the intelligence agencies of the UK, Canada, Australia and New Zealand, has established a global surveillance system aimed at tracking and collating information on every internet and telephone user on the planet.

And as elsewhere, such laws, far from being temporary in nature as they were claimed to be when introduced, have remained in place and, worse, expanded into other areas of law, with Australian states applying anti-terror-style laws to motorcycle gangs and trade unions. And the very definition of terrorism expands to fill the space available to it. Protests by pacifists and people complaining about water quality have been labelled 'terrorism' in the United States, and groups targeted by the Department of Homeland Security's intelligence 'fusion centres'—whatever they are—include Ron Paul supporters, the Occupy movement, the ACLU, pro- and anti-abortion activists and gun ownership advocates. In the UK, in attempting to justify the detention of journalist Glenn Greenwald's partner David Miranda, the UK government argued in court that simply publishing documents that might influence a government was 'terrorism', and that the motives of the publisher didn't matter. 'Terrorism is terrorism,' the British government's lawyers averred, meaning one could be a terrorist without even knowing it (the most dangerous *kind* of terrorist, presumably?). What they really meant was not that 'terrorism is terrorism', but that anything they wish to deem 'terrorism' is 'terrorism'.

Anti-terrorism laws are thus like untreated cancers: they grow relentlessly and metastasise, infecting unconnected areas of law, undermining basic rights wherever they can find purchase. Aviation is a particular cluster point. Airports are now the legal null zones of the Western world: step into an airport, indeed even drive up to one, and your rights start vanishing. Security personnel can scan you, interrogate you, strip you of your possessions, detain you, use an (admittedly adorable) dog to sniff you and explore your belongings. If you choose to fly, your basic rights become dependent on the good temper and goodwill of bureaucrats and security guards.

But despite the ferocious and ever-expanding nature of these laws, their benefit is negligible. How so? Because (just as Mueller and Stewart show with security spending) they are *in addition to* already comprehensive criminal and anti-terrorism laws that enabled law enforcement and intelligence agencies to infiltrate, prevent and investigate the activities of terrorists, and thus provide only a *marginal* risk reduction.

This is another key aspect of War on Terror Stupid that people fail to grasp: there was no low-hanging regulatory fruit when it came to terrorism before 9/11, no gaping holes in criminal law and intelligence-gathering regulation that allowed terrorists free rein, or prevented agencies from doing their jobs properly. Rather, 9/11 was the result of agencies like the CIA, the NSA and the FBI *failing* to use the powers they already had, despite possessing detailed information about the attack and the attackers, and the failure of existing airport security measures which may have stopped the attacks.

Nor has this lesson been learned since. The review panel Barack Obama was forced to establish in the wake of the Edward Snowden revelations reported that it couldn't find any evidence that the extraordinarily expensive, and intensely invasive and damaging, mass surveillance conducted by the NSA in recent years had thwarted a single terrorist attack. Indeed, terrorist attacks like those of the Neo-Nazi Miller couple in Las Vegas in 2014, clearly signposted on Facebook days in advance, aren't even regarded as terrorist acts.*

---

*   Mass shootings are, strangely, not considered terrorism events despite usually being carried out by, for example, Neo-Nazi white males.

Terror and Nothingness: The existentialism of the War on Terror

Why does such palpable and expensive Stupid flourish in absurd national security policies costing trillions and damaging the fabric of Western countries while going virtually unnoticed?

Western societies managed to get through the Cold War without much of the rampant Stupid of the War on Terror, despite our foe in that conflict being a sophisticated, modern dictatorship with the capacity to completely destroy us. Western governments spent more on defence then than now—the US was spending well over 5 per cent of GDP on defence in the 1980s compared to around 4.5 per cent until recently—but spent far less on 'homeland security' and intelligence (Cold War intelligence agencies were, in any event, notoriously riddled with double agents and profoundly incompetent). They had no need for mass surveillance of the kind East Germany established, now replicated in electronic form by the NSA, GCHQ and other Anglophone agencies. Nor did they need laws that dramatically curtailed basic rights: indeed, it was the very economic, political and social freedoms of Western liberal democracies, in contrast to the oppressive conditions of the Soviet Union, that played a key role in undermining the latter.

One reason for the difference is a toxic mixture of risk aversion on the part of politicians and risk incomprehension on the part of voters and journalists. As any number of economists, psychologists, neuroscientists and statisticians have demonstrated, humans are wired to make rapid, rather than accurate, risk assessments, given early humans needed the former more than the latter. We thus tend to overstate the risk to ourselves of things that are unusual, that we can see affecting us personally, that are beyond our control, that aren't associated with anything positive and which are unfamiliar. Contrarily, we underestimate the risks from things we are familiar with, over which we have a degree of control or which are a by-product of positive things. The prospect of dying in a car accident—which in Australia is around ten thousand times more likely than dying as a result of terrorism—is apparently far less worrying to people than perishing at the hands of violent religious fanatics; ditto the chance of being murdered, which is about forty times greater than dying at the hands of a terrorist. Our different reactions to the Cold War and the War on Terror are thus partly a difference between a world in which the chief threat, the Soviet Union, was a familiar part of our mental furniture, while Islamic terrorists are a sinister and unfathomable Other.[*]

That your average citizen doesn't understand risk, or how additional security laws or spending only provide marginal reductions in already negligible levels of risk, isn't surprising. But, political leaders, if dim-witted, still have access to high-quality advice on those subjects and many others, and thus have no such excuse. But their probability calculus is a political one: the remote chance of a major terrorist attack (in contrast to the much higher chance of ordinary low-casualty events like road accidents) must be treated seriously because of the political ramifications if one occurred.

During the early stages of the War on Terror, politicians and security officials around the world repeatedly referred to terrorism as an 'existential' threat. Its repetition suggested the

---

[*] But see, for example, Michael Herr's *Dispatches* (1977) for how the Vietcong and North Vietnamese Army did many of the allegedly unprecedented terrorist acts of Islamic extremists.

word was in danger of coming free from its actual definition and drifting off, like 'decimate' and 'genocide', into a far vaguer meaning—in this case, 'really bad'. Terrorism is by definition *not* an existential threat, but limited in impact even compared to conventional war. The Cold War was an existential threat, given all of humanity could have been obliterated through one small error, as nearly happened in 1963 and 1983. But terrorism *is* an existential threat for politicians, since any major attack would inflict, beyond the death toll or economic impact, serious political damage on those in power at the time.

Skilful politicians, however, also see opportunity in threat (the Chinese word for 'crisis' also means 'opportunity').* The War on Terror has thus been ruthlessly exploited by politicians both to extend government powers and for electoral gain, most famously when the Bush Administration pressured Homeland Security Secretary Tom Ridge to elevate the terror threat level just before the 2004 presidential election in order to boost Dubya's chances in a tight race.

The Stupid produced by the War on Terror is thus a repulsive combination of voter ignorance of the basic rules of probability and politicians' awareness of self-interest. That's why anti-terror policies so strongly emphasise security theatre—elaborate and often very expensive measures, like airport body scanners, that create an *impression* of greater security without adding significantly to it. The primary effect of the airport X-ray body scanners used until recently in the US (they've now been replaced with millimetre wave machines) seems to have been irradiating people, given the evidence of cancer clusters among TSA staff, and the invasion of privacy—a former Transportation

---

* In fact it doesn't, that's a Western myth, but whatever.

Security Administration official admitted that TSA staff racially profiled passengers and routinely gathered to mock passengers' body images on scanners. However, politicians are evidently convinced the public rates scanners highly: during the swine flu hysteria of 2009, the Australian government installed thermal scanners at airports, insisting they would detect people with elevated body temperature.* Hundreds of millions of dollars have been spent in the United States and Australia installing body scanners at airports, without a cost–benefit analysis ever having been done, money that would have been better spent separating traffic at well-known highway blackspots, or providing better health services in regional communities, if the intention was to save lives rather than create the illusion of greater security.

A system designed for Stupid

Stupid isn't a rare exception when it comes to the War on Terror: the primary institutional tools of national security are automatically predisposed towards absurdity. Intelligence and law enforcement agencies in Western countries are subjected to far less oversight than other government agencies, meaning corruption, incompetence and unauthorised or illegal activity are far less likely to be exposed than elsewhere in bureaucracies. (Contrary to the traditional conservative view that government bodies must be subjected to the most forensic scrutiny in the way they spend public money and regulate industry, it is usually the left that pushes for security and intelligence agencies, and

---

* An elegant example of Stupid in which a strain of flu not demonstrably worse than normal seasonal strains, and possibly less dangerous, sparked billions of dollars in spending by worried politicians to erect 'protective' measures like thermal scanners and rush into production vaccines that were never needed. The UK alone wasted £150 million on unnecessary swine flu vaccine.

the companies they keep in business, to be subjected to public and political scrutiny.) Instead, they operate with minimal scrutiny except via rubber-stamp secret courts or parliamentary oversight committees that work behind closed doors, meaning the evidence and arguments about the activities of intelligence and security agencies can never be publicly scrutinised.

As a consequence, intelligence and security agencies are particularly prone to misjudgements that result from a lack of concern about how internal decisions and policies may be viewed externally. It might be small things, like Australia's foreign intelligence service using an aid program as cover for bugging the Cabinet of East Timor for the commercial advantage of Australian companies.* It might be serious blunders, like the FBI's cross-border gunrunning operations, only exposed after a law enforcement official was killed as a result. Or it might be something profoundly wrong, like the CIA spending millions of dollars trying to develop mind-control drugs via monstrously unethical experiments—frequently on unwitting subjects—that resulted in a number of deaths over nearly two decades. Lack of scrutiny creates fertile ground for Stupid.

It also leads to abuse and mission creep. In the wake of Edward Snowden's revelations, the NSA admitted that a number of its staff had confessed to using its vast surveillance apparatus to stalk women—though it only knew of those who had admitted doing it. Snowden also revealed that intimate photos picked up by NSA internet surveillance were often shared among staff. This comes on top of previous revelations that NSA staff

---

* The whistleblower who revealed the bugging was then raided by Australia's domestic intelligence agency and had his passport revoked to prevent him leaving the country to give evidence about the bugging to an international tribunal.

had listened in to the intimate conversations of US defence personnel and journalists for titillation a decade ago, and that NSA staff broke US laws thousands of times in the operation of the Obama Administration's mass-surveillance programs. Edward Snowden's revelations have also demonstrated how the NSA and other Anglophone intelligence agencies, despite the 'War on Terror' hyping of their role, in fact devote vast resources to economic espionage against even close allies.

Abuse of the intelligence-gathering powers that have been dramatically expanded in the War on Terror are thus not the problem of 'a few rotten apples' but an *inevitable* outcome of a culture of secrecy, which fosters abuse and incompetence. When there is no fear of oversight and accountability of the kind that lurks in the minds of most bureaucrats, incompetence, corruption and abuse follow more readily. It also leads to misjudgements and a tendency to use power merely because it is available to be used, not because its use is the most sensible means to achieve an organisation's goals: NSA spying on the leaders of most of the US's allies, and the efforts of Australia's intelligence agencies to listen in to the phone calls of the Indonesian president, have inflicted significant damage on the national interest of both countries, for no clear gain. In a direct parallel with the Iraq War outcome, the NSA's deliberate strategy of degrading internet encryption standards has actually made us *less* secure, by helping the cybercriminals who are supposed to be one of its targets, while the revelations of its surveillance have inflicted major economic damage on US IT companies, which have demanded that its activities be curtailed so that they can restore trust in the eyes of their customers.

Lack of, and resistance to, accountability is also a reason why humour is regarded with such malice in national security operations. Humour is, at least in part, realising the incongruity between what should be and what is—that is, it is a basic form of human scrutiny that identifies what doesn't feel right in others' behaviour, or that exploits the difference between what others say and what they do or what actually exists. As the identification of *The Onion* as possible evidence of treasonous intent, and the prosecution and conviction of people for joking about bombs at airports (sometimes not even when they're at an airport) suggest, national security isn't merely not humorous, it is anti-humour, a kind of humour black hole sucking everything around it into a singularity of zealotry. To joke at the expense of national security is to immediately signal your unwillingness to accept at face value the claims of those who purport to be providing it, and thereby to immediately place yourself under suspicion. National security officials reflexively resent scepticism and treat it as a direct threat.

Like politicians, security and intelligence agencies have seized the opportunity of the War on Terror to increase both their budgets and their powers. The budget of Australia's domestic intelligence agency increased 600 per cent during the War on Terror, and it also received a glittering new headquarters on the shores of Lake Burley Griffin in Canberra that cost $700 million and was, aptly, 25 per cent over budget; the Australian Federal Police budget increased 160 per cent and that of Australia's foreign intelligence agency by over 200 per cent. The powers of such bodies, and especially ASIO, have undergone a similar rapid inflation, with almost annual extensions of its legal powers, which often receive minimal parliamentary scrutiny.

But another group has similarly benefited from the War on Terror without even the risks faced by security and law enforcement agencies, which are at least exposed if a terrorist attack occurs: corporate America. Stupid is big—very big—business. Defence contractors obviously benefit from US military action (the share prices of several major US defence contractors surged in mid-2013 in anticipation of US military action in Syria and surged again when the Obama Administration announced air strikes aimed at Islamic State militants), but more than a third of Australia's $70 billion-odd defence acquisitions budget over the last decade has flowed to foreign defence contractors, nearly all of it to US defence companies like Lockheed Martin and Boeing Defence. Even more has gone to those companies indirectly via local subsidiaries.

However, defence contractors aren't the only, or perhaps even the biggest, corporate beneficiaries of the War on Terror. Ten US firms earned $72 billion between them from the Iraq War, with more than half of that obtained *not* by a defence contractor, but Dick Cheney's former firm KBR, which secured nearly $40 billion worth of US government service contracts in Iraq. The really big bucks in the War on Terror aren't so much in weapons as in cleaning, and catering, and construction, and administration and transport to service the military and intelligence machines. Oil companies earned billions from supplying the armed forces of the US, the UK and vassal states like Australia in Iraq and Afghanistan; healthcare companies that manage veterans' services for the US military have tripled their profits as a result of over a decade of war. Homeland security spending, which in the US is still over $40 billion a year, also provides a strong revenue stream for both defence contractors and IT companies like IBM.

The corporate beneficiaries of the War on Terror, which stretch across IT to defence to services to health care, form a potent public and private lobby for continued expenditure on national security. Military personnel, politicians and national security bureaucrats often take board or executive positions at firms that work in national security industries after leaving their former profession, and sometimes go back to their old careers after a stint in the corporate sector. Northrop Grumman, Boeing and Lockheed Martin are fixtures in the list of top-twenty lobbyists in the United States; former and current defence contractor executives played a significant role in institutionalised lobbying efforts like the US Committee on NATO, which lobbied for the expansion of NATO in the 1990s, and the Committee for the Liberation of Iraq, which aggressively pushed for an attack on Saddam Hussein in the lead-up to the Iraq War.*

In such an environment, governments and highly influential industries have at best little incentive in ending the War on Terror and some agencies and companies may even seek to perpetuate it. Defence industries, in particular, must be concerned about repeating the disaster of the West accidentally winning the Cold War, which precipitated a big drop in military spending—over 20 per cent in the US alone between 1990 and 1997. Military spending in the West has already reduced because of fiscal pressure in the wake of the global financial crisis; victory in the War on Terror would be a bitter blow indeed for arms manufacturers and companies providing services for military and intelligence operations, and a fate to be avoided at all costs. Thank goodness the Islamic State came along when it did.

---

* A particularly unsubtle example of military-industrial-complex lobbying is former Republican State Department official and Iran-Contra survivor Richard Armitage, who has attacked Australia's allegedly low level of defence spending without divulging that his firm, Armitage International, is a Washington lobbyist for US defence contractors.

Manufacturing terrorism

Besides the Iraq War encouraging terrorism against Western targets, the conduct of the wars in Iraq and Afghanistan have created other positive feedback loops for terrorism. The destabilising effect of the Iraq War and massive expenditure on oil by Western armies in their campaigns helped drive oil prices to record highs: one oil analyst suggested the Iraq War was responsible for oil prices trebling. This has been a boon for Saudi Arabia and other repressive Middle Eastern autocracies, which promote fundamentalist forms of Islam that provide fertile soil for Islamist alienation and resort to violence.

The more significant feedback loop is the direct radicalising effect of the United States' extra-judicial killing program involving drones, which have killed at the very least hundreds of civilians, and many children, in Pakistan, Yemen and Afghanistan, as well as an Australian, a New Zealander and several US citizens, including Anwar al-Awlaki and his son, Abdulrahman.* Drone strikes that kill civilians enrage target communities and directly create the conditions for radicalisation and anti-Western anger. This isn't just the view that Malala Yousafzai, the brave Pakistani schoolgirl who was shot by the Taliban, put to Barack Obama in her White House meeting with him, but also that of the former US commander in Afghanistan, General Stanley McChrystal, who explained that drone strikes 'are hated on a

---

* The drone strike that incinerated the sixteen-year-old Denver-born Abdulrahman, who was eating at a cafe with friends while looking for his (by then dead) father in Yemen, killed no militants. The man who ordered the strike, Homeland Security Advisor John Brennan, was rewarded by Barack Obama with promotion to head of the CIA. The killing of this boy has never been investigated by any authorities, and was dismissed by one source close to the Obama Administration as a case of 'wrong place, wrong time'.

visceral level, even by people who've never seen one or seen the effects of one' and that they threaten the achievement of broader goals. As it turns out, the direct manner in which the attack on Iraq increased the terrorist threat to Western citizens is being continually replicated via drone warfare.

However, it's the FBI that seems most committed to perpetuating the War on Terror, and if there are no terrorists, the FBI will invent them. The great majority of people prosecuted for terrorist plots in the United States since 9/11 have been caught in FBI stings, usually involving plots initiated or advanced by the FBI or its informers themselves, not those prosecuted. In one case, an FBI informant convinced a homeless man to sell two old stereo speakers (sic) to an undercover FBI agent for grenades to use in a plan, suggested by the informant, to attack a shopping mall. The homeless man is now serving seventeen years for terrorism. In another case, that of the 'Newburgh Four', four drug users living in poverty, including a mentally ill man, were recruited by an FBI informant and promised holidays, cars, businesses and huge amounts of cash—up to a quarter of a million dollars—to carry out a plot; one of them was told he would be killed if he backed out. All four are serving twenty-five years for terrorism.

The FBI isn't alone in this type of behaviour. British police, in league with the UK's febrile tabloids, entirely invented an Islamic extremist plot to blow up Manchester United's Old Trafford ground in 2004—there was no plot, no explosives and no extremists. Another Islamic extremist plot, said to involve the biotoxin ricin, turned out to have no ricin, and four of the five people charged were acquitted.

Three of the key features of the War on Terror thus demonstrate how it can be a vast, self-perpetuating cycle of

Stupid: the Iraq War actually made us less secure by radicalising civilians in target countries and increasing the incomes of fundamentalist Middle Eastern regimes; drone strikes continue to enrage and radicalise target communities; and undermining encryption as part of mass surveillance degrades internet security. And if terrorist plots don't exist, they are invented by police agencies.

And while we have incorporated the low-level Stupid of the War on Terror into our daily lives—enduring the security theatre of the airport scan, assuming our governments are spying on us, tolerating the waste of billions of dollars on pointless conflicts—we're oblivious to the greater absurdity: that the fixation with national security comes with a body count, not merely of foreign lives lost in distant wars, but in the consequences of infrastructure not built, health services not provided, prevention programs not funded, social services cut back, all in the name of strategies that in fact make us less safe. The desperate and draconian effort to make Westerners more secure is killing them too, not just the nameless victims of violence in places like Iraq. And this form of Stupid will continue as long as governments, intelligence and law enforcement agencies and large corporations benefit from it.

BK

Entr'acte—*From Dallas with Love* to *Moonfaker*: the lost films of Stanley Kubrick

JFK was paralyzed by poison contained in the flechette in less than two seconds—so paralyzed that the first rifle bullet that hit him did not knock him down, but left him in a nearly upright position. A second volley of shots fired at JFK a few seconds later struck a stationary, visible target. The paralyzing flechette shot was fired by a man holding the umbrella launcher.

—Richard E. Sprague and Robert Cutler,
The Umbrella System: Prelude to an assassination (1978)

As it turns out, we know the identity of one of the (many) alleged participants in the plot to murder President John F. Kennedy. He outed himself in 1978: his name was (so he said) Louie Witt, and he was the Umbrella Man. There he is in that original found-footage horror movie, the Zapruder film, a blink-and-you'll-miss-him bystander holding an umbrella as Kennedy drove past on That Fateful—and sunny—Day. His umbrella, Witt said, was a Neville Chamberlain-based reference to the support for appeasement of the president's father, Joseph Kennedy, when Ambassador to London in the 1930s. But while you might have missed him, he didn't miss the president—he launched a CIA-developed poisoned dart at Kennedy for the purposes of paralysing him so he could more easily be shot. Or, at least, that's what some JFK conspiracy theorists believe.

Oliver Stone, in his exhausting tribute to stunt casting, *JFK*, more soberly suggested Witt in fact was signalling the assassins on that most sinister piece of topography, the Grassy Knoll, rather than firing flechettes.

Witt's cover story isn't as silly as it sounds, if you think about it. The whole concept of appeasement is a little hard to sum up visually, unless you could re-create Chamberlain's hangdog features and what we'd now term his Walter White moustache. And that's no good if the target of your protest is actually Joseph Kennedy, who was indeed, like many of his fellow Americans, a strong supporter of appeasement before the war. On the other hand, precisely what his son was supposed to do about that in 1963 isn't clear, especially given his father had been disabled by a stroke two years before. Witt could have waved some shares, in reference to how Kennedy *père* made his fortune from insider trading; he could have waved some steroids, or women's underwear, in reference to two of JFK's many pathologies, but that would have looked less interesting and, in the case of the underwear, might even have been mistaken for cheering. A Chamberlain-style umbrella makes some sense.

And the umbrella-launched paralysing flechette has its problems. Yes, umbrella weapons had a rich Cold War history—the Bulgarians once used a pneumatic umbrella to kill a dissident with ricin in London. But if you could fire a paralytic agent from long range into the presidential blood stream, why not fire something, well, a little more lethal? Why such an elaborate assassination? Was there a kind of demarcation dispute between the assassins? Did strict union rules, or a particularly zealous interpretation of the CIA's offshore mandate, require that the CIA only be allowed to *paralyse* the Philanderer-in-Chief, while other conspirators from domestic agencies got to actually kill him?

On reflection, there's a certain comfort in this thought—that even assassins plotting one of the most infamous crimes in history had to follow strict bureaucratic rules about areas of operation. You could almost imagine a *M*A*S*H*-style comedy as the conspirators fight intelligence bureaucracy and bumbling paper-pushers insistent that all hell will break loose unless a presidential assassination is conducted strictly in accordance with the rules.

And for that matter, what *is it* with the CIA and convoluted assassination methods? Some of an apparently endless stream of CIA plots to kill Fidel Castro involved exploding or poisoned cigars, poisoned wetsuits and—the one that makes you wonder if the CIA's LSD experiments went all the way to the top—an exfoliant that would, Samson-like, destroy Castro's political authority by removing his trademark beard. In that context, maybe an umbrella-launched paralytic flechette isn't too much of a stretch.

Welcome to the remarkable world of conspiracy theories.

No one has died as a result of JFK conspiracy theories, unless you count Lee Harvey Oswald, slain before his guilt or innocence could be properly determined (*conveniently!*). But some other conspiracy theories come with a vast body count. The oldest recorded conspiracy theory—forget the Illuminati, they're Johnny-come-latelies from the eighteenth century—is the 'blood libel' directed at Jews, who allegedly conspired to kidnap and murder Christian children for the purposes of ritual murder. This first emerged in the twelfth century, and for the following seven centuries it saw thousands of Jews murdered either by mobs or after 'trials' for killing Christian children or, more accurately, for being Jews. The blood libel was known at the time to be false—several pre-Reformation popes, starting in the thirteenth century, attacked it as merely an excuse to murder and steal property from Jews, but to no avail; indeed, the blood libel was only the beginning of a long list of anti-Semitic conspiracy theories that continue today.

Such theories, and others based on racial, religious or ethnic stereotyping, relate to an identifiable group, easily targeted for violence or theft and easily demonised as the Other by white, Western societies. But there are different types of conspiracy theories, so a system of classification is needed. For example, in addition to theories involving groups easily identifiable as separate from the rest of society, some theories postulate the work of fifth columnists or domestic cabals, people indistinguishable from Us, who could be our friends and neighbours, who can operate undetected in plain sight.* But since the Enlightenment, and especially in the industrial era, conspiracy theories have focused on small groups of powerful figures—anti-Semitism began focusing on a finance industry elite, for example, and in the twentieth century it centred on large corporations,

---

* In its Cold War form, this theme produced three of the greatest science fiction films: the original *Invasion of the Body Snatchers*, Howard Hawk's *The Thing From Another World* and then John Carpenter's remake, in which the most faithful human friend of all, the humble dog, turns out to be—spoiler alert—One Of Them.

secret powers within governments or even supra-governmental bodies, which either kill key figures that pose a threat, stage dramatic events to extend their power or use technology to control some or all of the populace.

Such theories aren't the preserve of any one ideology or side of politics. Left-wing conspiracy theories focus on wicked governments and evil corporations a little more than right-wing theories, in which the UN, atheists and internationalism are the villains, but libertarians are as eager to target overreaching governments as progressives are. Indeed, the revelations by Edward Snowden of the very real conspiracy of systematic intelligence agency surveillance of the internet and telecommunications have produced an unlikely and at times tense coalition of support between conservative libertarians and left-wing progressives, both opposed to governmental surveillance.

Now, the internet seems to have been a great enabler for conspiracy theories, with its capacity to empower and connect communities of like-minded users and the dramatically expanded research capability that it offers, enabling anyone to access a trove of data from which to cherrypick whatever information affirms their beliefs. At least one popular conspiracy theory, about chemtrails, is a wholly internet-era creation, although it only barely qualifies as a fully fledged conspiracy theory since no one has ever clearly explained exactly what the chemicals dispersed at such high altitude are supposed to do and why such an expensive and elaborately inefficient method has been chosen to distribute them when, say, you could chuck some stuff in the local water plant.

The internet is wonderful for conspiracy theories because back in the analogue era, theorists had to settle for amateur magazines or pseudopeer-reviewed journals devoted to their conjectures, or the *Fortean Times*, samizdat for the paranoid circulating on the fringes of publishing or sent like contraband through the mail system (for conspiracy theories about which, see Thomas Pynchon's *The Crying of Lot 49*). They did, just before the early internet let a thousand alt.conspiracy newsgroups bloom, get their own TV show, *The X Files*, a drama based on the simple premise that not one or some but pretty much *all* conspiracy theories were right, thereby delivering a weekly stream of villains for the credulous detective duo to battle. 'I want to believe' was a key slogan of the show, encapsulating the basic problem of conspiracy theories in four words.

On the other hand, if you look closely at conspiracy theories, other than chemtrails (which is akin to that staple of the Cold War, the fluoridation conspiracy theory), there are very few genuinely new plots: 9/11 truthers reprise the FDR-knew-about-Pearl-Harbor theory with a dumber but even richer president;[*] corporations are still either holding back utopian technology or trying to kill us, as always; Muslims are less likely to be murdered by their fellow citizens than Jews used to be, but the alleged plot to 'impose sharia law' (aka 'creeping sharia' aka 'jihad-by-stealth') is a less grisly version of the blood libel, with halal food taking the place of blood-soaked matzo bread.

Indeed, there's a case for the 1960s, not the internet era, being the heyday of conspiracy theories, not merely because of assassinations, social upheaval, the Cold War and Vietnam, but because of the feedback loop created by popular culture. Even before Kennedy's death, *The Manchurian Candidate* (starring none other than Kennedy pal Frank Sinatra, the centre

---

[*] Gore Vidal long claimed that FDR was complicit in Pearl Harbor, and was a 9/11 truther in his last years, demonstrating that Vidal was less America's Biographer than its Dream Diarist.

of many a Mob-based conspiracy theory himself) had played with the idea of patsies used for presidential assassination. Stanley Kubrick had made *Dr Strangelove*, a satire of nuclear war all the funnier and more discomfiting for being an entirely plausible characterisation of the military mindset (Kubrick had to change a Slim Pickens line to remove a mention of Dallas after the death of JFK). The hugely popular Bond films were ritualistically, even archetypally, conspiracy theories featuring a procession of well-resourced cabals and super-villains. In 1967, the spoof US government paper *The Report from Iron Mountain* argued that extended periods of peace were bad public policy and governments needed a variety of lurid social controls to cope; the satiric nature of the work wasn't clear to the media at first, and later the text would, inevitably, be adopted by conspiracy theorists as actual evidence of a New World Order plot rather than a clever piss-take.

Then there was the Apollo project conspiracy: it was only possible to maintain that the moon landing was faked after *2001* had made space travel look realistic; inevitably, it was Kubrick who was alleged to have filmed the fake moon footage. That wasn't the only way the Apollo conspiracy oozed into Hollywood: in 1971's *Diamonds Are Forever*, Connery-Bond (sadly sans umbrella weapon—that would get a mention in the Moore era), in the course of investigating an elaborate Howard Hughes-inspired conspiracy, actually interrupts what appears to be a restaging of the moon landing in the villain's lair in the Arizona desert.* The whole of the sixties seemed to teeter on the brink not merely of social chaos, but of some bizarre admixture

---

* Proper Kubrick conspiracy theorists, of course, can see that the director left any number of clues pointing to the earlier conspiracy in *The Shining*, thereby giving us a conspiracy theory about a conspiracy theory inside a movie.

of farce, tragedy and conspiracy, all invariably played out on screen, from where it seeped into popular culture.

The emergence of conspiracy theories at such times of social stress suggests they have a valuable psychological role. Indeed, conspiracy theories have multiple important uses. For starters, they're a great mechanism for disposing of unwanted information. This is why denialism inevitably and logically ends up in conspiracy theory: while cherrypickers try hard to explain away the vast reams of data from the world's climate scientists showing a warming planet, or how vaccination saves lives, ultimately the only satisfying explanation is that scientists or the medical profession or drug companies are colluding in secret to push an agenda.

So, at its most benign, the warmist conspiracy theory is supposedly that scientists have faked global warming to maintain government funding for their research. Most versions are a little more melodramatic and tend to involve the United Nations' plans for one world government (seventy years of trying and still nothing!), a left-wing plot to de-industrialise the world—there's no soy latte on a dead planet, after all—or even, more rarely, a right-wing plot to promote nuclear power.

But conspiracy theories are less about the epistemological challenge of inconvenient data and more about the human need to find meaning in randomness. The human brain reflexively finds patterns and structures in its environment, a skill immensely useful in the days of primitive humans competing with other predators (as portrayed by Kubrick in the early, funny scenes of *2001*): try hunting and gathering without an ability to make sense out of the sights, sounds and smells around you, much less more complicated tasks like farming, building or, speaking of pattern recognition, writing scripts for Bond films. Better to be predisposed to make Type One errors—false positives—than Type Two errors—false negatives—since the latter will get you killed much more quickly out on the early Anthropocene savannah.

The hypertrophying of this intellectual capacity to identify patterns—apophenia*—can lead to tendencies like thinking you're hearing things when you play records backwards; satanic backmasking is a charge levelled at artists as varied as the Beatles, Britney Spears, Hall and Oates, Judas Priest and the Bee Gees, of whom it might be said that it's satanic enough to play them forwards, let alone backwards. But it also enables sufferers to skilfully fish out every piece of evidence that appears to confirm a conspiracy while failing to see, or explaining away, every piece of contrary evidence.

This surely is one of the reasons why there's a well-established correlation between belief in one conspiracy theory and belief in others. It may be that if you distrust governments enough to think they're poisoning us with chemtrails, you're likely to think they killed Princess Di (although for what reason has never quite been explained). That's especially the case if you live in a culture that is predisposed to conspiracy theories—as Richard Hofstadter argued in the 1960s in *The Paranoid Style in American Politics*, even since colonial times Americans have seemed predisposed to seeing plots all around them. This reflects not just a tendency to mistrust government, but a mental predisposition to spot conspiracies, which means your brain will constantly spot evidence that some nebulous They is engaged in perpetrating a collective crime.

---

* The term began life as a description of a form of psychosis, but has since spread more widely—quite rightly given what a cinematic term it is.

But conspiracy theories are more than group inkblot tests: they fulfil the need of many people to wish away the unpleasantly messy nature of life and the essential purposelessness of the universe. Believing that some cabal somewhere—Jews, climate scientists, the CIA, Big Pharma, the Illuminati, the Bee Gees, whoever—is in control and doing things for their own motives, however sinister, is a more comforting thought for many people than that bad things merely happen, often for no larger purpose, that the universe is a cold, indifferent place in which chance plays a far greater role than human design.

In that sense, the sheer ineptitude of so many conspiracies, by any credible measure, is irrelevant. Fluoridation has been a spectacular failure as a mass-poisoning scheme. False flag gun massacres intended to provide the basis for greater gun regulation in the United States have likewise failed. The death of JFK ushered into the White House the most aggressively liberal president on domestic issues in US history. If the Jews or the Rothschilds or the Masons or an international drug cartel headed by the Queen of England controlled the world's financial system, they did a terrible job in 2008 with the destruction of trillions in wealth in the global financial crisis. But none of that matters. What matters is that someone, somewhere is in control—in secret, and with evil designs (if plainly incompetent), but at least there's *someone* in charge. This is a more appealing idea than that there might be something profoundly wrong with your society, or that US intelligence and law enforcement agencies are inept, or that a beloved figure could be killed in an entirely meaningless accident or act of violence. More appealing than the idea that things, even big, dramatic, epoch-making Things, do not, necessarily, happen for a reason.

Conspiracy theories are also a readily obtainable marker of status, at least in the eyes of the theorists themselves. To believe in a conspiracy is to understand the way the world *really* works, to have privileged access to information that the rest of society doesn't have or refuses to acknowledge, to be an *insider*, part of an information elite self-selected because of their intelligence and scepticism. This information snobbery enables the theorist to look down on the rest of us who are too dumb or too sheep-like to recognise reality, who've been gulled by the cover stories of the conspirators: 'That's what they want you to think.'

This can lead to a certain exasperation if a conspiracy turns out—as some do—to be correct. 'There's nothing new there; everyone knew that' is the annoyed reaction of many experts to the revelations about National Security Agency surveillance, seemingly angered that everyone else has now acquired what some previously used as a personal marker of distinction. Conspiracy theories are a club that becomes unappealing if too many people join, their members epistemological hipsters who knew 9/11 was a con, that Big Brother *was* watching us, that the moon landings were Stanley Kubrick's finest work and that LBJ killed JFK *before it was popular to believe it.*

A decision to believe in conspiracy theories, and what conspiracy theories you choose to believe, is thus similar to a consumer decision to buy one particular product or another based on its advertising and what the product says about you. In Australia, affluent inner-urban families are significantly less likely to vaccinate their children than in lower-income areas, and a similar phenomenon has emerged among affluent, well-educated mothers in California and the UK. Deliberately refusing to vaccinate one's children has thus become a marker of social status, a lifestyle accessory that marks one off from the broader herd, the immunity of which is so important. For older right-wing males, belief in a giant UN-controlled global-warmist conspiracy demonstrates their individualistic, capitalistic mindset. More traditional-minded conspiracy types might prefer the Old Faithfuls of the conspiracy world, JFK and fluoridation, while scholarly theorists embrace the Illuminati, the Knights Templar and plots involving the Catholic Church, ancient texts and historic figures—although, God help us all, Dan Brown might have come dangerously close to popularising those.

But while conspiracy theories notionally give the theorist a greater, more authentic understanding of the world by explaining *what is really going on*, they're often predicated on ignorance. At the heart of many conspiracy theories are howling errors of fact or absurd non-logic. The blood libel, for example, is said to have derived from apocryphal tales of the behaviour of Jewish families during the Crusades; in the face of forced conversion to Christianity, they preferred to die or kill themselves and their families. What would, in a Christian context, be interpreted as martyrdom was considered evidence that Jews were disposed to murder children. The Knights Templar were disbanded because the King of France saw it as a way of evading the huge debts he owed the order. Rather than being an incipient dove, JFK was every bit as signed up to escalating the war in Vietnam as his successor.* The claims of 9/11 truthers about air interception and controlled demolitions of the towers have been repeatedly debunked. *The Protocol of the Elders of Zion* is a fabrication. The lawyer for drug trafficker Schapelle Corby admitted simply

---

* And for the same reasons—JFK had poor advice from both the State Department and the military about Vietnamese nationalism, and the Democrats couldn't stomach a reprise of 'who lost China'.

inventing his claim that corrupt baggage handlers planted the cannabis she tried to import to Bali. Andrew Wakefield falsified data in the paper he used to claim a link between autism and vaccination and planned to make money from scaring people off vaccination; he's been struck off the medical register in the UK and a US judge threw his libel suit out of court.

But conspiracy theory factoids are the cockroaches of epistemology, capable of surviving even a nuclear blast of contrary evidence. Indeed, the act of disproving them often *reinforces* their validity in the eyes of adherents. After all, if you're bothering to try to discredit their theories, they *must* be on to something, especially if you work in the media and are therefore in on all the conspiracies because you need to cover them up.

Another core theme of most major modern conspiracy theories is a belief in the unity and competence of governments. Most of the challenges confronting governments around the world—keeping economies growing, delivering services effectively while struggling to convince voters of the desirability of paying tax, the looming impact of ageing populations—look a doddle compared to the superhuman feats of organisation required to poison the entire population without anyone knowing, tightly control thousands of climate scientists around the world or use swine flu to declare martial law as a prelude to a New World Order. Disillusioned voters the world over can only dream of governments with the organisational genius required to pull off the conspiracies with which they are so often charged.

The sordid truth is that governments aren't especially competent even in the areas they directly control, and nowhere near as unified as conspiracy theorists make out. If multiple US government agencies *had* conspired to kill JFK, they almost certainly would have had problems of interoperability and demarcation. Bureaucrats everywhere protect their turf. Some like to build empires. Some like to avoid responsibility of any kind. All look with scepticism at the activities of other agencies. Tribalism is still tribalism despite the PowerPoint presentations and bureaucratese. And information is harder to control than conspiracy theorists realise. There's always someone who gets caught and spills, or a whistleblower, or an agency that won't cooperate, or even if a secret is kept close, the passage of time tends to out it. Climate change denialists like to compare global warming to Lysenkoism, the absurd agricultural and genetic theories that became legally enforced orthodoxy in the Soviet Union in the 1930s and 1940s. But in fact Lysenkoism demonstrates how hard it is to enforce quackery even with a state apparatus dedicated to surveillance and thuggery—it took full-blown Stalinism to suppress opposition to Lysenkoism, and only in the Soviet Union itself; in other Eastern Bloc countries, it was criticised and rejected. After Stalin's death, criticism of Lysenko re-emerged despite the Communist Party's control mechanisms and within a decade he was denounced and his theories abandoned.

But in the minds of conspiracy theorists, democratic governments operate with Stalinist brutality and remarkable efficiency, moving at top speed to execute their plans flawlessly, like in a Hollywood film: the black helicopters materialise at a moment's notice, the men in suits all act as though part of a hive mind, decisions are made in a split second, plenty of resources are always available. But as anyone who has worked in government knows, bureaucratic reality is messy, and laborious, and frustrating: half the black helicopters are being refitted because of a poor procurement decision, there aren't enough pilots on duty to fly the rest, and poor intelligence caused by agencies refusing to share information has sent them to the wrong location anyway.

This can be seen in the best recent example of a conspiracy theory that turned out to be true: that a US government agency, in league with its counterparts in the UK, Canada, Australia and New Zealand, has a giant internet and phone surveillance and computer-hacking system that it uses to monitor everyone in the world with a phone or internet connection. This was an actual, real-world conspiracy of exactly the kind portrayed in movies, in which the US government, from the president down, implemented a vast, secret plot to spy on their own people and the rest of us. But the core problem was the vast nature of it—it was so huge that the plot extended beyond politicians and government officials and men and women in uniform to private contractors, cleared by a privatised former government security vetting agency. It only took one contractor among hundreds of thousands to decide that the illegal, secret mass surveillance being conducted by the NSA needed to be exposed for the conspiracy to fall apart. Even in the America of Barack Obama, in which whistleblowers are jailed as spies and journalists are regularly spied on, it proved impossible to keep secret a giant government plot to turn the planet into a panopticon.

And as it turns out, secrecy is a highly inefficient way of conducting affairs. Julian Assange has written of a 'secrecy tax' that makes organisations trying to operate in secret less efficient, less internally communicative and less adaptable. The response of the US government to the Edward Snowden revelations has been a sublime demonstration of the secrecy tax in operation: despite knowing that more revelations were to come, and thus preparing for them, or even being proactive in pursuing a debate about surveillance that was going to happen anyway, the Obama Administration and its agencies remained, for months, painfully reactive and relied for an extended period on denial, evasion and casuistry that has left officials, Congressional figures and the president himself embarrassed.

Another logical fallacy at the heart of conspiracy theories is the straightforward *post hoc ergo propter hoc* ('after this, therefore because of this'). For many theorists, what comes after a major event, and who benefits from it, provide an insight into who caused that event. But merely because Western governments have exploited 9/11 to justify a significant reduction in their citizens' basic rights and funnel money to defence contractors does not mean 9/11 was an inside job; merely because the Vietnam War rapidly accelerated after 1964 does not mean JFK's death was a factor. The proper question isn't 'Who benefited?' but 'Who best exploited it?'.

The problem is, when governments behave as if they *are* engaged in conspiracies, they enable conspiracy theorists. The War on Terror has encouraged conspiracy theories because governments have given themselves more power, decreased accountability, engaged in extra-judicial killing, kidnapping, torture and unjustified imprisonment, and reduced transparency. A government that by its own admission abducts people and transports them to 'black sites' for torture, taps the entire internet or breaks into the systems of major internet companies even after those companies have given them access to their data, can easily be assumed to be doing much worse besides that we don't yet know about; indeed, it may be *sensible* to assume that they are doing much else that hasn't been disclosed. Even a government like Australia's secretly approved its citizens being ferried about for torture while publicly denying any knowledge of them, and used its intelligence services to bug the Cabinet rooms of a vulnerable micro-state to benefit a resources company.

This furtive behaviour of governments, their continual arrogation of power, their attacks on whistleblowers and their treatment of their own citizenry as (to use the National Security Agency's own term) 'adversaries' to be constantly monitored seem designed to confirm the worst biases of the paranoid and make belief in conspiracy theories look like a sensible precaution rather than seeing them as the delusions of tinfoil wearers. Real-world governments behaving like governments in movies do worse than blur the line between fact and fiction, they undermine the basic compact of trust between elec-tors and those who, at least notionally, serve them as elected leaders. It becomes much harder to argue that governments are not conspiring against their own citizens when, in fact, that's exactly what they're doing.

BK

7

Reason and unreason: How we've all gone Stupid-mad in an age of absolute sanity

To think of Dr Freud as that guy who wrote about dicks is to think about Bruce Springsteen as that guy who helped Courteney Cox out with her career. If you care to listen to The Boss or Freud, you'll find they both told us with great intelligence how we're just dancing in the dark. Although, of course, many people think we're dancing in the sun of reason. We should all be made to listen to Springsteen and read Freud to remind us that this age, in many respects, is as dark an age as any and, in fact, quite a bit darker than most. Mostly because we think it is so illuminated.

This is a feature of every age. Generally, we tend to presume that this time is the most enlightened time and even if we romanticise the past—and I fully intend to glorify Freud or at least redeem his reputation as That Penis Guy—we do so through the enlightened filter of the present. We know that nostalgia is never a longing for a real thing lost; it's more of a romantic way of avoiding the present. It is probably worth mentioning that in the Good Old Days, nostalgia was actually a mental disorder.

Nostalgia. It ain't what it used to be. What it first was, in fact, was a medical disorder recognised in soldiers deeply troubled by their longing for the past. During the Thirty Years' War, some men were discharged from the Spanish Army of Flanders with the condition that was first described in a 1688 medical text. Up until the American Civil War, this illness was treated.

Of course, now we are so much more enlightened and we know that soldiers were just suffering the effects of war. They had post-traumatic stress disorder, silly! Thank goodness we know that.

And thank goodness we can now recognise depression. Did you know that Willy Loman from *Death of a Salesman* was depressed? Well, Arthur Miller, who wrote the play, didn't and he was a bit, um, depressed by the news that for a 1999 Broadway revival, director Robert Falls gave the script to two psychiatrists. Willy was diagnosed as depressed.

'Willy Loman is not a depressive,' Mr Miller said to the *New York Times*. 'He is weighed down by life. There are social reasons for why he is where he is.'

Willy Loman was weighed down by life. Soldiers were weighed down by death. Diagnosing any of these men, either in the terms of their own era or by ours, just seems silly. External forces impacted on them and it would be, surely, as Stupid to get Willy some Prozac as it would be to take men forced to kill other men into family counselling. Or Lady Macbeth into a treatment program for obsessive-compulsive disorder.

But. We are very enlightened. To remove Willy Loman from his broad social context and to give him a narrow psychological diagnosis is the work of our age. But it wasn't Freud's work, now discredited and darkened by the false memory of a big penis. Psychiatry as it is now—organised and immense and as detached from the world that produced it as Willy is from life—is very often very Stupid. And not only is this iffy branch of medicine itself Stupid, but it has begun to endorse our individual Stupid in a way that extends well beyond patient care. It is, after all, the science of the self. Psychiatry has not only itself become a Stupid science decried by some of its own most respected practitioners; it is now very useful in enhancing our everyday Stupid.

It seems stupid to say that a soldier is suffering the internal illness of 'nostalgia' and not the external impacts of war. But, what we say about Loman, or what we might say about ourselves is just as stupid. This is an era that makes its influence felt. Which is to say, there has never before been an instant where we have been so intimate with the institutions of the state and the market. Opting out is not a realistic option in a time that demands our participation in and consumption of social and electronic media, goods, organised labour and all of those exchanges that create a 'normal' and socially viable person.

We tend to think of our time as one that celebrates the uniqueness of the individual. And, in some ways, there are greater freedoms to behave in ways that are not orthodox; for example, living in a homosexual relationship will not make you a pariah. Neither will failing to show up on every Sabbath to your temple. But what will mark you indelibly is, for example, a refusal to engage in social media. In 2012, both *Forbes Magazine* and *Time* ran articles proposing that an individual without a searchable social media history was far less likely to gain employment in white collar industries. Drawing on the experiences of a former Facebook employee, Katherine Losse, who left the company and cashed in her options, the articles concluded that non-participation in the profit-seeking social media sector not only made life difficult, it was almost impossible. In a piece in the *Washington Post* that same year, Losse, who deactivated all her own social media profiles for a time, explained how Facebook kept 'dark' profiles of those who had not yet joined the big blue giant. 'The moment we're in now is about trying to deal with all this technology rather than rejecting it, because obviously we can't reject it entirely', Losse told the *Post*.

The internet knows that you are absent. And the realms of work and of consumption and health could be said to develop something very like a 'dark profile' if you 'choose' not to participate in their conventions.

One cannot simply not participate in a range of institutions. Not, at least, without a superhuman effort. To describe one's involvement in the world as 'social pressure' doesn't really begin to describe the demands of life which is formed in large part by institutions. Not only our self-esteem but our livelihood is contingent on participation in and some adherence to a dizzying set of norms in the workplace, in the way we look and in our physical health.

In short, there's a lot of stuff we are supposed to do. And it is pretty easy to fail a lot more in the face of so many daily tests. Yet, we naturalise all of these standardised tests and we naturally believe it is our shortcoming when we screw them up. When we fail at life as it is so broadly and meticulously prescribed, we call it mental illness. We have failed life. We are not permitted to think it is the conventions of life that have failed us.

Of course, mental illness can be a useful category. There are those who seem beset by what we would have once called demons. There are certainly people in urgent need of patient care. Even if we have trouble with the sort of extreme medicalisation that leads us to diagnose Willy with depressive disorder and not a bad case of life, we can still agree that it might have been nice if he could have talked through his issues with a professional; maybe even taken some drugs. But it is unlikely that Willy would get much more than drugs even if he did seek help today. Medicalisation, a process that characterises and treats some problems or conditions in medical terms, doesn't have much time for the kind of talk that Freud proposed.

In a complex era that produces complex problems, we are forced to rational solutions. Instrumental medicine might not be ideal in the way it treats the results of life experience as illness, but it's what we've got. Perhaps treating, as we do, things like libido or alcoholism or a lack of socially sanctioned beauty is not the best approach. Perhaps it would be better to reform the world, or to reform the patient's understanding, as Freud suggested, of her place within it. But sometimes it's just more efficient to recognise and treat a problem as a disease. Get your nose fixed. Dry out in a hospital. Take Viagra as prescribed. These may not be ideal solutions to problems we can argue only exist because of social forces and could be fixed by drug-free years in the therapist's suites. But, they are, sometimes, solutions.

But I don't know if we can be quite so permissive when it comes to the medicalisation of Willy Loman. That people are improved by a one-size-fits-most treatment of the 'symptoms' described as anxiety and depression is quite uncertain. The pharmaceutical solution, which is so overwhelmingly and easily offered—in the 2004–2005 financial year, more than twelve million prescriptions for antidepressants were written for Australians—is no solution. In fact, it comes from Stupid. (Actually, I personally found that it produced Stupid. I have never been more Stupid than when I was taking one of the SNRI class of drugs.)

Again, it would just be foolish to reject medicine in its treatment of psychiatric disorders. And this is in no way an account of the Evils of Big Pharma. (Although, like a lot of large institutions, the pharmaceutical industry may fall into patterns of evil.) What I want to do is to take, like Freud would, a patient history of psychiatry itself. Perhaps we can talk out its problems when it comes to treating 'everyday' illnesses such as the anxiety and depression of Willy Loman.

There have been moments in history where we were almost admiring of mental illness; according to one of psychiatry's best-known critics, Michel Foucault, seventeenth-century Europe was 'hospitable' towards the mad. In *Madness and Civilisation*, he takes us on a tour of those moments when the mad have been identified romantically or worshipped as prophets, through those where they have been confined and tortured as devils, to a time (now) where they are medicated and known as 'mentally ill'. Foucault's big book of mad is long and difficult and one I can only recommend to the studiously insane. But its central idea that madness as we now know it is in fact a product of the Age of Reason is a really good one.

Even if you have no time for Foucault—and, man, he is an effort—you probably know about history's idealised madman. Even now, some hopeless romantics think of the mentally ill as seers; as people whose view is not so much impaired as it is enhanced. But this view has all but disappeared. Today, depression—the most common form of recognised madness—is typically seen as limited vision and not at all as something that can give anyone any particular insight. Every now and then, some nutty scientist will tell us that depression has an upside; that there is a benefit to depression in that it seems to create the conditions for deep thought. Certainly, Aristotle thought of it as a useful pest. In *The Problems*, he notes that 'all men who have attained excellence in philosophy, in poetry, in art and in politics, even Socrates and Plato, had a melancholic habitus; indeed some suffered even from melancholic disease'. In 2009, a paper in US journal *The Psychological Review* called 'The bright side of being blue: Depression as an adaptation for analyzing complex problems' (Andrews, Thomson and Anderson) caused a fuss when the authors advanced the possibility that depression has some cognitive benefits.

Mostly, though, the view of depression is that it is bad thinking that needs to be fixed. If you have had an experience of the collection of symptoms psychiatry calls depression, you will agree that it is something that needs to be fixed. But perhaps you might also agree—if not now, then a little further along—that if it does need to be fixed, then we are certainly going about fixing it in a Stupid way. There is an argument to be made that depression, and mood disorders in general, aren't getting a whole lot better. Which is to say, maybe this is one of the things that our enlightened age has not illuminated but darkened.

Even if we are not ourselves told by our doctor that we are mentally unwell, there is a very good chance someone in our lives will be afflicted by what we call 'mental illness'. And in the very rare case that you do not have the experience of knowing someone with a diagnosis of mental illness, you will have certainly heard a statistic like 'one in three Australians' or the World Health Organization's declaration that mental illness will be a major health concern in coming decades.

Now, there are many good practitioners who will critique this view of mental health and remind us that what we often have when we are diagnosed with 'mental illness' is a perfectly logical reaction to life. Psychiatry has long been Stupid. Well, to be fair, it has been Stupid on and off. It wasn't Stupid where Freud was concerned. This is the guy who gives us the useful idea of the unconscious mind. Before Freud, we heard preludes to the idea that we have a big numb beast inside us. Jesus is thought to have said, 'They know not what they do.' Marx, who half described the unconscious mind as 'ideology', said, 'They don't know what they are doing, but they are doing it.' Nietzsche saw something very close to Freud's idea of the unconscious mind. He called it the 'will to power'. These accounts of how and why we are so often so fucked up and out of our own control appear throughout history. There's stuff inside us that we are very good at keeping in the dark.

Let's just pause to shine a little light on Freud, the Prince of Psychiatric Darkness. Freud talked about the conscious mind being like a stronghold in a great city. This 'ego' is the thing we need, and the thing that develops in most human children, to make us social. If we were solitary creatures, we'd have no need of ego (nor super-ego, the semi-conscious part of us that stores away morality and 'conscience'); we would just need our id, or our unconscious. Our unconscious, of course, is the city. The big messy ancient city that stores unexamined memory in the darkness. At another point, Freud describes the unconscious mind like a horse and the ego, or the conscious mind, as its puny rider.

We don't know what we do but we are doing it. The biggest part of us is always in the dark. Actually, I think the city describes it best. If we think of the dark city, we can begin to see how this development of consciousness is reflected in history.

The city of the self is in darkness at childhood, so let's say that the Dark Ages are something we remember as our intellectual infancy. We build the garrison at the Enlightenment. And from this little stronghold of conscious thought, we form the ability to engage in all kinds of complex social interaction. It is here, in this tiny space, that conscious miracles are made. We learn to describe and govern ourselves and others. Our capacity to think and to organise and to reason evolves at speed. We have grown into and built a conscious social adult world that gives us powerful principles like science, reason and liberal democracy. We no longer need God to assuage the dark fears felt by the barely conscious child and we feel that our world is bathed in light.

But what we consciously forget while we're in this small garrison full of light is that the city full of darkness sustains it. The process of psychoanalysis is one that acknowledges the darkness. Freud may not have succeeded in finding a way into the dark unconscious, but he certainly knew it was there. What our modern age did, however, was grow to suppose that everything was bathed in the light of reason. The great fault of the Enlightenment was to make us believe that we were entirely enlightened. In our eagerness to believe we could shine a light on everything, we committed a fundamental act of adult Stupid. We repressed the unconscious darkness in which every conscious life begins.

If we are to entertain this Freudian view of Enlightenment history, we can see how what was once just seen as the darkness of uncontrolled human emotion now becomes the opposite of reason. You are no longer emotional or mad or a prophet or a demon. You are just unreasonable. And the way we treat unreason is with reason.

Freud wanted to treat patients with some crazy techniques. Dream interpretation; word association; an analysis of 'slips' or mistakes. Psychoanalysis doesn't believe that mental illness is the opposite of reason. Rather, it's the thing that reason leaves behind and fails to acknowledge. Of course, you might still think this idea of the unconscious as an actual thing is a crock. But you might acknowledge that it is also a very powerful crock in terms of explaining mental illness. There are few of us who can say we understand our own behaviour fully. There are fewer still who can say they understand the behaviour of the world. Unless we actually stop believing that we are all completely rational enlightened beings in full command of all our actions and nations, there really is no hope for our journey out of Stupid. And perhaps there is no hope for treating the large numbers of people who feel real and keen pain. If there is no moment where we say that psychiatry simply does not know, then the suffering we call 'anxiety' and 'depressive' disorders are bound to continue.

We can do better as an organised species that acknowledges its own Stupid and so can psychiatry. It is the perverse hope that we will think more ably in the future than we do right now that prompts me—and other more qualified people—to ask questions of the branch of medicine that defines reasonable and unreasonable behaviour in the present. As we've said about a thousand times elsewhere in this book, it is *crucial* for us to examine the idea of 'progress' if we want to stop being so stupid. We tend to assume that things are just getting better.

Come on. Lots of things are absolute shit and one of them is the fact that a large number of people having, like Willy Loman, perfectly logical reactions to life are being treated with drugs.

Psychiatry won't admit it, but the psychiatric view of science is actually mystic and dark. A great deal of science is not at all mystic. A great deal of science happens entirely in that well-lit garrison. But psychiatry is not science. There are no blood tests for psychiatric disorders. There are no brain scans. No pathology has yet been found. All we have is a checklist of symptoms as evidence for depression, ADHD or binge eating disorder. We have a checklist of symptoms and some drugs littering the streets of an unconscious city now growing more uniformly fucked thanks to the idea it knows how to organise itself.

Concern about job loss, the death of one's child or physical dismemberment can all be diagnosed as depression. Actually, grief can now be diagnosed as depression, too. I remember reading that in the news and wondering to myself if, perhaps, love would also one day become a mental illness.

This will almost certainly be the case. There is 'an involuntary interpersonal state that involves intrusive, obsessive, and compulsive thoughts, feelings, and behaviours that are contingent on perceived emotional reciprocation from the object of interest' identified by psychiatry (Albert Wakin & Duyen B. Vo, 2011 *The Wakin–Vo I.D.R. Model of Limerence*). One is no longer 'love sick'. One has come down with something called 'Limerence'. This involuntary and frequent affection is pretty much what I feel for my partner.

One can easily suppose in such a rational and illuminated century where even talk shows shed 'light' on the darkest corners of the psyche that psychiatry has progressed. I began to suspect that this may not be the case when, in 2008, my ninety-seven-year-old grandmother, who was widowed, in pain and about to die, was prescribed an antidepressant. A young doctor called her 'depressed'. As if death wasn't already sufficiently medicalised.

I'm hardly the only one shocked by psychiatry's irrationally rational authority. Some of the twentieth century's most respected voices in psychiatric medicine have denounced a system that can no longer make room for the sadness of death. There are guys who, quite literally, wrote the book on madness who now find it mad; we'll meet them in a minute. First, let's look at that book; it's one where normal sadness is rewritten to become depression.

The most influential document in psychiatry today was not written by Freud; a difficult voice muffled for its insistence that the world had something to do with the darkness of individuals and that an unconscious mind governs so much of this individual will. It is *The Diagnostic and Statistical Manual of Mental Disorders*, or the DSM, a book that turns much non-normative behaviour into a series of symptoms that come together to give us diseases. The DSM, first published in 1952 and currently in its fifth revision, is both the major funding source and the raison d'être of the American Psychiatric Association. In it, you'll find all the mental and mood disorders for which we can be treated and a few for which we cannot. There are some diseases-by-committee so dumb and made up that even psychiatry can't be bothered to invent a way to fix them. Honestly, read it. Some of the diseases look like they were put in there for kicks or on a dare. Among my favourites in the new edition of the DSM is binge eating disorder (BED). It is basically like very mild bulimia without the throwing up and it has, like so many of the disorders in the book do, pretty generous criteria. To wit:

eat to excess more than twelve times in three months and feel a bit bad about it. So if, like me, you have eaten a pizza on your own once a week, possibly in your underwear, and felt a bit crap about how fast you rammed it into your greedy pie-hole, congratulations: you're not just a lazy pig who has fallen into a bad habit because things have been shitty lately and/or you like pizza; you're mentally ill.

Actually, in researching this chapter—surely a 'rational' act—I have shown symptoms consistent with BED. I ate an imperial pound of Cadbury Dairy Milk Marvellous Creations Jelly Popping Candy Beanies when I was trying to understand Foucault's account of madness and I ate a whole barbecued chicken while I was reading just one chapter of Freud's *Civilisation and its Discontents*. When Freud compared my conscious mind to a garrison in the city of the id, I thought I felt bad because I knew that most of humanity represses most of itself most of the time. Now I know it was because I ate an entire bird while I was alone in my underpants. I also ate the parson's nose. I am not even going to tell you what I ate when I was reading the newest revisions to the DSM. Let's just say that I should probably be in sectioned care for greedy lunatics.

Thanks, psychiatry. Thanks for turning my erratic eating habits into unreason. Thanks for BED, which turns 'eating even when feeling full' into something that can be medicated with Topmirate, an appetite suppressant, or with antidepressant drugs. Let's not think about talking it through. Let's not say that overeating is a normal response to a culture that encourages it or, worst of all, just fun.

We should make brief mention of the influence of pharmaceutical companies on DSM revisions. Certainly, this topic is widely discussed by psychiatrists. There are a few blockbusters on the subject, including David Healy's *Let Them Eat Prozac: The unhealthy relationship between the pharmaceutical industry and depression*. There is a wealth of study on economic rationalism and how it plays its part in creating 'mental illness' that is, in fact, just a reaction to life. You can read many compelling arguments against the business of a psychiatry that would create a 'disorder' like BED in order to medicate it. But my argument is more about how the idea of reason is used to make us ill.

There are many reasons why one might overeat, not the least of which is that consumption itself is seen by so many of us as an antidote to the despair of the everyday. I mean, this despair is produced and then milked as surely as psychiatric illnesses are invented and then medicated. Listen, for example, to the music played at any major supermarket chain. It will be Coldplay, U2, Snow Patrol, REM. Mournful music played in the key of minor consumption. Even if psychiatry has dispensed with the idea of the unconscious mind, marketers still know how to work it.

It strikes me that if one is overeating, one is behaving in accordance with the temptations and frustrations of our era. And no, I am not saying that people have no choice. If I said that, Bernard, a real free-will guy, would demand a creative divorce. But I do believe our choices are limited by the diminishing size of our conscious minds and the encroaching size of our BED appetites. Every day, this rational world makes our big, dumb ids just a little bit bigger and dumber.

The era is mad and it is not unreason to act in accordance with its demands. If one is overeating and feeling bad about it, one is probably driven by unconscious desires. The correct way to illuminate these unconscious desires might be, say, a Freudian approach. That is, we would set about illuminating the unconscious and actually shining a light on the individual experiences that led us to repeatedly enact this unwanted behaviour. Psychoanalysis is the process of giving light to individual darkness. We are mostly made of chocolate-eater, says Freud. The chocolate-eater is the city and the conscious mind is the tiny dieter in the garrison. The city stores all of the history and is, in fact, the foundation for this tiny little room to which the city is hostile. The conscious us can be seen as an unwelcome soldier in the city of the self.

In *Civilisation and its Discontents*, Freud described how this internal conflict plays out in the social. And he talks about how the psychoanalytic approach is a long, and quite unreasonable, process of illumination. From the garrison, we learn to view and even command some of the city. This remains a powerful idea. And it is one that stays with us in a very contradictory form. We absolutely agree with Freud that 'repression' is a bad thing and that we MUST talk about our problem; we must shine a light on all the dark. And we do this on talk shows and in newspapers and on our deathbed. But really, in thinking we have conquered the chocolate-eating city, the chocolate-eating city conquers us. Freud would be 'depressed' to know that he gave us Oprah, and Stupid people who think that 'mental illness' is an explanation and a cure for unwanted behaviour. Mine is a whole generation of twits with a psychiatric industry to support them in the belief that we know about the ugliness of the unconscious city because we see it on TV.

What is that thing Keyser Söze says about the devil in *The Usual Suspects*? The greatest trick the devil ever pulled was convincing us all he didn't exist. We believe ourselves, in this age of psychiatric reason, to be emptied of the devil and filled with rational light. But the city is now even darker and our idea of the devil remains. It's a wasteland filled with chocolate wrappers and electronic memories of suffering. The unconscious is devouring us with a melancholy soundtrack and the delusion it has disappeared.

Psychoanalysis is the attempt to throw light, to take us carefully through the rubble and make sense of it. Whether we have suicidal thoughts or a chocolate problem, it is an approach with value on both a philosophic and individual level. But there is so little demand for it in a world that sees itself as so enlightened.

Now, there are still a handful of psychiatrists who will embark on this individual exploration of the unconscious with a patient. But mostly, there are psychiatrists and general practitioners who will prescribe a one-size-fits-most cognitive or drug approach. And what this supposes is not, as Freud posited, that the individual unconscious needs illuminating but, in the process started by men like Descartes and mutated by an increasingly rational Oprah Age that feels it has absolute knowledge, that we have *already* illuminated everything.

If I happened to have a serious problem with binge eating—and I know this can be a serious problem; I live in the world's most obese nation—I think I would benefit more long term from a discussion of the factors that led me to cram things into my face. If I can genuinely see the problem truly illuminated, as Freud would have recommended, and not just falsely illuminated by a GP going through a list of symptoms and prescribing me a factory-made solution, then I think my chances of overcoming the bad behaviour would be much improved.

Here is a case where real enlightenment might work; where really tackling that Stupid that lives in your big, dumb, pleasure-craving, death-loving id and exposing it to light could change your behaviour. Instead, the more common end is to take a mass-produced solution. And for the patient, this is almost as much a faith-based cure as any snake oil. We trust that the professional knows what he is doing and has a fine understanding of the very complex research and theorising that led him to give us a Selective serotonin reuptake inhibitor (or SSRI, such as Prozac or Zoloft). But what we emerge with is no real understanding of the darkness inside us and no way to really illuminate it.

Accepting a standard cure, in which I have no understanding, just doesn't strike me as a good way to bounce back from an undesirable mental state. This is not to say the new drugs have no place. I was prescribed medication to recover from the ongoing attentions of a stalker. I was also instructed in Thought Field Therapy, an idiot-fringe treatment that required me to tap my 'meridian points'. My understanding of meridians is about the same as my understanding of how serotonin inhabits the neural cleft; which is to say, hazy-to-none. But I underwent this therapy, which I had no choice but to trust, for a year and I just wish, given that I still feel the effects a decade later of the conditions that the psychiatrist called post-traumatic stress disorder and major depression and generalised anxiety, that I had walked into the office of a good Freudian.

I think what I got was some urgent care that stopped me killing myself. But what came after that was false enlightenment. The diagnosis did no good to anyone but my insurance providers. I got a false cure just as easily as I might get a false diagnosis of BED if I chose to explain my recent eating habits to a doctor.

Just why the DSM-5 felt the need to add a regular feature of my Friday nights to its taxonomy of unreason is uncertain. And not illuminated much by its own explanation. 'A primary goal is for more people experiencing eating disorders to have a diagnosis that accurately describes their symptoms and behaviors,' they offer as a justification for BED.

The chief function of psychiatry's pseudo-science is diagnosis based on symptoms. Diagnosis based on symptoms, usually described by the patient, is all that psychiatry has. It is an improper science behaving like a proper science. It is totally full of shit.

But we buy this idea of the illuminated self and we accept that 'mental illness' is itself a rationale for much of our unwanted behaviour.

The editor of the third revision of the DSM is Robert Spitzer. Described by *The New Yorker* as 'one of the most influential psychiatrists of the 20th century', the man diagnosed the DSM itself with delusions of progress. In the foreword to an excellent book on the history of depression, *The Loss of Sadness* (Horwitz and Wakefield, 2008), he said he had been 'forced to rethink [his] own position' on the habits of a medicine that made ordinary sadness a medical concern.

The editor of the fourth revision of the DSM was even more broadly critical of the publication of which he had once been chief architect. Allen Frances called the defence by the American Psychiatric Association of its book a 'meaningless mantra' in the *Huffington Post*. In the journal *Annals of Internal Medicine* he described an urgent 'crisis of confidence' and advised that the revised DSM be used 'cautiously, if at all'.

There are men and women of science pleading for the DSM to be remade.

If one shows evidence of distress upon a fatal diagnosis and those 'symptoms' extend to a period longer than two weeks, one will be diagnosed with depressive disorder. Yes, you can and most likely will be diagnosed with depression along with certain death. These are the plain instructions in psychiatry's most influential handbook.

Psychiatry may not be rational, but it is certainly rationalised. It may not be medical, but the conditions it purports to treat are certainly medicalised.

There is a widespread belief that there is a stigma associated with mental illness. I have found that the reverse is true. There is a stigma in saying: 'Hey, maybe something else is going on here that has nothing to do with "mental illness". Maybe I am not mentally ill but just responding to a life that pumps waste into my brain and does not permit its outlet.'

I believe in reason. But I don't know if I believe that if the psychiatric version of reason is much good at treating 'mental illness'. A great deal of the time—and again I want to be clear that there are obviously people beset by terrible pain who require meaningful therapy—'mental illness' is unconsciously defined by psychiatry as the opposite of reason. So if we think about Freud's city of the unconscious as being a good idea, then psychiatry itself is a rejection of this territory. Psychiatry wants to make us live entirely in the reasonable garrison of the conscious mind. In other words, the reason of the Enlightenment has begun to believe in itself so completely, it does not allow for anything outside it. If psychiatry continues to see unreason as something to treat rather than something that can be explained or even accepted, then it will continue its program of widespread Stupid.

Psychiatry has a great history of imposing its irrational diagnostic reason on people who really didn't need it: Willy Loman. My grandmother. Nostalgic soldiers. Homosexuals—a disease category that was removed from the DSM in the seventies not thanks to scientific evidence but because of political pressure.

In other words, homosexuality ceased to be a disease for exactly the same reasons it was classified as one in the first instance. Scientistic, moralising, half-arsed Stupid.

Occupied for so long with the unambitious and harmful work of normalising people who are not ill and of making illness normal, psychiatry has fallen into darkness. It has abandoned even the pretence of science in its mania for finding a disease to fit a cure rather than finding a cure to fit a disease.

'Mental illness does not discriminate,' say the organisations that support the view that nearly everyone is mentally ill and not just, perhaps, in need of a talking cure or a better life. Mental illness does not discriminate and neither does psychiatry. It provides a narrow range of drug therapies for an ever-increasing range of made-up diseases. And in its mania to treat Willy Loman-itis or the sadness of death and other inevitable human states of confusion, it has much less than it should to offer those suffering disorders that might truly have an identifiably medical basis. In other words, how about a little bit less looking for drugs to treat binge eating disorder and a bit more research into suffering that cannot be socially explained?

Practitioners and patients must become more cynical about the false light of psychiatry. There is no branch of medicine which gets away with so much profitable mischief with so few biomarkers. But what it lacks in laboratory evidence or any account of its underlying scientific principles, it makes up for in profit and a broad public enthusiasm for diagnosis. To claim that mental illness may not be as widespread as routinely suggested is not unkind. Nor does it discredit the very real agony people feel or the very real need for its remediation. This is not a moralising claim. It's just a simple conclusion that even a basic understanding of what is meant by scientific method allows. Psychiatry's method, by the admission of some of its most notable practitioners, is not scientific. It is a pseudo-science that got lucky with the development of some drugs that changed moods. The hypothesis that low serotonin levels cause depression is losing traction. No one has a good idea of how these drugs work. In 2011, Marcia Angell, a former editor of *The New England Journal of Medicine*, wrote of psychiatry's vague ideas of chemical imbalances that 'researchers have still come up empty-handed'.

This is a science without theories and without any real shifts in its theorising. This is a medical practice that, unlike cardiology, does not have a uniform set of guidelines on what life practices a sick person might embrace or avoid. Of course, a good shrink might dare you to consider that changing your life is a more effective route out of a depression that, meta-studies suggest, in a mild form is resistant to drug treatment. But a profession working to sustain itself in the half-light of reason is too preoccupied to produce that many good shrinks.

Freud may have been dancing in the dark with ideas that bore more relation to philosophy and art than they did to reason and science. But perhaps this approach is what psychiatry needs to save itself and the many, regardless of their 'diagnosis', who need it. As much as psychiatric diagnosis might provide some short-lived comfort to desperate people, it has been shown to be an impotent practice. It is not moralising to say that our idea of mental anguish as a disease needs redress. What is moralising is a system of hunches masquerading as theory that can transform non-normative behaviour into a problem.

Depression and anxiety are not beautiful. 'Mad' people are not prophets. People in pain need relief. But they're not going to get it from mysticism in scientific drag. The belief that we are enlightened and not benighted is a poison. It is not a remedy.

The Stupid of failing to acknowledge our ignorance will get us every time.

Pass the fucking chocolate.

HR

8

Political arithmetic, or, Slack hacks lack facts when flacks stack the stats

You know that I have little faith in political arithmetic and this story does not contribute to mend my opinion of it.

—Adam Smith, 1785, after Alexander Webster revised his estimate of the population of Scotland by one-sixth.

Much of the Stupid we discuss in this book is easily spotted by anyone with a functioning brain, even if sometimes we've become so inured to it, even if it takes some effort to separate it from its surroundings. But some forms camouflage themselves successfully as the very opposite of Stupid, masquerading as scientific and mathematical evidence, hiding behind numbers, lurking within data, requiring more than just close attention to identify. Some forms of Stupid take some work to unmask and expose, making them all the more dangerous. One of them is the systematic misuse of numbers to mislead and misinform public debate.

Let's start with a contemporary example, one torn from the headlines of Sydney newspapers. It deals, after all, with an alarming problem. Violence on the nocturnal streets of Sydney was growing worse, caused by an epidemic of alcohol abuse— binge-drinking teenagers and aggressive, alcohol-fuelled males travelling into the city's entertainment areas and looking for trouble, lashing out, assaulting others, often at random. Young men died, struck down with a single punch. The city's doctors, sick of treating the victims of this rising tide of damage caused by alcohol, demanded action. The media joined the campaign, calling for tougher laws, heavier sentences and tighter restrictions to curb the epidemic of violence. Eventually, after an intense debate in the city's newspapers in early 2014, the state government agreed and brought in a set of hard-line laws and new restrictions on alcohol consumption in Sydney. Informed public debate had led to the successful resolution to a vexing public policy issue.

There was only one problem: it wasn't true. There was no rising tide of violence in inner Sydney—quite the opposite: the actual number of assaults (not the incident rate, which accounts for population changes) in inner Sydney had last increased in 2010 and had fallen more than 20 per cent since 2008. In particular, alcohol-related violence, crime statistics showed, had fallen precipitately in the city. The deaths of young men as a result of 'king hit' attacks, tragic and painful as they were, as agonising for their families and friends as they must have been, were increasingly atypical in a city and a state where violence had become significantly less common over a number of years— except for domestic violence, which remained a too-common feature of crime statistics and a too-rare subject of media interest. Moreover, as we saw in an earlier chapter, Australians' alcohol consumption has been generally declining for nearly thirty years, and data showed more young people weren't drinking at all and fewer were binge drinking. Data from the Australian Bureau of Statistics showed alcohol consumption in Australia in 2013 was at its lowest since the mid-1990s.

Journalists engaged in the media campaign avoided mentioning the contrary data about falling violence and less drinking, or declared it 'confusing' in a 'lies, damned lies, and statistics' way. One campaigning doctor admitted that the *level* of violence might not be getting worse, but its intensity was, a claim difficult to verify or even assess accurately. But nonetheless, public health lobbyists welcomed the tighter restrictions on drinking that resulted, and called for a national summit to discuss increasing the level of tax on alcohol, which in Australia is already high by world standards. Alcohol was 'cheaper than water', journalists and commentators repeatedly said, a claim that, like most of the others made in the course of the debate, could be easily proven false within thirty seconds online.

The whole campaign, in fact, had been invented by Sydney's major newspapers—both of which, while we're on the subject of statistics, had lost 15 per cent of their circulation in just one year prior to the campaign—in league with paternalist public health groups and anti-alcohol campaigners. The result of this media-induced wave of Stupid was some very ordinary policies: the government proposed the demonstrably flawed policy of mandatory prison sentences, introduced arbitrary restrictions on inner-urban drinking venues and planned to make the penalties around steroid selling the equivalent of hard narcotics offences.

Now, it would not be a major revelation in this history of Stupid to note that the media beat up stories around the topic of crime. And, it should be noted, as new forms of crime emerge, they receive the same Stupid treatment by the media as more traditional law-breaking. Take 'cybercrime', which is frequently labelled 'the fastest growing form of crime' by the media and politicians. In the same way as public health lobbyists earn a living offering solutions to 'problems' like alcohol, the media hype cybercrime with the aid of companies that make money from selling protection against it. In fact, there have been so many wildly overstated reports about the cost of cybercrime that in 2013 one cybersecurity firm, McAfee, apologised for and retracted a claim that cybercrime cost US$1 trillion globally, after issuing a new report suggesting the cost was less than a third of that. Not long after, Microsoft claimed the cost of cybercrime was actually $100 billion a year. And genuinely independent reports (that is, those not produced by firms that make money from selling cybersecurity products) showing the cost of cybercrime is falling, and falling significantly, are increasingly common.

As for the 'fastest growing crime' tag, the FBI used that description of cybercrime in the US a decade ago, and they haven't used it since (because it's not true), but it has taken on a life of its own since then, an unkillable factoid still to be found in politicians' speeches, law enforcement statements and media reports.

And the Stupid gets worse—much, *much* worse—when it comes to one specific type of 'cybercrime': software and content 'piracy'. File sharing has by itself generated a mini-industry dedicated to proving its profoundly damaging economic effects, despite content industries continuing to perform strongly. The US broadcasting industry's revenue has risen 22 per cent since 2009 to hit a record US$121 billion in 2012. Worldwide movie ticket sales have soared in recent years—in 2013 they set a new global record of US$36 billion and ticket sales have risen

22 per cent since 2009—and while the music industry has seen steady decline in sales of recorded music in recent years, global live music sales have smashed previous highs, with an all-time record $4.8 billion spent in concert ticket sales in 2013, a 30 per cent increase on 2012. But according to a litany of industry-funded studies, file sharing is on the verge of destroying those industries. According to a study prepared by an economics firm for an Australian film studio body in 2010,* file sharing would result in the loss of more than 8000 Australians jobs in content industries that year and cost those industries $900 million. 'Nation of unrepentant pirates costs $900m' was the scolding headline in an ensuing media report.

But some basic checking would have raised significant questions about the report. Rather than falling, employment in both the creative and performing arts and motion picture and sound recording industry subsectors had, according to data from the Australian Bureau of Statistics, steadily risen over the decade to 2010, despite the alleged impact of movie piracy (first via pirated DVDs—a now almost-forgotten form of crime, like wreckers luring ships onto rocks—then online). In 1999, employment in Australia's creative industries averaged 27,000 people over the year and motion picture production 22,000. In 2013, they averaged 41,000 and 27,000 jobs respectively. More Australians are employed making films and in the creative industries now than when, courtesy of a dirt-cheap Australian dollar, George Lucas made those wretched *Star Wars* prequels here.† Further, the numbers were different to those in another

---

* Australian studio bodies are simply subsidiaries of Hollywood bodies, and parrot exactly the same lines on file sharing.

† In a similar period, employment in the US arts and entertainment industry has risen 16 per cent.

report by another economics firm for another content industry group mere months earlier, which concluded movie piracy cost Australia $551 million and caused the loss of 6000 jobs across the whole economy.

Okay, so you say 6000, I say 8000—there's not such a big difference . . . but there had been *another* report four years earlier showing piracy cost the Australian movie industry just $230 million annually in Australia. However, the US authors of that report later admitted they'd got some basic calculations wrong and inflated their estimates. And when that first report, the 8000 jobs one, was eventually released for public scrutiny—the journalist who wrote the story at the time hadn't seen the report, just been told what was in it—it was revealed the report was simply the application of data from a European report to Australia, without any attempt to use local data or take local circumstances into account. Worse, the source report—the European report, yes, I know it's hard to keep track, but as I said, there's an entire mini-industry producing these—had been discredited, particularly its prediction that piracy would cause the loss of 1.2 million jobs in creative industries in Europe. In 2013, the EU was lauding its creative industries as an important and, for the Europeans, all too rare, source of economic growth.

All right, all right, the blur of numbers is getting too much. And a generous soul, seeking to explain such inconsistencies, might think that there's just something innately difficult to calculate about the internet, what with it being *cyber* and *virtual* and *borderless* and everything having to be calculated, presumably, in binary numbers. But increasingly we have a broader environment of all kinds of public debate in which statistics and economic data are routinely invented or manipulated, and contrary data ignored, in the service of a preferred narrative that suits specific interests, including the media's. Across dozens of diverse public policy issues, we're awash in all kinds of rubbish numbers about jobs and costs gleaned from misused data, absurd economic modelling and nonsensical reports produced by vested interests and handed to a gullible or collusive media for reporting.

Like ever-rising levels of crime, there are some numerical claims that draw their strength from being incessantly repeated despite being contradicted by reality, and these routinely feature in the media and in political polemic. Like crime, suicide is regularly claimed by the media to be rising to 'epidemic' levels, when, as we have seen, it has fallen dramatically in Australia over the last two decades in the non-indigenous community, and remained at about the same (far too high) level among indigenous people. Since the Howard government's hard-line industrial relations regime was replaced by a more employee-friendly system by a Labor government in 2008, employer groups and conservative politicians have been regularly warning that it would lead to fewer jobs, lower productivity, unsustainable wage rises and union militancy. In fact, 2010 and 2013 both saw the second-lowest level of industrial disputes since records began in the 1980s; labour productivity grew significantly faster under the new system compared to under the Howard government, when it stagnated or fell; 2013 was the lowest year for wages growth in Australia on record; and over 700,000 jobs had been created under the new system. Nonetheless, the claims continue to be made regardless of their inaccuracy, with claims of a 'productivity crisis' and 'wages explosion'.

But the primary abuse of numbers in public debate relates to their manipulation and invention. And so persistent and widespread is this form of Stupid that we can list the dodgy techniques that are used over and over again in public debate by those who try to use numbers in their own interests. These are just a few:

The reverse magic pudding

Norman Lindsay's beloved Magic Pudding would always re-form into a pudding no matter how often he was eaten, providing a handy metaphor for generations of Australian economists and politicians, who would often accuse their opponents of 'Magic Pudding economics'. But a staple of bogus economic numbers is a reversal of this—a peculiar form of commerce in which money lost from one industry (invariably, the industry that has paid for the report concerned) *never goes anywhere else,* but instead entirely vanishes from the economy, a pudding that magically consumes itself if no one else does.

Thus, the money lost from content industries because of piracy, for example, is assumed to simply disappear, unspent. A consumer who had downloaded something for free rather than paying the content industry's inflated prices forever retains the money they might have spent buying the CD or DVD or going to the cinema. They don't put it in the bank, where it might add to savings that can be used for investment; they don't spend it watching other movies or buying other music (in fact, there's evidence file sharers spend considerably more money buying music than those who don't also download it for free), nor do they spend it elsewhere, creating jobs and growth in other industries. It just sits there in their pockets, never touched again, or perhaps they bury it every time they download something, so it never flows to any other part of the industry or the economy.

A variant on the reverse magic pudding is the type of report that argues government spending in a particular area would create thousands of new jobs both in that industry and, because of *multipliers*, in other industries as well—without mentioning that similar spending in other areas or industries might via other multipliers create *more* jobs, or that there may be greater benefits for the economy in governments reducing support for industries, curbing expenditure or cutting taxes.

Economists debate the issue to this day, but some say *multipliers* are a branch of . . .

Major event mathematics

This is a special branch of applied mathematics, studied closely not in the halls of academe but in consultancies working for governments and sporting bodies. This area deals with the remarkable properties of major event numbers, which do not comply with the ordinary laws of maths but instead have, rather like the additional dimensions of string theory, further layers of multiplication and an innate capacity to erase negative symbols. This is because, unlike conventional maths, major event maths works backwards from the answer you want to give you the numbers you need.

Only in the arcane world of major event mathematics, for example, can the Melbourne Formula One grand prix, which costs the state of Victoria $50 million a year, somehow generate a net $30 million in economic benefits. Likewise, by employing major event mathematics, bidding cities always ignore the fact that nearly every host city ends up spending at least twice more than budgeted to host the Olympic Games and loses money doing so. It's major event maths when builders of big road projects start from the traffic levels they need to make the project viable, then work backwards to their traffic forecasts. And when FIFA announces that 26 billion people have watched a soccer tournament on a planet with only 7 billion people, them's major event numbers, presumably delighting advertisers who are reaching not merely every human on earth, but tens of billions of aliens as well.

The inapt comparison

This trick's a clever one, because spotting it requires quite specialist knowledge or a willingness to go digging for information: use a comparison to make your case for you while not explaining all the ways in which the comparison is meaningless. Say you want to argue that costs in Australia's construction industry are too high. But too high compared to what? Comparing them to Chinese or African building costs will alert even casual readers that you're making a dodgy comparison. Why not the United States? It's a developed country, just like Australia, and will make your point that Australia should reduce wages and introduce greater 'workplace flexibility'. The only problem will be if someone bothers to check and spots that you're comparing costs in something entirely inappropriate. You might compare Australian construction costs to costs in the Texas building industry, which is half the size of the entire Australian industry and thus benefits from huge economies of scale, and which relies on immigrant labour, much of it illegal, for more than a third of its workforce, and which has a workplace death rate many times higher than Australia's. The comparison in fact is a proposal that Australia massively scale up its construction sector using illegal immigrants whom we don't mind seeing killed.

On the other hand, there are times when industries insist that it's everyone *else* who is making the inapt comparisons. In response to a parliamentary inquiry into why software, content and IT products cost more in Australia—often 50 per cent more—than in the United States and other markets, companies like Microsoft, Apple and Adobe and the copyright industry argued that international comparisons, even for software and content that could be delivered online, were meaningless. Such comparisons were, in the words of Microsoft, 'of limited use, as prices differ from country to country and across channels due to a range of factors'. There's no point comparing prices internationally, you see, because they might be different.*

The unrepresentative poll

You're an industry body eager to influence policy, but unfortunately you just can't get the numbers to work for you, even with a reverse magic pudding or major event maths or using an inapt comparison. What to do? There's always the opinions of your own members, which can be sampled at minimal expense if you've got their contact details: surveys of business

---

* Now, peculiarly, one of the Australian employer groups that incessantly argues that Australian costs are too high, the Australian Industry Group, takes a somewhat different view when it comes to overpriced IT products. AIG told the parliamentary inquiry into the differential that large companies like Microsoft shouldn't have to adjust their local prices downwards to reflect currency fluctuations because of 'the desirability for consumers, suppliers and retailers of having relatively consistent pricing of goods'. That wasn't very long after AIG had argued for a tiny minimum wage raise because small businesses were struggling with the impact of the high Australian dollar. Naturally its position had nothing to do with the fact that Microsoft is an important partner of AIG.

executives on their expectations inevitably yield concerns about the rising cost of regulation, taxes and wages. That's even the case when it is businesses themselves that have been bidding up the cost of labour, as happened during Australia's resources boom, when resources firms competed with each other for a limited pool of skilled labour to build new mining and extraction projects.

Or you're a PR firm looking for a cheap'n'cheerful way to generate some coverage for a client. How about a quick survey of their customers, preferably on something inanely 'fun' or related to sex so that the media will pick it up? Who knows, it might be a slow news day or get picked up on social media and 'go viral'.

Not that such exercises have to be the preserve of hard-up industry bodies or inspirationless PR firms. The prestigious World Economic Forum Competitiveness Report is regularly cited by chin-stroking business figures and commentators from around the world as an important insight into how different economies compare when it comes to how governments can make life easier for business. What's never mentioned is that much of the report is based on the responses of a handful of business executives in each country, rather than any objective assessment of regulatory practices. This meant that in the 2012 report, a small number (fewer than seventy) Australian executives rated Australia, then under a Labor government, worse for government nepotism than Saudi Arabia, which is run by a single family; they rated Australia lower on 'trust in government' than Bahrain, where anti-government protesters are butchered and jailed; and they rated Australia's judiciary as less independent than that of Qatar. Of course, given that senior Gulf state business executives are usually related to, or are themselves, key government figures, such results aren't surprising.

Adventures in time

Want to discredit a policy that has no significant impacts in the short term? Two of the most widely used tricks in Australia involve time-travel economics. Don't be intimidated, it's dead easy: compare the industry employment outcomes from a modelled scenario with a business-as-usual scenario (employing the reverse magic pudding of course) and declare that a particular policy will 'cost thousands of jobs', as though thousands of workers in an industry will be sacked tomorrow, even when the relevant industry will in fact grow, just at a slightly lower rate than under the business-as-usual scenario and thus produce slightly fewer *additional* future jobs than otherwise.

Alternatively, compare the GDP outcomes from the modelled scenario with the GDP outcome of the business-as-usual scenario, do so over a period long enough to generate a substantial difference—say, fifty years—and then use the difference in GDP fifty years hence to claim that a policy will 'shrink the economy by X per cent', as though we'll immediately enter a prolonged recession rather than have a minutely slower growth path over decades.

Better yet, the really clever will calculate the per capita or per household GDP 'loss' and use that figure to warn that a policy will cost each household—cost *you!*—thousands of dollars, giving the impression families will somehow be stripped of income or have assets seized in a midnight raid.

Both of these tricks have been repeatedly used to attack climate change policies in Australia, and have made a comeback under Australia's new climate change denialist conservative government, which since its election in 2013 has claimed a carbon price will reduce GDP by $1 trillion 'over

the next few decades'—without mentioning that's actually
a difference of 1–2 per cent of total GDP between now
and 2050.

Social costs

Jealous that business groups and large companies were having
all the fun with dodgy modelling, in recent years NGOs,
research institutes and non-profit lobby groups decided to get
into the action themselves and created a new sub-industry
around modelling the 'social costs' of various undesirable things
such as alcohol or illnesses deemed not to be attracting sufficient research funding from governments. 'Social costs' in this
instance isn't used in the narrow economic sense, but consists
of a more nebulous mix of externalities, economic costs (lost
productivity, mainly), fiscal costs to taxpayers via the health
system or criminal justice system, estimates of economic loss
associated with illness and premature death, and reverse magic
pudding costs that are actually expenditure for other sectors of
the economy—out-of-pocket medical costs for unfunded treatment for illnesses, for example.

In Australia, economists working for public health groups
have thus estimated that the costs of various problems run into
the many hundreds of billions. Drug use, for example, is said
to cost Australia $56 billion a year. Eating disorders have been
estimated to cost $70 billion a year; obesity was calculated to
cost over $50 billion a year in 'lost wellbeing' (the comparable
US estimate was $190 billion). Alzheimer's disease is predicted
to cost Australia over $80 billion a year in the 2060s (adventures-
in-time alert!). Depression costs $13 billion a year, illiteracy is
said to cost $18 billion, stress nearly $15 billion—even insomnia
costs nearly $15 billion, we're told.

All of these are real problems affecting the lives of people and, indeed, possibly reducing their productivity or sending them to early graves. But the procession of claims about their 'social cost' has the cumulative effect of suggesting that the best way to massively expand the GDPs of Western economies would be to send the entire population to the gym and counsellors.

The politics of political arithmetic

Concerns about this form of Stupid long predate the emergence of economic modelling and polling in the twentieth century. As the quote from Adam Smith that begins this chapter indicates, the provenance and accuracy of the calculation of statistics have been disputed almost from their inception. Moreover, the original name, 'political arithmetic', was enormously significant—'statistics' as a name didn't catch on until an enterprising Scotsman, John Sinclair, rebranded 'political arithmetic' using a German term for qualitative (as opposed to quantitative) descriptions of the characteristics of states (states . . . statistics . . . geddit?).

But statistics, right from its very inception, was always about power and politics. It had been an Englishman who first referred to 'political arithmetic'—William Petty, an early demographer (among other things, in the pre-twentieth-century tradition of polymathy) who followed in the footsteps of another Englishman, John Graunt. Graunt had produced the first work of demography, *Natural and Political Observations on the London Bills of Mortality* in the 1660s.

Graunt and Petty, who was also an economist and who urged better statistical information to improve tax collection, correctly understood that accumulating demographic data was an inherently political act. The growth of statistics was an inevitable consequence of the growing dominance of monarchies in the early modern period, even if government did not yet have many of the recognisable characteristics of the modern bureaucratic form.* In particular, the demands of warfare—of which monarchies were very fond—the shift to permanent (and increasingly national, rather than mercenary) armies and economic policies like mercantilism that conceived international trade as a zero-sum, competitive game drove the emergence of the centralised state. Such entities needed to understand the size and structure of their population so as to know how many men of military age they could butcher, their economic resources to pay for wars and even how long their citizens lived for, given the early modern habit of granting leases, awarding pensions and selling annuities for several lives rather than a set period of years.

The early growth of statistics was accompanied by the beginnings of probability theory by English and European mathematicians—in particular, the work of Thomas Bayes, which would re-emerge in the twentieth century—thereby providing the tools to start better using the data being collated. But while that was occurring, the English grappled with the politics inherent in political arithmetic. A bill to conduct the first national census in England in 1753 was defeated by 'country' opponents of the government—conservative landed aristocrats who claimed to defend the traditional liberties of Englishmen (mainly property rights) from a central government bureaucracy—aka the 'court'. The 'country' opposition

---

* Marshall McLuhan argued the development of statistics in the sixteenth and seventeenth centuries was an inevitable consequence of the arrival of printing and the more centralised, visually oriented world it enabled.

wasn't just opposed to a centralised bureaucracy in theory—they themselves controlled the local bureaucratic, law enforcement apparatus and ecclesiastical apparatus that would have collated census data across England.

As a result, the first national census wasn't conducted in the UK until nearly half a century later, after the first census had been conducted in the United States. In the US, contrarily, despite a similar antipathy towards centralised power to that which thwarted the UK census, censuses were not merely considered non-threatening, they were written into the Constitution as the basis for taxation and state representation in Congress. But back across the Atlantic, as if to prove the point of the 'country' opponents, the transformation of France from *ancien régime* to Napoleonic empire via revolutionary chaos saw a dramatic rise in governmental statistical compilation, even via basics such as Napoleon's standardisation of measurements throughout France. Statistics and centralisation of power went hand in ink-stained hand.

The innately political nature of the compilation and use of data continued to be demonstrated as political arithmetic—now rebranded as the shorter, but harder to pronounce, 'statistics'—and probability expanded in the nineteenth century. Statisticians and mathematicians developed key tools of probability, such as the law of large numbers, the least squares method and normal distribution, and re-argued the medieval debate about nominalism in determining categories and classifications of data, while data collection played a bigger and bigger role in public debate. At the same time, complaints that statistics were being exploited inappropriately or by vested interests to pursue self-serving agendas grew. The French medical profession bitterly divided over the meaning of data from cholera epidemics in

1820s Paris. New statistical techniques combined with data collected from English parishes was used in the debate on Poor Law reform, with some statisticians arguing that tough welfare laws were correlated with lower poverty rates. And a big spur to debate over statistical methods in the late nineteenth and early twentieth centuries were the efforts of eugenicists and social Darwinists to identify links between heredity and intelligence. Much of the hard work of merging social statistics and probability into a single subject area was done by men eager to argue non-white races were intellectually inferior.[*]

A form of that eugenics argument was still going on in the 1990s with the most notorious recent example of statistical Stupid in the service of an agenda, Richard Herrnstein and Charles Murray's *The Bell Curve*. The book was named after the curve of normal distribution, on the left side of which, the authors suggested, African Americans and immigrants were to be disproportionately found. The coverage of the book prompted criticism about the failure of many US journalists to identify the poor methodology underpinning its conclusions about the links between race and intelligence, as scientists, psychologists and statisticians raced to show the profound flaws in the book.

The discovery of normal distribution curves in sociological and medical data accompanied the earliest data gathering, but it was the Flemish statistician Adolphe Quetelet who made them famous in the early to mid-1800s. In particular, Quetelet claimed that the normal curve that represented, say, the distribution of human height or weight, was also applicable

---

[*]   The reader will recall from an earlier chapter that William Jennings Bryan, in the Scopes Trial, was doggedly opposed to Darwinism, not merely because he believed it incompatible with the Bible and Tennessean folk wisdom, but because he believed it promoted conflict.

to human morality, measured by marriage, crime and suicide statistics. Quetelet was thus a 'moral statistician' as much as any other type. He considered the average human, the one closest to the mean at the centre of the normal curve, to be an ideal of moderation, with all others a kind of imperfect copy, too tall or too short, too heavy or too light, too unethical or too officious, all small departures from the will of the Creator for the perfect being found at the apex of the curve.

Quetelet's view initially informed the sociology of Émile Durkheim at the end of the nineteenth century, albeit from a different perspective: for Durkheim in his early work, the mean human was the product of social forces, the most representative creation of the society in which they had been born and raised. But later, the mean became instead synonymous with mediocrity; the average human for Durkheim was average indeed, lacking strongly positive or negative qualities, a compromise, moderate in everything and good in nothing, including talent and ethics.

This shows how inherently political statistics are: the shift in characterisation of those on the left-hand side of the normal curve to 'below average' led to that segment of the population being deemed by some to be a threat to Western societies. Francis Galton was a cousin of Charles Darwin and an eminent late-Victorian polymath across many fields, including statistics, in which he devised the concept of standard deviation. Galton also invented the terms 'eugenics' and argued for the 'weak'—those on the left side of the curve—to be kept celibate and for eminent families—the right-siders—to intermarry in order to improve the racial stock. His protégé, Karl Pearson, one of the key figures in the twentieth-century development of statistics, also advocated race war and rejected the utility of trying to improve social conditions. 'No degenerate and feeble stock will ever be converted into healthy and sound stock by the accumulated effects of education, good laws, and sanitary surroundings,' Pearson insisted. Pearson believed himself to be a stickler for intellectual rigour, telling the *British Medical Journal* in 1910 that social scientists ought not to prostitute statistics for controversial or personal purposes.

Herrnstein and Murray's arguments were thus simply a reiteration, almost verbatim, of the arguments of eugenicists a century before. They used their statistics to call for less welfare, lamenting that America was subsidising 'low-IQ women' (i.e. African American and immigrant women) to have children rather than encouraging high-IQ women. The eventual result, they argued, would be a kind of IQocalypse in which the intelligent (whites and Asians) lived in fortified compounds shielded from the teeming slums of low-IQ masses.

The economics of political arithmetic

An important development in statistics in the twentieth century was the development of input–output models and the pioneering of econometrics, and their use once computers became available after World War II to help process large amounts of data. A key driver of the proliferation of this kind of Stupid in public debate has thus been the spread of computable general equilibrium (CGE) economic models that use real economic data to model the likely impacts of policy changes or economic reforms.

These once required significant IT power to run—the 'computer' used to model the British economy in the early 1950s was a two-metre tall machine that used coloured water. This limited their use to academic institutions and official policymaking bodies like central banks. But even small computers can now run such models easily, and anyone can download simplified versions of widely used economic models like that of the Australian economy developed by Monash University. Economic consultants and academic institutions now advertise their models, either self-developed or bought from institutions with a proven track record, as a key part of their service offering to potential clients.

And there are more economists than ever before to run such models. Since the 1980s, Australian higher education institutions have seen a dramatic increase in students choosing to study business administration and economics, increasing their numbers per annum almost threefold between 1983 and 2000, by which time business admin and economics was, despite slower growth in the 1990s, the most popular field of study for Australian students. The US saw a similar rapid rise in the number of economics undergraduates from the mid-1990s onwards, while all Anglophone economies seem to have seen increases in the numbers of economics students since the global financial crisis showed the profession in such a favourable light. The English-speaking world appears to be suffering from a plague of economists, far in excess of what banks and governments need, leaving the rest to wander the streets holding 'will model for food' signs.

The other key ingredient such models rely on are input–output tables put together by the government statisticians that detail the relationships between and interdependence of different industries and sectors of the economy. But input-output tables themselves, without the labour or expense of CGE modelling, are often used to generate output, jobs and income multipliers for particular industries, thus providing the ingredients of the reverse magic pudding used by industry lobbyists to demonstrate the case for assistance.

So rife had the misuse of these multipliers by economic consultants, industries and governments arguing for handouts become in Australia in the 1990s that the Australian Bureau of Statistics actually stopped providing multipliers in its input–output tables, in essence saying that if people were going to misuse them they could produce them themselves. 'Users of the I–O tables can compile their own multipliers as they see fit, using their own methods and assumptions to suit their own needs from the data supplied in the main I–O tables,' the ABS said. 'I–O multipliers are likely to significantly over-state the impacts of projects or events. More complex methodologies, such as those inherent in Computable General Equilibrium (CGE) models, are required to overcome these shortcomings.'

Magical multipliers and fictional industry reports about the huge benefits or costs of particular policies or misused data should have little direct impact on policymakers, who have access to more reliable and genuinely independent assessments of policy impacts. That doesn't stop governments from pursuing bad policy, of course, but it means they have less excuse—the NSW government, for example, repeatedly pointed to evidence of declining violence in Sydney before caving in and agreeing to a get-tough reform package on alcohol-related violence. But dodgy reports can be effective at influencing the media and voters.

Reports, or extracts from them, are thus often given ahead of release to journalists or outlets regarded as sympathetic, because it complements an outlet's ideology or partisanship, and then offered to readers under that most abused term 'exclusive'. Alternatively, journalists too innumerate or too time-pressured to subject reports to basic scrutiny get them. Few journalists outside science and economic rounds have sufficient grounding to subject economic modelling to rigorous scrutiny, and few have the time to dig through evidence that would undermine material served up to them by lobbyists, NGOs and industry. Moreover, it enables the media to create the illusion of journalism. The classic description of news is what somebody does not want you to print, and the rest is advertising. Bad maths is advertising masquerading as news, filling column inches and the minutes between ad breaks in news bulletins, and without even being paid for. The benefit to media outlets, instead of revenue, is a saving, generating the appearance of journalism without the need to invest in the resources required for actual newsgathering, leaving the consumer to do the work of critically examining what's been offered.

The discomfort or lack of interest of many journalists when it comes to numbers is a cliché that has been the subject of complaints for decades—journalists were, it's long been said, the kids at school who topped English, not maths or science. But it becomes plain when they write more traditional stories where hard data is available but needs to be researched and explained, rather than handed over as a gift. Stories about crime trends, for example, rarely contain actual evidence about crime rates, even though crime statistics, which have been trending downwards in many Western countries in recent years, aren't hard to unearth. Instead, journalists prefer anecdotes over data: anecdotes are harder to discredit and provide an immediate human hook for media consumers, regardless of how meaningless or unrepresentative personal stories may be. Actual crime data is likely to provide an unappealing counterweight to individual stories of out-of-control thugs, alcohol-fuelled violence or rampant cybercriminals.

Lies, damned lies and opinion polling

Different problems arise from numbers that journalists should be more comfortable with: those produced by polling organisations. Opinion polling was a nineteenth-century creation of American newspapers and magazines—the first one was for the 1824 presidential election—until polling became professionalised and more statistically rigorous in the twentieth century. That was after a magazine called *Literary Digest* predicted a landslide to Republican Alf Landon in the 1936 presidential election. The reason you've never heard of President Landon is that he actually lost in a landslide to FDR and the *Digest* shut soon after, setting an example of media accountability that, alas, has rarely been followed since.

In most democracies, the media continues to be a key customer of polling companies, particularly around elections, although it is now rare for a media company, rather than a marketing company, to own a polling organisation, as News Corporation does with Newspoll in Australia. The relationship tends towards one of interdependence or, perhaps, symbiosis, though it's unclear whether the media or marketers are the parasite. A polling company without a media outlet struggles to match the influence or profile of companies that are linked to national media. For media companies, which invest in the costly process of polling either by owning a pollster or contracting with one, a poll provides influence and precious column inches for its political journalists.

Historically, Australia has had relatively good-quality polling, mainly because we force people to vote, which removes the challenge of predicting voter turnout that bedevils US polling, and we refuse to let them exhaust their vote on minor parties, removing the lottery of first-past-the-post psephology in the UK. And there's a lot of polling, too, for such a small country: until recently, there have been around ten national polls a month in Australia outside elections.

But problems arise in the interpretation of the results by journalists. Partisanship among journalists and outlets plays a role—my side edges down 3 points, but yours plummets 2—but more common is the practice of retrofitting narratives onto polls. Having invested in the expensive process of polling 1000 people (usually riding on regular omnibus marketing polling conducted by the pollster), media outlets feel obliged to get their money's worth by dramatising the results, regardless of what they are.

This yields the sight of even very good journalists being compelled to explain small changes in polls, including those within the margin of error of the poll (around 3–4 per cent for a sample size of 1000), as arising from specific political events or a change in tactics by a party, establishing a narrative even when none exists. Thus, rises or falls in polls, even those resulting purely from statistical noise, generate their own positive or negative coverage as journalists rely on *post hoc ergo propter hoc* logic and scour preceding political events for explanations of shifts that may be entirely random.

Sometimes even this doesn't work, when polls go in a direction not anticipated by journalists, thus requiring 'government has failed to benefit from . . .' narratives. Testing of such explanations is never undertaken, and the many assumptions embedded in them remain unrevealed: not merely that the change in polling results is statistically significant rather than random variation, but that voters have paid sufficient attention to politics to react to events that precede the polling outcome and that the reaction has occurred in a time frame that has been detected in a poll.

Even if polls and polling interpretation don't have a lot of influence on voters—in fact, there is little evidence that polls change voters' minds, such as via any bandwagon effect—they do have an impact on politicians, especially in countries with a short political cycle, like Australia, where a federal election is never more than thirty-six months away and parties have taken to removing even electorally successful leaders at the first hint of trouble. The result is a strange feedback loop of Stupid, in which meaningless numbers are interpreted as meaningful and influence the behaviour of those ostensibly the subject of the numbers.

One man's story of debunking and desperation

As someone paid to write about public affairs, I have a certain professional as well as personal interest in the Stupid that hides in numbers. Having written for years about polling, I've decided that voting intention other than immediately before an election is of limited interest except to the extent to which it seems to influence the views voters express on other issues. I also get my share of 'independent reports' from publicists, NGOs and other purveyors of such things, although not nearly as many as some other people in the Australian media, much of whose entire journalistic output consists of 'exclusives' about new reports commissioned by major industry groups. But mostly my interest is centred on trying to debunk bullshit reports, a task that feels like King Canute trying to whack aquamoles while holding back the waves.*

---

* Yes, I know, Canute got a bad rap—he was demonstrating the stupidity of trying to hold back the waves, not seriously attempting it. Call it the Caligula effect—sarcastically threaten to make your horse a senator because actual senators are such duds, and the next thing you know you're being portrayed as barking, or more correctly neighing, mad.

It can be a tedious task—going straight to the methodological explanation of a report, if it has one, checking the data and assumptions, checking the results of other reports, consulting independent sources of data, putting together your own data. There are certain tricks you can use. There is often a remarkable difference between what companies involved tell investors and stock market regulators and what their 'independent modelling' says, like the foreign-owned power companies who produced 'reports' stating that a carbon price in Australia would see them shut down generators and go out of business, while they told foreign shareholders Australia would continue to be an excellent market for them. And sometimes there are surprises—I once encountered a report from one of Australia's best-known economic consultancies that significantly understated the case they were making for the client who had hired them. Another time, the data in a report outright contradicted the conclusion in the executive summary, which is all most people ever read.

But mostly it's the same weary trudge through Stupid, often from the same consulting firms, via media spokespeople and PR firms who mysteriously don't yet have a report to give you despite a media release or an 'exclusive' article about it being carried in a newspaper that day. Such reports are inevitably 'probably available next week', that being a Friedman Unit-type period in which corporate communications people think you'll forget you wanted a copy of the report. In fact, one ends up feeling less like Canute than Travis Bickle, God's Lonely Man, walking through streets filled with statistical depravity and mathematical filth, hoping that one day a real econometric rain will come and cleanse the place.

To be sure, this form of Stupid isn't as deadly as some. People don't die from biased modelling or inflated claims, at least not in the way that people die, say, from vaccination denialism or the War on Terror. But this kind of Stupid offends, offends egregiously, producing a stench that combines the sickly odour of people on the make with the rot of intellectual dishonesty. It dresses itself in the garb of rigour, and quotes data at you; it purports to adorn public debate by adding to our understanding of economic and social impacts. In fact, it is collations of lies, generated for the purpose of skewing, not informing, public debate, and leaving us misinformed, not better informed.

After three centuries of collating statistics, developing the probability techniques to use them and building the econometric tools to understand how we interact economically, there has never been more mathematical Stupid. In fact, most of us are worse off than Adam Smith, who at least knew to be sceptical of statistics even before they were called that.

BK

9

Postmodern nausea: Derrida, vomit and the rise of relativity

'Let me tell you what postmodernism isn't.'

This was the reliable beginning of just about every Stupid lecture on the postmodern condition I attended in the 1990s. This made it very difficult to know what to do in exams. And when you mentioned this to your Stupid teacher, they would say, 'Ah—the text is just like life! Decentralised and confusing with no real purpose.'

But the fuckers still made us do exams.

Look. I got so annoyed by this I am just going to break all of the rules of postmodernism and tell you what it is rather than what it isn't. Because it's a useful term to describe some stuff that has, quite justifiably, gained a reputation for maximum bullshit.

Postmodernism might be used to refer to two things. (At this point, all the postmodernists say, 'But it is so many more than two.' They can fuck off.) The first thing it refers to is the current era. That's quite simple. It's just called postmodern because we used to call the period modern. It describes a period in time characterised by certain things. Which mostly involve increased complexity and the failure of the Enlightenment to deliver on its promise of enlightening.

The second is the 'practice' of postmodern philosophy. My favourite of these guys is Jean Baudrillard. My least favourite is Jacques Derrida. In the habit of postmodern confusion, we'll go with Jacques.

Derrida is the deconstruction guy. What is deconstruction? Every lecture I ever attended started with, 'Let me tell you what deconstruction is not.' I'm not going to do that. Instead, I am going to show you deconstruction. Here goes.

On 8 January 1992, US President George H.W. Bush vomited on the prime minister of Japan. Well, he didn't actually vomit *on* so much as *around* PM Miyazawa. The video is blurred and it is hard to assess exactly how much the guy was showered in free-world sick. What is clear from footage is Bush barfed more copiously than in the recorded banqueting of any statesman since Seneca took notes from the long tables of Rome. (Soon you will see what I'm doing. I am taking an arbitrary moment in history—8 January 1992—and elevating its importance. I am taking little details and blowing them up in order to show you, as deconstruction does, that everything is meaningless! Yay!)

Within days, the incident was widely documented and analysed. This alleged product of intestinal flu was broadcast on ABC in the US and parodied the following week on *Saturday Night Live*. It was later referenced in *The Simpsons* when a fictionalised Bush threatened Homer he would ruin him 'like a Japanese banquet'. It appeared in a *USA Today* roundup of The

25 All-Time Most Memorable Meltdowns and would enter the Japanese lexicon: Bushu-suru is slang still used to convey the act of public vomiting in Japan.

I remember hearing that a satirical play and a painting were inspired by the executive chunder. That there is no hard evidence these works exist does not diminish the plausibility of their creation. Which is to say, as one's parents often will at a gallery: they'll make art about anything these days. (Okay. I have stopped deconstructing for the minute.) The man often held responsible in intellectual circles for legitimising art about vomit is Derrida. Or, to be more general, the man often held responsible for legitimising everything is Jacques Derrida. The guy whose most quoted sentence is 'Il n'y a pas de hors-texte' or 'There is nothing outside the text' (in Of Grammatology) was, himself, a vomiter on the emperors of reason.

Nothing. There is nothing outside the text. There is no God, no reason, no taste and no morality. There are only words, words, words which, in turn, only relate to other words. This statement is helpful to an understanding of the two previously mentioned things: both the postmodern era and the philosophy it spewed.

No one finds Derrida appealing, and if they say they do, then they are ill or they are liars. Let's just start our painful date with Derrida in understanding that the declaration 'There is nothing outside the text' means: all meaning is relative to other meaning. And therefore meaningless. It is all just text; or, it is all just words we utter and pointless discourse we make.

This idea is pretty hard going. And unfortunately, once you see what he is saying, it is also pretty hard to dismiss. The repercussions of saying that all meaning can only be compared against other meaning are great. It means that there is no dependable truth, morality or ethical way to govern. This is an immense break with the past. But, as we will see, it is one that is currently being enacted in my Stupid deconstruction, which now begins again.

In 1992, the year we repeatedly visit, Cambridge was one of many storied universities that honoured this important man. Not everyone was pleased about his honorary doctorate, and a number of academics wrote a letter of protest to *The Times* of London, beginning, 'M. Derrida's work does not meet accepted standards of clarity and rigour.' It went on, 'M. Derrida's career had its roots in the heady days of the 1960s and his writings continue to reveal their origins in that period.'

If I am not mistaken, these guys are calling Derrida a dirty hippie. Such was the man's infamy in 1992.

There are plenty of ways we could write about post-modernism other than using Derrida, the dirty hippie. But if George H.W. Bush has taught us nothing else, it is not to over-stuff ourselves.

There are many postmodern philosophers we could greedily consume here. But we need to be picky or we might be sick. I actually did chuck before an exam in the Department of General Philosophy at Sydney University in 1992. Postmodernism actually made me spew.

So, we have confined this buffet to two simultaneous courses. We have Derrida as the primary way to understand what is meant by postmodern philosophy, and we have the year 1992, in which George H.W. Bush vomited on the prime minister of Japan and I vomited on the flagstones of the university quadrangle.

In the interests of declaring my bias—itself a Derridean habit—I should say that I liked Derrida a lot at university, upchuck notwithstanding. This is chiefly because (a) he was very fond of cats, and (b) he was, and is, so difficult to understand, it's quite acceptable, if not actually useful, to give up the chore of understanding him and say, 'Ah, Derrida . . . so playful!' and have your peers not think of you as an absolute tool.

This helps to explain why people who did *not* ponce about doing cultural studies think that Derrida is a tool. The point is, he's not a complete tool. But given that people like me, and curators of art shows with vomit as a central theme, spent the better part of the 1990s saying, 'Ah, Derrida . . . so playful!', it is perfectly reasonable to think of the man and his work as a waste of good French.

There is a lot of good postmodern thought to read. But if we have to choose one guy, let it be Derrida—for three reasons. First, for the sake of brevity. Second, Derrida is currently enjoying a lack of popularity; I therefore conclude you may be less disposed to boredom in reading the name of a man currently resting in theory's lavatory. Third, Derrida 'invented' deconstruction.

And, even overlooking that 'deconstruction' is one of the most abused words in the philosophical vocabulary and can often be seen on menus or in colour magazines on Sunday preceding the names of actresses who offer glimpses of themselves no more candid than 'sometimes I don't feel that pretty', it also permits us to 'deconstruct'. Which is to say, focus on an arbitrary thing.

Like, The Year My Non-Vomit Streak Broke: 1992.

So I am selecting a postmodern way of describing postmodern thought and postmodern life. You might find it useful to get an understanding of the thing called deconstruction, if only because you can dismiss it in the future as Stupid.

Deconstruction is often used to mean a revelation; a kind of stripping back to a foundation. Woody Allen famously misused it in the title of one of his worst films, *Deconstructing Harry*. Here, Harry is 'deconstructed' through Allen's customary lens of psychoanalysis. We see Harry's dreams and his past and this is not at all Derrida but Freud. It is true that deconstruction is a way of investigating a text—and text can even mean a person. It is also true that deconstruction, like the talking cure, might employ methods like wordplay or concentrating on elements of a thing normally considered unimportant. But it is not true that deconstruction, unlike psychoanalysis, strives to get at any sort of truth. Because, and this is where you might justifiably spit at the page, deconstruction does not believe in truth. I'll tell you what deconstruction does believe in (spoiler: nothing!) in just a little while. But we do need to look briefly at the long history of the death of truth.

I have about as much time for the claim that there can be no truth as I do for middle-period Woody Allen. Which is to say, it's depressing and it's not very useful. In the absence of truth, we may as well just all pretend we were always totally fine with Woody shacking up with Soon-Yi.

(DECONSTRUCTING AGAIN!)

Allen, quoting the poet Emily Dickinson, said of his 1992 separation from Mia Farrow, 'The heart wants what it wants.' It is only in matters of the heart that I can accept such absolute relativism. The heart is permitted to bang out its independent truth. Everything else, as far as I'm concerned, has a responsibility to truth beyond itself; to truth outside the text.

While it is Stupid to call Derrida Stupid, I am actually going to say that I believe that he is wrong. There is something outside the text. I think as an assessment of life as it is currently lived, his deconstruction is pretty much spot on. But I think that as a grand theory of how meaning has always been and will necessarily be, it is probably the most depressing thing I could imagine.

I am so angry with Derrida for saying that life is necessarily meaningless that I am going to give some meaning to his.

Derrida was a French Algerian philosopher who was born in 1930, set Anglophone philosophy aflame in 1966 by declaring the death of meaning at John Hopkins University, and died in 2004 shortly after he had written about feeling embarrassed to be naked in front of his cat.

Deconstruction is not a set of instructions, necessarily. It is not a way to look at the world, but it is the way in which the world reveals itself to us; or the way the world, to use the maddening phrase of Derrida, is 'always-already'.

In other words, he's saying we're fucked. Or rather, always-already fucked. Always-already fucked.

It's true that a lot of the language of postmodernism is really hard to follow and/or take in with a straight face. It's my hope, though, that I have done some of the heavy lifting on your behalf and that soon we'll move towards an understanding of something that is not, actually, all obscurantism and does serve to describe the current shape of the world.

I believe in truth. This is not an extreme statement. Unless, of course, you are a devout postmodernist in which case, it's heresy. But for the rest of us, there is at least the idea of some foundation on which we can rest our knowledge.

But it's slipping away. With or without Derrida.

Still, for some people, a deity is the foundation of all knowledge. But it is often and quite compellingly argued by His critics that God has ceased to function in the way that He once did, even to those practising religion. The 'common sense' of humanism is now shared by most people who believe certain secular truths to be self-evident, such as man is by nature reasonable or has a particular essence.

In recent years, superstar atheists like Richard Dawkins have been making much of humanism as a thrilling new way to live. Dawkins, who had started to get antsy by 1992—when he wrote in the *New Statesman*: 'Religion is no more than corrupted software of the mind. God sits in people's brains like a virus'—borrows heavily if selectively from the humanism of Kant and other theorists of the eighteenth century. He just gussies it up.

Some of us also borrow from the truths of the nineteenth century. We don't have to be socialists to believe Marx when he tells us that the foundation of being is to organise the materials necessary for life. We might believe Nietzsche when he tells us it is the 'will to power' which is, more or less, the drive to live. Then Freud tells us it is the drive to have sex and then, later, the drive to die that is at the foundation of everything. And then we meet a whole lot of guys who think it is the need to make meaning through language and there is always something and so it has been back and back and back since Thales, who believed in the sixth century BCE that the foundation of all life was water.

I believe in truth; or I believe in several truths, including some of Kant's reason, some of Marx's economic determinism and some of Freud's foundational psychiatry. But when I start watching the serpent of truth slither through history, I get a little nervy and cover my eyes in case the truth-snake changes shape again. The problem is, Derrida did not cover his eyes and went on to intellectualise the slippery end of truth. The truth wants what it wants, he says. And then, without a minute's warning, we have no foundation, nothing to believe in, and suddenly, Mia Farrow is no longer anywhere in sight.

So what Derrida wants us to believe is that the truth has not just died but that it never lived. We are no longer made of water, souls, history, reason, money or an id. We are nothing.

Derrida says we have always been nothing and it is with this that I cannot bring myself to agree. But I can agree that his deconstruction is a good enough snapshot of the increasingly meaningless era in which we currently live a bold new Stupid.

Derrida says that our understanding of existence is structured in terms of oppositional pairs. He says that these oppositions are structured with one half being understood as dominant and the other being understood as subordinate. These might include man and woman; good and evil; reason and emotion; speech and writing. Our entire principle for organising reality is structured in this way so that we can point to anything and look at it in terms of what it is not. This could include the quality of being Australian. This is actually a particularly good example because Australians usually describe themselves in terms of what they are not: an Australian is not un-Australian.

An Australian is not American. An Australian is not a communist. An Australian is not unfair. An Australian is not easily angered.

We define Australian-ness by looking at what it is not. This is how we organise all meaning: in relation to what it is not. But those other things against which we are writing the 'text' of being Australian are themselves defined in terms of what they are not. So an Australian is not American who is not English. And an Englishman is not a Frenchman who is not fond of bad food. And on it goes, until the bad food ends up being eaten by

President Bush the Elder, who deposits it on the Japanese prime minister, who is not American but who is covered in vomit that has now acquired meaning throughout the world. Or at least as much meaning as anything can have because, baby, it's all relative.

Derrida, I have neglected to mention, was a linguist and had studied the traditionally understood relationship of the signifier, or the word for a thing, with the signified, or the thing. It had been previously supposed that the signifier bore a static relationship to the signified; that when I said something was 'Australian' it was clear what I meant. But Derrida proposes that what I mean never becomes clear and is always (and already) a case of articulating absence when I say Australian. The signifying chain depends only on itself for the production of meaning and there is nothing that is truly Australian, just a whole lot of things that being Australian isn't, which in turn are things that aren't other things that bear any relationship to anything outside the chain.

A common reaction to this is 'bullshit', because it seems so obvious that Australian is a knowable quality that exists independently of the word that describes it. But then, when you try to explain Australian with Derrida's hypothesis in mind, you might find yourself, as I did, in freefall.

We have always thought of language as an instrument of meaning. But with Derrida, we begin to suspect that the opposite is true: meaning is the servant of language.

In the beginning, there was the word. And then there were just more words. And now, there is nothing outside the text.

As he advances toward complete meaninglessness, Derrida becomes more of a sickening threat. He challenges, quite convincingly, the idea that there is nothing in our minds before language and that language is not something we make to fit our needs but we are something for language to rest on.

There is a passage on meaning I remember reading in Virginia Woolf's *Orlando* before I was old enough to realise I was really bored by Virginia Woolf: 'There is much to support the view that it is clothes that wear us, and not we, them; we may make them take the mould of arm or breast, but they mould our hearts, our brains, our tongues to their liking.'

Orlando, by the bye, is a lady-man lost in time. I couldn't really say as I didn't finish the book and the movie with Tilda Swinton was out the day I went to hire it. But it is a book about the fragile nature of identity and gender; at least I said so in my deconstruction exam. And I think this observation saved me from a fail. The book is certainly full of the idea that people are made of the things that constitute their opposite.

We don't wear clothes; they wear us. We don't use language; it uses us. Our identity is a performance; an effect of all the oppositions in the world. If we try, like the hero/heroine Orlando, we can move beyond the idea that we, or anything else, is one thing and allow the parts of the thing that we are not to become more present.

Orlando would be an example of a conscious deconstruction.

But deconstruction happens all the time. According to Derrida, we are always-already involved in deconstruction. Deconstruction is something one can perform deliberately, but even then, one is simply making explicit that which was already implicit. So deconstruction is something that we necessarily perform in the creation of meaning. You're talking, baby, you're deconstructing.

This practice of uttering meaninglessness is neither good nor bad; although it is presumed to be healthier, I guess, if it is clearly identified. At a very basic level, deconstruction is the admission that there is no foundation to meaning. So it finds another way to explore the foundation of meaning. It meanders when it is intentional because that is all anyone can ever do. (Not that 'anyone' exists, maybe, as a unified speaking subject.)

Deconstruction remains a minor pastime of literary scholars who will privilege a small part of a text. They might take the subordinate or suppressed element in a binary pair (say, the girlish fragility of Ahab in *Moby Dick*) and blow it out of all proportion. You could, say, really study the creation myth of *Terminator* which has a man going back in time to give birth to a future Eddie Furlong and make the entire movie about men feeling alienated from the process of childbirth instead of the apparent meaning of the film which is, of course, that Arnold Schwarzenegger is the greatest man-bot of all time.

This stuff is fine in literary criticism. And it is, for me, fine as a critique of our times. But the idea that meaning is always (and already!) a closed system more powerful than Skynet is just too much for my tastes. I need to see life as a possibility lived beyond the singularity of language.

Everything is equally meaningless? Always? And already? I haven't got a great argument beyond 'fuck that shit', but you may be pleased to know that other well-regarded thinkers, including Foucault and Jürgen Habermas, do. To be honest, I don't have the intellectual temerity or rigour to try to understand these guys' refutation of Derrida. Because Derrida, who 'playfully' describes deconstruction mostly in terms of what it is not, makes it difficult enough to understand what he is saying without throwing some extra continental philosophers onto the grill.

Everything is meaningless. There is nothing outside the text.

This sort of relativism is quite dreadful not only for the pessimistic headache it confers—if nothing has any meaning, then we might as well just smoke a bowl and light it with the pages of Plato's *Republic*—but because it forces us to assess everything in the world as having equal merit. Even the very Stupid.

Derrida may currently be unfashionable. He was highly influential, though, and made a significant contribution to Stupid in the areas of literary and cultural studies and the thing we now call 'journalism'. Even people who couldn't tell you his name are influenced by his methods.

High school students of English will now 'read' *Big Brother* as a 'text' that has, apparently, all the richness of Shakespeare. Well may you ask WTF. Now, I earn a partial living as a television writer and have a keen interest in defending good interpretations of reality TV. I actually don't believe that an erudite reading of mass-media entertainment is necessarily a bad thing and not just because it pays my rent. I know that a critical reading of television can provide a good look at art and anyone who doubts this should read Clive James. But what I don't believe, and I am now underemployed and alone among my peers as a result, is that television is very often a good way to make statements about the society that produced it. When you allow yourself to believe that a bunch of drunken twenty-somethings living under surveillance in a fake house in the middle of a theme park can produce something as meaningful as *Titus Andronicus*, you're fucked.

And we are fucked. A colossal amount of 'commentary' with the belief that everything is meaningful is spewed into our brains daily. People say that 'positive' homosexual characters on television show that homophobia is disappearing, but figures on suicidal ideation and homelessness among queer youth ascend. People say that skinny models make women starve themselves, a claim that has all but been refuted by those who specialise in eating disorders. People say that in a time where everything is meaningful, we can look to anything for meaning.

This is the impulse of cultural studies: to look for evidence of whatever you fancy in whatever you have at hand. In my view, this is a kind of Stupid that has all the gravitas of glitter-and-glue craft collage. You use materials at your immediate disposal to make a pile of shiny shit that is work better left for five-year-olds. It is not a 'pure' expression of Derrida but is still very much in his debt. Derrida made it okay for people to privilege the overlooked elements of a text and he must take some responsibility for the cheap French franchise that goes on in his absence.

Pretending that it has social justice as a central concern, a new writing that 'calls out' evil or praises progress in low entertainment has become common and perfectly acceptable. What was once the work of art critics has become a central political project, even for politicians. In 1992, G.H.W. Bush's vice-president made a speech about moral values. Of the television program *Murphy Brown* Dan Quayle said, 'It doesn't help matters when prime-time TV has Murphy Brown, a character who supposedly epitomizes today's intelligent, highly paid professional woman, mocking the importance of fathers by bearing a child alone and calling it just another lifestyle choice.'

In a longish and madly racist speech, Quayle talked about poverty. He did concede that poverty was, in part, the cause of poverty. But, he said, it really had more to do with poor morals as exemplified by Murphy Brown. Of black America, he observed, 'There is far too little upward mobility.' And this was not because people didn't have access to money. Rather, it was 'because the underclass is disconnected from the rules of American society'.

So Murphy Brown, the whitest fictional woman in America, was responsible for poverty. After all, she was the one who enjoined members of America's black female underclass to have children out of wedlock. It was Murphy who devalued the American father and it was not economic conditions that forced him into unemployment or that tore apart traditional family structures.

Dr Anne Summers, an Australian feminist academic, popular writer and political adviser to the Keating government on women's issues, has a similar understanding of the culture. Having freshly delivered a speech on how 'misogynist' depictions of then Australian prime minister Julia Gillard on the blog of an unemployed cartoonist engendered 'misogyny', Summers was interviewed by the *Sydney Morning Herald* on the matter of some urinals in a high-end Sydney restaurant that were shaped like mouths. The urinals, by the way, were modelled very clearly on the Rolling Stones logo; if porcelain could be said to have a gender, it was male. The urinals, in fact, are still installed in a Rolling Stones museum in Germany. They remain undisturbed in a homosexual men's club just a few kilometres away from the high-end Sydney restaurant. But the fact of their maleness did not stop Summers from calling the latrines 'misogynist' and suggesting to others via Facebook that campaigning for their removal was worthwhile work.

There is nothing outside the toilet. There is nothing outside *Murphy Brown*. For the right and for the left, the culture can show us what is wrong better than, say, actual statistics can, because it's all relative. Neither Summers nor Quayle are the sort likely to concede to the impact of Derrida, but it is here as clear as urine. In a world where everything is held to be of equal weight, we are free to be crushed by the heft of a bold new Stupid. This postmodern century is one that holds all 'text' as equally influential and celebrates the democratisation of intellectual merit; or our enslavement by the feudal lords of Stupid, depending on how you choose to see it. These days, every child wins a prize. Even Dan Quayle and Anne Summers, who are hailed for the courage of their Stupid. These days, the scandalous blog post is held to be as worthy as the most cautious journalism. These days, political news is no more significant than celebrity news. These days, one's self-esteem need have nothing to do with one's real-world achievements. These days, the average is elevated and the excellent is met with a 'meh'.

Derrida is, in some part, responsible for a meh-world that can no longer be arsed using the energy required to declare, 'This thing is more important than that thing.' He describes a world where meaning is only ever relative to other meaning and where there is no central meaning. Now, as we will see, Derrida gives us absolutely no hope of escaping from the dreadful truth that there is no truth.

But sometimes what Derrida sees is a fairly accurate picture of a world that causes some of us to throw up our hands and say, 'Nothing means anything anymore'. My chief problem with Derrida, save for the fact that he enabled people to make stupid arguments about sit-coms and urinals, is that he says meaning is always absent. I believe this absence is real but it is an event that belongs to the present.

Whether or not you agree with Derrida's view, and the broader postmodern view, of nothing meaning anything, you might concede that ours is a world from which meaning has largely drained and continues to drain apace. A loss of meaning is a pretty serious event. And it is for this reason that Derrida's difficult-to-understand but impossible-to-shake-once-you-do theory of meaninglessness is worth our attention.

I want you to think about our very common avoidance of meaning for a minute. Think about how we are inclined, as a mass, to remember George H.W. Bush as a man who vomited on a prime minister and not one who was silent on apartheid, noisy about war and who drove US citizens into poverty in proportions unmatched for thirty years. And then had his deputy blame it on television. Think about how Bush's detractors would rather remember him for an instant of embarrassment at dinnertime and not his policy; how his supporters would rather think of him as the great foreign policy president who was so conscientious in his diplomacy that the poor old guy was sick on a prime minister. Here, we shun real argument by letting comedy and tragedy stand in for facts.

We are eager to love or hate, to worship or deride. But we are rapidly losing the inclination to examine our reasons for such strong emotions. This doesn't mean we are by nature lazy and stupid. It just means that the once reliable chain of meaning that would tell us that this instant is important and this instant is just a guy vomiting is wrapping around itself. There is nothing outside the text, the vomit, the urinal or the sitcom.

We get quite het up about things. We sling insults around like 'hater' and we tell people with whom we disagree to 'go die in a fire'. We are easy with hyperbole and we say that we 'love' and 'worship' people with whom we agree. Certainly, as we'll discuss in a later chapter on compassion, we are given to very grand emotion. But we are now more rarely inclined to make passionate intellectual criticisms than we are to react to presidential emesis. When it comes to problems that require understanding that transcends 'good' or 'evil', we will shrug because, hey, it's all just relative. A vomit is as good as a complex critique in an age where it's all more text.

The vomit begins to reveal a little more about what is meant when we talk about the postmodern era. There is a lot more 'text' being generated and fewer ways to sort it. There is no centre to our conversations and our knowledge because everything acquires the appearance of having equal weight. And so everything has acquired equal weight. Starved of the nutrition provided by real meaning, we gorge on any junk. We'll even take vomit. Urinals. Cancelled sit-coms. There is now an acronym to describe the anxiety that one might overlook something important: FOMO, or Fear of Missing Out. One can live in FOMO. Or one can accept that one cannot possibly know the difference between important things and trifles. Becoming Stupid in a world where there is increasingly 'nothing outside the text' is a pretty valid reaction. Sometimes, it is better not to react than to react and say something Stupid. I am a very talkative person and it took me many years to realise that one could simply not investigate all 'text' all the time.

•

I remember as a young woman visiting southern California and being unable to detect meaning in the easy grunts of its citizens. I remarked to a liberal American with whom I was doing business that she must be pleased about the Clinton Administration's plans for universal health care. 'It's awesome,' she replied in a way that could have been exhausted or cynical or glad. A few days later, I was in a bar and news of Rodney

King, the African American victim of a vicious beating by officers of the Los Angeles Police Department, was being discussed again on the television (the riots which followed this brutality, by the way, were described by Quayle as the work of Murphy Brown). I remarked to my host that such things were awful. 'It's awesome,' he replied in a way that could have been exasperated or mocking or delighted.

What did they mean? I didn't know what they meant.

The word 'awesome' hung in the smog above Los Angeles for the duration of my stay; it became fused in my memory with the wheeze of the hydraulic 'low-rider' cars I saw crawl along the city's great boulevards and the hiss of the faulty Viper roller coaster at Six Flags Magic Mountain. It drifted out of a broken machine and into the dirty air where it stayed and made no sense. 'Awesome' had become waste.

I was lost in this decentralised, postmodern city that fancied itself as a relaxed paradise of smooth rides and enlightened Americans but to me looked, rather quickly, like a hell of dented vehicles and people who couldn't commit to an idea. When the Qantas plane left LAX for Sydney, I looked down until the city was lost in smog. 'It's awesome,' I said. And I wasn't even sure what I meant.

Los Angeles is, in the most literal sense, awesome. Or it was at least to Australian eyes shortly after 1992. Most obviously, it is a place whose primary business is producing the appearance of meaning and it was, in fact, on entertainment industry business that I first visited.

I travelled to Los Angeles to interview the musician Courtney Love who was, at the time, extraordinarily famous, and when one approaches celebrity, as I once did often, one can feel very postmodern. Which is to say, I think it must be very much like a tour of a nuclear power plant. On the approach, you feel a little nervous to be visiting the place where dangerous energy is born. You imagine you feel the hum of the plant and you wonder— most particularly if you are interviewing Courtney Love—if you might not visit on the very day the core melts. You have a sense of the deterrence of the place at the same time as you feel excited to be visiting its centre. And then you get there. And there is no hum and no evidence of the thing of which you were so afraid. It's a tiny thing that doesn't look as big and explosive as you'd hoped and feared, and you can't help wondering what all the fuss was about. But you never doubt for a minute that this centre, that doesn't feel at all like a centre, is the centre.

I should say that Courtney never showed; her husband, Kurt Cobain of the band Nirvana, whom she had married just eighteen months before in 1992, had committed suicide. This left me alone for most of a week on the margins of a tragedy, which I was trying to find meaningful, looking for Los Angeles' centre.

Los Angeles has no centre. It is difficult to navigate and even when one has a driver—and Courtney's record company had provided me with one—the car moves slowly through wide streets and even wider freeways that are only differentiated by the amount of money they cost to build. Classless California where Anyone Can Make It has visible signs of both wealth and poverty but is democratised by the pace of the traffic. Rich and poor alike spend much of their time stuck in cars. Los Angeles is a really inefficient place whose residents have given up on civic activity because it takes too long to get there (even though Angelenos will always insist that travel time is twenty minutes). Los Angeles is too big and too individualised to make any shred of sense as a city.

I am not the first person to try to describe depthless post-modern life through the murk of Los Angeles. Thousands have talked about the meaninglessness of its entertainment industry and how its appetite for profitable mediocrity creates zombies. Hundreds have commented on the primacy of the automobile and the way in which one finds oneself always on the way to something and never actually there. Dozens have written about its theme park attractions and how these are, if not just as real as the city itself, then actually there just to give us some kind of reassurance that what is outside them is, in fact, real.

Of Los Angeles' Disneyland, French theorist Jean Baudrillard wrote in *Simulacra and Simulation*, 'Disneyland is presented as imaginary in order to make us believe that the rest is real, whereas all of Los Angeles and the America that surrounds it are no longer real.' Literary critic Fredric Jameson has a sense that he has not yet evolved to the postmodern future as glimpsed in a popular LA hotel. Its mirrored external walls reflect the city back at itself and its entryways are unmarked. It suggests a continuity of a city that doesn't exist and it defies the guest to find his way to rooms that are, he writes in *Postmodernism, or, the Cultural Logic of Late Capitalism*, dark and miserable bins in contrast to the light-box lobby. The hotel destroys the 'capacities of the individual human body to locate itself' and there is nothing outside the hotel, or the text. The hotel is Los Angeles. Los Angeles is the hotel.

This is what comes to us after the modern era of certainty, centrality and efficiency. It's a time of doubt, confusion and systems that have begun to break down. Jameson observes that the boutiques of the hotel are, like everything else in the place, impossible to find. The place was built as a last-gasp architectural statement that would attract visitors and shoppers in droves. And it does. But no one can find the fucking entrance and even if they do, the boutiques behind it are invisible. Capitalism, like everything else, has begun to take place in a world that can no longer accommodate it.

These are not metaphors but accounts of an actual experience of postmodern life in Los Angeles and in the world. There are, as people will often say, no longer any rules. Things move very fast and appear to lead to nowhere. No one can even find the fucking shops. So of course there is no hope for the survival of meaning.

These are interesting times but these are devastating times. As one system (say, a global economy) eclipses another (a domestic economy) we are stuck using old rules to explain new practices. And when these rules don't really work to explain and govern the new systems, one of the many casualties—and these include workers and marriage and living close enough to one's school or work to walk there—is meaning.

So we give up and say FML or FOMO or we continue using old routines to explain new stories. Or, if we are quite unusual, we do what Derrida did and say, in a very complex way, that meaning is all bullshit anyhow.

Eventually, Derrida would return to material concerns. He and his cat enjoyed many conversations about ethics before his death. In the meantime, the great thinker left the world just a little worse off than he found it. With a new language to describe the crisis in meaning.

Personally, I believe this crisis will play itself out. I believe that at some point, people will become so sick of conversations about nothing that they will vomit on the new, radical emperor and let us know, as is their wont, which philosopher best described their movements into a time that demanded reality.

For the minute, though, we are very much enamoured of life trapped inside Derrida's 'signifying chain'. Matching sign for sign, we declare our disdain for unsound lavatories and sit-com characters with the use of an awareness ribbon. We use an unreal thing to condemn an unreal problem. We draw rainbows on the pavement to signify our support for sexual difference that we actually want to make the same. We change our Facebook avatars to 'increase awareness' of a paedophilia that everyone already (and always!) condemns. We say a black president is a 'symbol' of 'hope' and don't really seem to mind that the most progressive thing he ever did was write legislation that would make health insurers more stinking rich than they had previously dreamed.

We are caught in a 'playful' game of deconstruction that I really don't think we can blame Derrida for entirely and one, I think, that would have surprised even him with its savage and self-reflexive meaninglessness.

I used to like postmodernism at university. And then, one day, it really happened.

HR

10

Hyperreality, authenticity and the fucking up of public debate

A Sydney newsreader solemnly intones a story about a future bid for a World Cup. He 'crosses live' to a journalist standing outside the city's largest stadium, for a thirty-second discussion that adds no new information. The journalist, standing alone but for a film crew in front of an empty sports arena, is thanked by the newsreader, who moves on to the next item.

•

A political leader dons a high-visibility vest and a hard hat while visiting a construction site. Across town, or in another city, a rival leader dons a high-visibility vest and safety goggles while visiting a factory, where she announces a policy relating to the relevant industry. Evening news bulletins carry images of both politicians talking to workers, or nodding thoughtfully while listening to them. 'This is about creating real jobs,' one of them says.

•

An email is distributed to journalists from a public relations firm offering the results of a survey about the products of one of its customers. In addition to the link to a media release, the PR firm has included links to graphics, 'case study' examples to support the survey, contact details for a blogger willing to comment about the product, a summary of the survey and suggested 'angles' for the story for journalists. The following day, major newspapers carry a short item mentioning the product and the survey.

•

A political journalist laments the unwillingness of contemporary politicians to go beyond carefully constructed talking points in their public statements, saying it is contributing to public disillusionment with politics. The following day, a senior minister's offhand remark on an issue is interpreted as evidence of division with the government, and declared a major gaffe.

That Australia's media is awful is an argument likely to unify a diverse group of people. Progressives complain of the right-wing bias of the mainstream media and of the dominance of News Corporation, a company openly and aggressively hostile to progressive political parties and, for that matter, much of reality. Conservatives complain about the left-wing bias of the Australian Broadcasting Corporation. Media aficionados talk of the decline of traditional journalism caused by a shrinking print media. Political junkies moan about the poor quality of political journalism; readers with a science background laugh and cry about the dismal quality of science journalism and other technical rounds.

And Australians don't trust their media; they rank journalists at about the same level as politicians in terms of trustworthiness and the only outlets they consistently trust at a high level are the national broadcasters. Nor are Australians alone in their distrust. In the US, trust in the media fell to an all-time low in 2012 and only slightly recovered in 2013. In the UK in early 2013, less than one-third of people said they trusted the media (albeit in the wake of one of history's greatest media scandals).

Okay, so far, so anodyne. Journalists have always ranked with used-car salesman and advertising executives in public esteem. But the Australian media, following international trends, is finding innovative ways to be more awful or, more correctly, to achieve a new kind of hollowed-out awfulness. This would no more be a cause for concern than the decline of any other industry, except that we rely on the media to provide a space for public debate about important issues and to hold the powerful to account. An intelligent, sceptical media is one of the core defences of a society against the kinds of Stupid that we've seen throughout this book. The fate of the media, therefore, is the fate of much of our public debate and our ability to fight Stupid, and increasingly our media isn't a defence against Stupid but part of the problem of Stupid.

One of the excellent conceits of Colson Whitehead's novel *Zone One* is his 'stragglers', zombies who don't seek to rend the flesh of the living in stereotypical undead style, but who remain fixed in place, forever poised to undertake some action from their past, some ritual or behaviour apparently randomly recalled from their days of living. It's an apt image for much of the Australian media, permanently re-enacting the journalistic rituals of the past, or at least the past as communally remembered by the industry itself. The live cross to a journalist with nothing to say, at a venue only vaguely related to the story at hand, mimics the traditional 'breaking news' report from a journalist 'at the scene'. The pre-packaged story from the PR consultant, complete with infographics, suggested journalistic angles and 'independent' commentary, mimics actual analytical or investigative journalism. Media conferences by politicians in which nothing of substance is said, and no questions answered, re-enacts traditional media scrutiny of political leaders. All are symptoms of, if not looming death, then at least serious and permanent damage to the news industry.

The live but meaningless cross is said by TV insiders to be an effort by news producers to counter the havoc social media has wrought on their business model. In essence, that model was gathering people who wanted to know what's going on— which used to be a large chunk of the population—together at one time so they could be advertised to. Television journalism is expensive, and subject to strict regulation, but can still garner large audiences and is traditionally seen as key to a strong prime-time line-up. But now, the people formerly known as the eyeballs can be informed whenever they want, and don't have to wait until 6 p.m. to be provided with information in between efforts to convince them to buy stuff. Worse, they may well get better live coverage of events via social media or online sites than via broadcasters several hours later. Moreover, online users now only have to consume the news they're interested in, whether it is sport, politics or entertainment, without any danger of being exposed to annoyingly irrelevant content, even to the extent of having to flip past it in a newspaper or wait for the next story in a carefully structured TV bulletin.

Faced with this mutiny by their once passive audiences, television news producers try to match the immediacy that online news reports or social media provide by offering the drama of live coverage, albeit coverage of empty stadia or deserted streets where a newsworthy incident occurred hours before. It's a ritualistic mimicry of traditional breaking news events where live coverage would be relevant.

Online competition is also the reason why PR companies are happy to issue pre-prepared stories for the media, confident that even if one journalist angrily throws it back in their face, there'll be someone, somewhere who will use it. Newspaper companies are under greater pressure than ever as a consequence of the erosion of their revenue by new media, and are employing fewer journalists and demanding that those journalists whom they do employ cover more rounds and produce content around the clock and across multiple platforms: a print journalist might now produce stories both for a morning print edition and, during the working day, do video segments, conduct interviews for affiliated radio companies, and is probably covering a number of rounds compared to analogue-era journalism, when they might cover one or two. Media companies are also becoming more editorially risk-averse: the pockets that once funded defences against legal action by those they sought to hold to account are now much shallower. This is one area where citizen-journalists and social media can never match the mainstream media: it is only large media companies that can afford to fight defamation actions and suppression orders. As media companies lose revenue, so they lose the capacity to hold the powerful to account.

As a consequence, there's been both a decline in expertise and in the time and effort journalists can physically bring to their craft, making them an ideal target for PR companies peddling fictitious 'reports' of the kind we've previously examined, or pre-prepared stories, even though they're of no news value. A survey in 2010 found that over 50 per cent of all stories in major Australian newspapers in a one-week period originated as public relations, with one senior News Corp editor explicitly blaming the shift of resources away from journalism and towards PR. In this particular front of the fight against Stupid, the resources Stupid can bring to bear are outmatching those of its opponents. And the result is more media self-mimicry, with outlets behaving in ritual fashion—even slapping 'exclusive' on a story if they've been given privileged access to it—without any actual news content or journalistic effort applied.

A history of the good times

Such mimicry is that of the straggler, representing the lingering race memory of what the mainstream media used to be like, in the analogue days. Before the internet and the bad times.

That media environment, which was in place for much of the twentieth century, had several important characteristics. It was, most importantly, a highly unified space: most consumers tended to consume the same products; they watched the same programs and read the same papers, no matter where they were or how they voted. Commercial broadcasters networked and affiliated their operations so that most people, even if they lived far apart, got the same radio and, especially, television programs; publicly funded broadcasters in countries like the UK, Australia and Canada provided national services to all citizens, and even though newspaper circulations fell over the course of the second half of the century in Anglophone countries, even as late as the 1970s three-quarters of Western households were getting a newspaper every day.

The environment was also controlled by a relatively small number of companies and national broadcasters that wielded substantial influence and often operated across some combination of newspapers, television and radio. Commercial mass media created a passive role for audiences and readerships, whose only function was to absorb the advertising directed at them, having been lured into the commercial firing range by the promise of content. And journalists, editors and producers played the role of gatekeepers, determining which information would be conveyed to people—particularly overseas news, which before the internet was heavily controlled by media companies with contracts with overseas media outlets.

In political journalism, this role was not so much gatekeeper as priest-like. Political reporters—usually men—worked in close proximity with politicians and then translated and interpreted their statements and actions for the masses; the only access to the pseudo-divine workings of power for voters was through such journalists, who alone possessed the training and wisdom to mediate and explain the doings of the high and mighty. As neoliberal policies took hold in the 1980s, political journalists also assumed a sacerdotal role in relation to the explanation of economic reform to voters, even if few fully comprehended the divine mysteries of economic deregulation.

Then the internet arrived, and this Edenic world fell apart. People fell out of the habit of buying a physical newspaper given they could read it online—newspaper companies having foolishly made their early online products free—and began using the internet first to do something other than watch TV, and then to download content they previously would have watched on TV (in Australia, usually months or years later, when broadcasters could be bothered showing it). Better yet, they could select the news sources they preferred, filtering out things they didn't want to hear rather than having no choice but to be exposed to them in a unitary media environment. Many media users prefer using news sources that they know they will agree with, rather than having to endure views and news they don't like.

Accordingly, the 'rivers of gold'™ from advertising that characterised the newspaper industry began to dry up, and what were for generations licences to print money in television became a less sure bet. Media outlets tried to keep up appearances, doing the same things they did when there was a unified media environment and they completely controlled both the content and the manner in which it was consumed by consumers, as if simply repeating the ritual would somehow bring back the analogue good times.

We're deep into the hyperreality of Jean Baudrillard and Umberto Eco here: these media rituals—the cross to nowhere, the pre-fabricated story, the rolling coverage of non-events— are simulacra of things that increasingly have no real-world existence, events simulated to look like the memories of earlier journalistic culture, but having no substance or reality.

Some media companies reach back further, to older traditions, in an effort to protect against the erosion of their revenues. Some—News Corporation's newspapers, and its Fox News service in the US, are the best but not the only example—abandon the pretence of objectivity and pursue a more aggressively partisan and campaigning line in their news reporting. For newspapers and radio, this tends to mean becoming aggressively right-wing, because those remaining users of print newspapers and radio tend to be old and conservative. This accounts for the get-off-my-lawn tone of much of, for example, News Corporation's newspaper coverage in Australia, which is dominated by a prostatariat of old white male journalists writing for old white male readers. Again, the rituals of journalism are carefully enacted—complete with 'exclusive' slapped on them, often for stories that are entirely fictional and heavily biased to suit the outlet's political agenda.

While this may infuriate those who disagree with the politics of, say, News Corp's newspapers, or MSNBC, it is a sound business decision: partisan media matches the demonstrated consumer need to select the news sources they prefer, it has a distinctive voice and cut-through appeal in a cluttered and fragmented environment, it allows better targeting of particular demographics, and it costs much less to run ceaseless commentary and ideological campaigns than to provide quality journalism. News Corp's newspapers in Australia are losing circulation very quickly—but certainly not as quickly as those of its print rival Fairfax, which is itself becoming more strident.

Moreover, such partisanship was one of the original media business models in the late seventeenth and eighteenth centuries, although much of News Corp's ideology might have been considered extreme even then. While weekly newspapers in England existed before 1700, the eighteenth century saw a huge expansion in this new industry as papers went daily and went local, multiplying and dramatically expanding their readerships—from around two million at the end of the seventeenth century to sixteen million at the start of the nineteenth, despite the relatively high cost of newspapers because of taxes. In a similar period, the number of London mastheads alone went from twelve to fifty-two, serving a population that went from about half a million to just over one million. In this crowded market, newspapers consciously adopted an oppositional tone in their political coverage, while others were subsidised by government ministers during the long period of Whig rule in the first half of the century.

Partisanship wasn't necessarily a guarantee of success, however, given it limited the potential readership of a masthead and many papers ignored, or had no capacity to report, local news anyway (even covering parliamentary proceedings was illegal until the second half of the eighteenth century, a restriction those regularly exposed to federal parliamentary proceedings in Australia might endorse). The early decades of newspapers resembled the early years of the internet, without so many cat gifs: papers relied strongly on commentary and on recirculating and repackaging news from other sources and newspapers. Colonial-era American newspapers, which were far fewer in number, also relied on second/third/fourth/fifth-hand news, commentary and literary efforts or humour—Benjamin Franklin, one of many printers who started or bought a newspaper to keep his presses busy, first achieved fame with his pseudonymous humour and political writing, which 250 years later would have been known as blogging.

After the American Revolution, however, American newspapers became intensely partisan. Founding Fathers like Alexander Hamilton and John Adams adopted noms de plume to excoriate their opponents (the pen names were always classical in origin, to give an air of republican virtue to the accusations of treason, imbecility and corruption they levelled at each other). Hamilton, Madison and Jefferson established and bankrolled partisan newspapers. Jefferson deserves some sort of acknowledgment for the rare political feat of establishing, using government funds, a paper with the explicit task of attacking a government of which he himself was a senior member, the first Washington administration. Not to be outdone, Alexander Hamilton wrote and encouraged attacks on John Adams, a

243

fellow Federalist, to undermine his prospects of succeeding George Washington.*

For most of the nineteenth century, there were low barriers to entry into the newspaper industry in the US, no copyright laws to stop the reuse of content and strong population growth that could support a constant supply of new titles in frontier communities and multiple mastheads even in relatively small cities. Newspapers reflected their editors' and proprietors' world views, and readily aligned with one or other of the major political parties; in the absence of rapid information networks like the telegraph, the emphasis of newspapers was still less on journalism and more on commentary. Also, crucially, neither political parties nor many editors felt any compunction about making and receiving undisclosed press subsidies.

It wasn't until the end of the nineteenth century that the growing concentration of newspaper ownership, changes in printing technology and pressure from politicians saw fewer newspapers and greater pressure for 'balanced' and 'objective' journalism of the kind twentieth-century citizens came to believe should be the norm in the media; the first schools of journalism began opening early in the twentieth century in the United States. But the tradition of a partisan press persisted in the UK, where to this day major papers are unabashedly politically aligned. It was the arrival of electric media—first radio, then television, both far more tightly regulated on content than

---

* The level of vituperation some of the most eminent Founding Fathers directed at each other in the press might give pause for thought to anyone who thinks the tone of modern-day politics is unusually rancorous. Dick Cheney might have shot someone but no one has ever matched the achievement of Jefferson's Vice-President Aaron Burr, who shot Hamilton dead for a perceived smear.

newspapers—and the rapid development of networks controlled by a limited group of companies (in Australia, the most powerful newspaper companies) that created, for seventy years or so, a cohesive media environment for citizens consisting of local and metropolitan newspapers, local radio and networked television and, except in the United States, a national broadcaster of varying levels of dominance.

Twenty-first-century partisan media, then, looks a lot like eighteenth- and nineteenth-century partisan media, albeit with less facial hair and slightly more diversity of journalists and editors.

Travails in hyperreality

While the coverage of politics in the media has undergone a cycle, political journalism itself has also changed: the rituals of the analogue era live on but are ever more hollow. Despite the growth of twenty-four-hour news channels, there are fewer journalists covering politics than there used to be. And politicians have long since found other ways to reach voters than via press galleries, even before the advent of social media; in Australia, mechanisms like FM radio, talkback radio or TV chat shows offer politicians a softer, less filtered environment in which they can deliver their message. But politicians are now also trained to face media scrutiny more effectively by sticking closely to a pre-prepared set of talking points, usually tailored with key phrases that form part of their parties' political tactics, and limiting opportunities for concerted questioning by the diminishing number of well-informed journalists. In Australia, political parties now closely manage not merely what senior ministers say but what backbenchers say as well, sending out key messages and daily talking points for use by any MP coming within range of a journalist.

This means political media conferences now consist of much the same hyperreality as the live cross to nowhere and the pre-packaged news story: the ritual of question-and-answer is observed, but little information is provided; rather than priests, journalists are reduced to the role of acolytes at a ceremony the purpose of which is not information provision or media scrutiny but a re-enactment of the memory of political accountability, a Holy Communion in which, sadly, no transubstantiation of rhetoric into responsibility ever occurs. Events such as a politician giving the media free rein to ask questions as long as they like, a politician regularly ignoring talking points in favour of intelligently responding to questions,* or, conversely, a politician being so poorly prepared that their discipline breaks down under journalistic probing, are now highly unusual.

In response, the media has also adjusted its thresholds for newsworthiness. Faced with politicians who rigidly adhere to talking points in Australia's tightly controlled party system, journalists now seize on the slightest deviation or slip from the anodyne as evidence of either division or an error (invariably a 'gaffe', 'stumble' or even 'debacle'). This in turn prompts politicians to confine themselves ever more doggedly to their talking points, aware of the febrile overreaction that will accompany even the smallest slip. Hyperreality begets hyperreality as the process of political scrutiny becomes ever less meaningful.

Another incentive for politicians to say less is the decreasing capacity of the media to adequately cover policy issues. Fewer journalists, with more rounds, more deadlines and poorer

---

* Of recent Australian political figures, only former senior Labor figure Lindsay Tanner and Liberal Malcolm Turnbull routinely spoke like both they themselves, and audiences watching them, have IQs above room temperature and are capable of grasping nuance and complexity.

resourcing, mean less coverage of policy issues, especially if they are complex or in areas regarded as dull. This is especially the case in television, where political journalists and their editors and producers have to compete for time in network news bulletins with hyper-local non-stories, car accidents and celebrity news. Labor's Lindsay Tanner has said that he increasingly found that talkback radio shockjocks were the only section of the broadcast media prepared to devote extended periods to discussing policy issues with a popular audience base.*

This tilts the incentives in political journalism as a whole away from policy coverage and towards personality-based political coverage, or what is derisively termed horse-race journalism (the best political journalists can do both well). Speculation about parliamentary party leadership, for example, or likely future presidential candidates in the US, is far easier than policy coverage, which requires background knowledge or good research skills, and consistently attracts more interest from readers and viewers than policy stories. Better yet, policy stories that can be interpreted through the prism of horse-race-style coverage can give the illusion of depth while requiring little policy understanding. A constant stream of opinion polls, many of them commissioned by the media themselves, facilitates this, providing political journalists with endless material with which to discuss which side, and which personalities, are winning and losing.

It also rewards politicians who offer simplistic messages over those with policy substance who lack the celebrated trait of 'cut-through', encouraging those with a skill for simple

---

* It was also on talkback radio that one of the most famous policy moments in post-war Australian history occurred: Paul Keating's 'banana republic' warning in 1986.

messages regardless of content and discouraging those who want to pursue complex policy in a contested environment.

This is one of the reasons for the success of Tony Abbott, now prime minister of Australia, who destroyed two Labor prime ministers in a four-year campaign of brilliantly effective political communication. Abbott, dismissed as a disaster waiting to happen by some commentators when he first secured the leadership of his party,* proved himself an immensely skilful political communicator capable of cutting through with targeted, negative messages to which his opponents had no answer.

Moreover, Abbott, a former journalist, understood that inconsistency was not merely the hobgoblin of little minds but irrelevant as well: he repeatedly and routinely changed his position on key issues. On climate change, for instance, Abbott publicly argued every possible position on climate change over a relatively short space of time in opposition. He variously claimed the world was getting cooler, that climate science was 'crap', that humans had little role in climate change, that he 'accepted the science' and that he wanted to 'give the planet the benefit of the doubt'. He also articulated every position on what action to take on climate change, from an emissions trading scheme to a carbon tax ('the intelligent sceptic's way to deal with minimising emissions'), which he then campaigned against, and a big-government style grants program. On another totemic issue, he went from opposing paid parental leave 'over this government's dead body' to supporting a scheme so extravagantly generous his own colleagues opposed it as a 'Rolls-Royce model'.

---

* In particular, me: I fearlessly predicted Abbott would in effect destroy his own party.

Abbott's genius for almost randomly shifting policy positions inevitably placed him at odds with the evidence relating to some important issues, but that too, he knew, was no impediment; contrary evidence was ignored, wished away or dismissed as a fabrication; eventually he claimed that his assertions were correct because 'they just are'. Abbott became the leader not just of his parliamentary party but of what could be termed the Assertion-Based Community, a philosopher-prince whose postmodern take on politics freed him from the shackles of consistency and evidence, allowing him to say whatever he liked, whenever he liked, unencumbered by the ordinary rules of political discourse. Abbott is the poster boy of the new media environment that favours cut-through over logic, simplicity over nuance and assertion over reality, the first postmodern prime minister for whom truth is whatever is politically convenient at that moment.

The level of Stupid in public debate has accordingly risen in Australia, and significantly so, given the media—whose traditional role it has been to enable debate about public issues—is increasingly fragmented and incapable of, or unwilling, to accurately report matters of any complexity.

Many in the media, however, lay the blame elsewhere. In recent years, the political class as a whole in Australia has been assailed by the media and interest groups for their unwillingness to embrace complex economic reform like the celebrated governments of the 1980s and 1990s. It's a criticism that ignores the greater difficulty of explaining complex ideas to voters when there is less interest on the part of the media in participating in that process, when significant sections of the media will launch partisan attacks regardless of the merits of a reform, and negative, simplistic politics are the most effective tactics in winning office.

Political journalists also lament the lack of 'authenticity' of modern politicians. They want more 'real' politicians, 'straight shooters' who don't communicate with talking points and the repetition of tactically appropriate phrasing but 'say what they think', plain-speaking politicians in touch with ordinary voters, who don't rely on an unrealistic public image, who are 'themselves', or perhaps even 'mavericks'. In short, politicians who will do their job for them of attracting eyeballs to political journalism.

Putting aside the irony that the media is itself creating the conditions that make it more difficult for politicians to behave with 'authenticity', there is some substance to this demand given how few politicians don't rely on talking points and back themselves to communicate intelligently. And it is not merely the ubiquity of media training that has bleached all the colour out of political communication, but the professionalisation of politics—professionalisation not in the sense of a lifting of standards—but in the establishment of politics as a career, complete with its own structure and promotional ladder.

There have long been dynasties for whom politics was the family trade; labour movement-based parties have long channelled people into parliamentary politics via trade union politics, politicians have often worked for others or in their parties before being elected themselves. However, increasingly in the UK and Australia, an entire career in some form of public life is possible—participating in student politics, taking a job as a political staffer, media adviser or trade union official, obtaining preselection, winning a seat, securing a frontbench spot, and then after retirement or losing one's seat, appointment to a statutory body, working as a lobbyist or taking a board position in an industry one regulated as minister to add to one's hefty parliamentary superannuation. One may even meet a partner in the course of such a career—a recent deputy prime minister of Australia is married to a former NSW deputy premier.

In the US, the professionalisation of politics has been seen more in the growing length of time politicians at the state and federal level now spend in office. This has been helped by gerrymandering by both sides to make electoral districts politically safer, so that they become lifelong sinecures for those who can get them, although they may face challenges from within their own parties to keep them. But compared to generations ago, contemporary politicians are less likely to have had another occupation prior to parliamentary politics, more likely have worked for other politicians or within their own parties first, more likely to have already established alliances or joined factions within their party, and more likely to have had long exposure to political techniques such as targeted communication. The result is more polished, less communicative and above all more cautious politicians, for whom politics is a career and income source, rather than a period of public service after a successful job in another field.

But if we understand what the media demand for authenticity is in response to, if we know what authenticity is *not*—it's not the bland careerist who has only ever worked in frontbenchers' offices since she left university—it's harder to know what it *is*. Authenticity can be faked—or, more correctly, its characteristics can be faked. A politician's language and lexicon can convey authenticity, but can easily be faked as well—at least sometimes.*

---

* While prime minister of Australia, Kevin Rudd (who actually grew up in poverty in a Queensland country town) tried to demonstrate his working-class credibility by robotically uttering phrases apparently randomly selected from the films of Chips Rafferty, like 'fair shake of the sauce bottle'.

If language can be faked, so too can inarticulacy, which in the US and Australia is linked to political authenticity every bit as much as a capacity for great rhetoric—so much so that many politicians have emphasised or cultivated their inarticulacy as a key tool of their image-making, contrasting themselves with their glibber, more polished rivals. George W. Bush, following Ronald Reagan, tapped into America's long political tradition of anti-elitism and cleverly used a propensity for malapropism as part of his folksy charm (Dubya, the third generation of his family to pursue politics, has a BA in history from Yale and an MBA from Harvard Business School). One of Australia's most effective political communicators was 1970s and 1980s Queensland premier and crook Joh Bjelke-Petersen, who pioneered a number of innovations in media management in Australia, as well as cultivating an aura of plain-spoken inarticulacy to the point of rambling self-parody.[*] Australia's least articulate and most authentic political figure of recent decades was Pauline Hanson, advocate of xenophobia, protectionism and a clutch of bizarre economic policies sourced from the remainders bin of right-wing bookshops. Hanson routinely insisted she was 'not a politician', an important part of her authenticity for the regional blue-collar people attracted to her politics; this non-politician went on to become a serial election candidate garnering extensive public funding each time she stood, even though she was never elected.

If not inarticulacy, what about ideological consistency? Doesn't authenticity include a willingness to stick up for certain principles regardless of their popularity? But rare is the

---

[*]   One of Bjelke-Petersen's staff, Clive Palmer, now a mining magnate and politician himself, uses similar techniques.

successful politician of any stripe who hasn't adjusted his or her position on significant issues or whose actions have never been at odds with their rhetoric. Those that don't in time look like relics, not politically savvy and authentic. And politicians with a reputation for authenticity are just as susceptible to such flexibility. Ronald Reagan (an actor before entering politics, and a better one than commonly given credit for) preached small government but presided over an increase in the size of the US federal government and a massive increase in US government debt. There was also a significant gap between the rhetoric of neoliberal icon Margaret Thatcher and her actions: the lady who was 'not for turning' presided over an expansion in the British welfare state, and the level of taxation as a proportion of GDP under the Iron Lady only fell from 40 per cent to 39 per cent.

More recently, John McCain, celebrated 'maverick' and passenger on, if not driver of, the 'Straight Talk Express', was wildly inconsistent in his position on major issues such as tax cuts, and seemed to veer between conservatism and moderate positions depending on whether or not he was running for the US presidency. Former Australian prime minister John Howard also liked to sell himself to voters as a straight shooter, declaring 'you may disagree with me but you know where I stand'. But he was also notorious for carefully parsing his own words to explain inconsistencies, and as a professed small-government free marketeer oversaw a dramatic rise in taxation, government spending and middle-class welfare while prime minister. So, one might conclude that ideological consistency is only properly 'authentic' when a politician can, regardless of what they actually do, create an *image* of stubborn adherence to principle, because the reality is unlikely to be there.

Worship at the altar of manual labour

The more closely we examine it, the more authenticity appears an entirely subjective judgement: one voter's authentic politician is another's inarticulate bully. Our own beliefs inform what we judge to be authentic, not merely in politicians but in others generally. Conservative voters will thus invariably find conservative politicians more authentic, while progressive voters will see a fake, and vice versa. Authenticity is a construct, another simulacra, generated not merely by a politician but by voters themselves, with all the epistemological rigour of 'I know it when I see it'.

This explains the risibly Stupid outbreak of Shopfloor Chic among Australia's major party politicians in recent years, in which they don high-visibility vests, hard hats, eye protection and other accoutrements of the factory floor at staged media events.[*] This elevation of labouring occupations as a key signifier of political credibility was borne out by an unusual speech by then Labor prime minister Julia Gillard in 2011, at that point trying to define her prime ministership as one focused on fairness and reward for hard work—preferably of the manual variety. Gillard, similar to her predecessor Kevin Rudd, liked to name-check 'tradies' as a favoured occupation in her government's eyes, and one type of tradesperson had a prominent role in her speech. '[W]e have always acknowledged that access to

---

[*] Shopfloor Chic seems to have at least momentarily supplanted the passion for 'noddies' at politicians' media events, where colleagues, staff or anyone who could be roped in would stand behind or beside a politician at a media conference and furiously nod in agreement as they spoke, as if that would somehow convince viewers watching the footage of the veracity of what was being said. Whether this actually worked, and what the cost of treatment for the resulting cervical spine damage was, is unknown.

opportunity comes with obligations to seize that opportunity,' Gillard said. 'To work hard, to set your alarm clocks early,* to ensure your children are in school. We are the party of work not welfare, that's why we respect the efforts of the brickie and look with a jaundiced eye at the lifestyle of the socialite.'

Not content with directing a sinister yellow gaze at the glitterati, Gillard also attacked the party nibbling away at Labor's left flank, the Australian Greens, who would, she declared, 'never embrace Labor's delight at sharing the values of everyday Australians, in our cities, suburbs, towns and bush, who day after day do the right thing, leading purposeful and dignified lives, driven by love of family and nation'.†

This apotheosis of manual labour, delivered, appropriately, at Sydney's Luna Park, had as much reality as the live cross to nowhere. The economies of Australia, the US, the UK and Canada have all seen big falls in manufacturing employment since the 1970s, as have other Western economies and Japan. Meanwhile, service industries have grown rapidly as employers of large numbers of workers. In Australia, manufacturing is a relatively small employer compared to a generation ago: it is now only Australia's fourth-biggest employer and on the verge of being overtaken by both education and professional services. Construction remains a key sector of the Australia economy in terms of generating growth, but it is still smaller than retailing and Australia's (and the United States') biggest employer, health care. Gillard holding aloft the calloused

---

* A phrase stolen/plagiarised/paid homage to by British deputy PM Nick Clegg, who briefly and worryingly claimed he was standing up for 'alarm clock Britain'.

† A minor oddity there is that the Greens are even more aggressively protectionist in their attitude towards manufacturing than Labor itself.

hand of the brickie as the champion of honest toil was about as authentic as a beer ad.

The politician in the high-vis vest sneering at the social set is thus an even more surreal simulacra than the mainstream media's news rituals; a person trying to portray themselves not merely as something they demonstrably are not, and most likely never have been, but aping an outdated representation of the real experience of ordinary voters, invoking a past that, to the extent it ever existed, has long since been replaced by an altogether different economic world.

Where this hyperreality becomes particularly ironic—hyper-hyperreality, perhaps—is when it is understood as a reaction not merely to historical changes like the arrival of the internet or the professionalisation of politics, but to the central message of Anglophone economic policy since the 1980s. The economic changes that have rendered politicians in the garb of manual labour about as meaningful as a carnival cut-out are the ones wrought by politicians themselves. All English-speaking countries have embraced liberal capitalism, to varying degrees, over the last thirty years, deregulating their economies, reducing taxation, privatising publicly owned infrastructure and service delivery and reducing industrial protectionism, accelerating the historic decline in Western manufacturing.

This abandonment of regulated economies that distributed the burden of supporting traditional public sector and blue-collar jobs across the whole community in favour of market-oriented economic individualism lifted living standards in deregulated economies for all income groups, although the main beneficiaries were high-income earners. But it also adversely affected some sections of the community, such as manufacturing workers—primarily blue-collar males, but female-dominated industries like textiles were also severely affected—who struggled in the transition to the service industries that increasingly dominate Western economies.

The message from political leaders who pushed these changes, and from the media that encouraged them, to those groups left behind by economic reform and to the whole community—never stated bluntly but built into the entire reform program—was that they were, henceforth, on their own. The days of a communitarian approach to economic policy, in which governments would support industries or continue to own assets in the name of maintaining traditional jobs, were over, unless your industry was particularly influential and could successfully demand continuing support, like the heavily unionised, male-dominated car industry. The days of maintaining some sort of handbrake on dramatic wealth inequalities were also finished: if you could make millions, good luck to you—the tax system was about enabling wealth creation, not redistribution. Economic assistance was now an entitlement that corporations and unions bid for, rather than the whole basis for a nation's economic policy. The individual was elevated over the communal.

This economic atomisation complemented that already achieved by the unified media environment of the twentieth century. The mass media created from newspapers, radio and television had worked to dissolve lateral bonds between individuals and replace them with a bond between individuals and the media, albeit a one-way bond in which the individual had two simple roles: to consume, and to choose what to consume, courtesy of the advertising delivered via the media.

The atomisation inherent in the liberal economic reform program, however, focused on the individual's role as a worker or producer rather than consumer, removing or reducing the community's support for uncompetitive industries or government-owned services, allowing areas like manufacturing or traditionally public-owned services like rail transport to fend for themselves in a global marketplace while service industries thrived.

Through the looking glass in pursuit of authenticity

The abandonment of communal economic values and their replacement with individualism—admirably summed up in Margaret Thatcher's declaration 'there is no such thing as society'*—also created a kind of values vacuum that different groups have sought to fill and/or exploit, creating a search for authentic social values and principles beyond those of the market, which have been deemed as socially insufficient by most non-libertarians. Individualism and consumer choice, it turned out, were insufficient as social glue, the philosophical equivalent of knowing the price of everything and the value of nothing.

Some on both the left and the right thus yearn for a return to a closed, protected economy and a traditional social order. In Australia, the most vocal parliamentary advocates for greater protectionism are found in the Greens and the rural conservative Nationals and ex-Nationals, and regional Australia has produced successive waves of right-wing protectionism coupled with conservative social policies and xenophobia over the last

---

* Often claimed by Thatcher's defenders to have been misquoted, or taken out of context, betraying a nervousness about the bluntness of Thatcher's message rather inconsistent with that prime minister's boots'n'all political style. But as we noted above, Thatcher's rhetoric was often a poor fit with her achievements in government.

two decades. More mainstream social conservatives, lamenting the rise of an entirely materialist and individualist society, tried to hold the line in privileging heterosexual, religious men and their dependents, advocating social regulation wholly at odds with their economic philosophy. As we explored in previous chapters, many progressives embraced paternalism as a replacement for large-scale economic engineering.

Conservative political parties also embraced nationalism and militarism, and did so much more successfully than progressive parties. The left, whether traditional or cultural, remains uncomfortable with nationalism, which is notionally antithetical to traditional Marxist analysis, but deemed useful during the twentieth century if it contributed to the class struggle. Accordingly, nationalism for the traditional left is good if it involves minority groups in other countries whose separatism may be contrary to the interests of Western countries or Western-aligned leaders (thus, Basque separatism good, Kosovan separatism bad). Domestic nationalism in Western countries, however, is seen as unpleasant populism and kitschy jingoism, at best an instinct with all the class of a flag bikini, at worst something subtly or not-so-subtly racist.

All of these replacement values try to mimic or return to the communitarian characteristics lost with the abandonment of regulated, protected economies, with varying degrees of success. Economic traditionalists can no more restore a closed economy than go back in time to the 1970s. Social conservatives struggle with the problem that their preferred family model, married heterosexual couples with children, doesn't reflect the reality of most Western households. Paternalism specifically proposes to demonise and alter the traditional behaviours of the community, not celebrate them. Militarism is now profoundly unpopular in the aftermath of two disastrous Western military ventures in Afghanistan and Iraq. Only nationalism has been successful, at least in countries where it isn't contested by indigenous groups.

Even nationalism, however, raises more questions than it answers when it comes to authenticity. What does it mean to be proudly Australian, or British, American, Canadian? The answer gets complicated once you go beyond a reflexive assertion that each is 'the greatest country in the world'. Nationalism in any meaningful sense must be code for other values and thus another simulacrum of a reality that doesn't exist for many, and possibly most, citizens. The American way is, stereotypically, about individualism, opportunity and innovation, however much that may contradict more than ever the experience of tens of millions of desperately poor Americans. But Australian nationalism still relies on values like 'the fair go' and 'mateship' (held, generously, to apply to women as well as men), which in any pragmatic sense derive from equity and communitarianism. In the UK, at least, 'British values'[*] come with a longer list and more depth, reflecting institutions, traditions and national characteristics long attributed to or specifically developed by the British. You don't get to develop political liberalism, parliamentary democracy and global imperialism without having some substance to your list of core values. But this redefines nationalism as institutional and historic pride. Either way, we end up chasing our tails in pursuit of 'authenticity' again.

And undermining this drive to find replacement values is that individualism is being reinforced and yet altered by the

---

[*]   Or, as they may become, English, Welsh and Cornish values, depending on whether Scotland elects to depart the Union.

internet. After sixty years of atomisation by the mass media and thirty years of individualism driven by economic policy, people are now being offered the opportunity to connect up to whatever relationships, values or communities they can find online. This reverses the atomisation generated by mass media but replaces it with something very different from the community ties undermined by the mass media in the twentieth century. Individuals use online interconnectivity to form their own communities—communities that differ significantly from analogue-era communities. Before the twenty-first century, the communities we formed were dictated almost entirely by geography and kinship: our relationships and our communities were based on where we lived, our families and our workplaces. To choose a new community, you had to move somewhere else or change jobs. Now, individuals can select from a global range of communities those they wish to directly participate in, reflecting their own ideological, personal, spiritual and recreational beliefs and world view. Individuals can, using the internet, choose which community feels most *authentic* to them, rather than having one imposed on them by virtue of where they're born, what they do and what media they're exposed to. Moreover, there are multi-billion-dollar corporations entirely dedicated to monetising this process of community selection: the individual is no longer materialistic—that's a banally analogue way of thinking. Instead, under digital capitalism, the individual is now the material itself, their very process of personal self-discovery and self-definition an online consumer transaction, if that's not too grandiose a term for an ad for that one odd trick to lose belly fat.

Older commentators ill at ease with the internet still like to argue that this online engagement is in some, perhaps indefinable, way qualitatively poorer than real-life interaction—real-life relationships and interactions are, they maintain, more *authentic* than online relationships and interactions. There's a decided tone of get-off-my-lawn and back-in-my-day to such arguments, and they tend to be made by people without substantial experience of social media, for whom, say, a like on Facebook and fully fledged online activism are the same thing. They're also ahistorical: that non-face-to-face relationships are less real than face-to-face ones would come as a surprise to, say, nineteenth-century frontier communities in the United States, where long-distance engagements and marriages were very common and held together by letter-writing, or for that matter to anyone who has endured a long-distance romance, particularly now that the internet enables much fuller communication between separated partners than the phones and letters of the analogue era.

It also overlooks that, particularly for people under forty, there is an increasing unity—not just complementarity—of online and offline worlds: when you're permanently connected to your community online, no matter where you go, via a mobile device, the online and offline spaces you inhabit become more difficult to separate, and claims that one is more authentic than the other become harder to understand, let alone verify.

The new era of self-selecting your community conversely reinforces yet another form of fragmentation, in which one's own personal experience is elevated to the apex of public debate as the narrative that trumps all others, no matter how soundly based they may be. For many social and political issues, this undermines the very capacity to have an intelligent debate: if you haven't lived (or lived through) something, your arguments are automatically less valid, less *authentic* than the arguments of those who have. Want to argue that crime is falling? Try wandering the streets of *insert name of major city* at night. Are you a white middle-class heterosexual feminist? Then don't speak about women of colour/gays/low-income earners—your analysis doesn't apply. Oppose regulation of junk food? Wait till you've lost a family member to diabetes. That is, you may have evidence, you may have logic, but unless you have lived experience, your arguments are automatically, well, *inauthentic*. And there is, ultimately, no logical response to such arguments: either you have the relevant experience or you do not.

Once this approach is teased out, however, its problems become clearer: experience isn't necessarily a guarantee of authenticity. Experience must be interpreted, and can be misinterpreted (thus, 'false consciousness', not to mention anyone who has ever enjoyed Nickelback) and subjected to dictation by others; most experiences central to identity politics are either innate or imposed, but some are a matter of choice, and increasingly so as the internet provides greater opportunities for interconnectivity for people who in analogue times might have been cut off by geography or culture from others with whom they identified. Nonetheless, this sort of thinking is part of the logic behind politicians' Shopfloor Chic—how can you announce an industry policy if you don't look like you've worked in a factory? And it's immensely appealing to the media as well, because individual anecdotes and personal opinion are automatically more appealing than hard data.

When you elevate lived experience to centrality in your socio-political critique and politics, you delegitimise the contribution to debate from other perspectives; if the traditional logical fallacy is appeal to authority, since the 1990s appeal to *experience* has come to rival it, creating a hierarchy of analysis with lived experience at the apex of authenticity. Moreover, as the phrase 'check your privilege' implies, it is not merely that a non-experience-based contribution to a discussion *lacks* legitimacy, the possession of other forms of experience creates an illegitimacy that is impossible to overcome: the scoring systems used to allocate 'privilege points' can be neatly flipped into a 'how illegitimate is your opinion' scale, depending on the colour of your skin, your sexual preference, your income and your gender.

The result is a further fragmentation of public debate on issues, with fewer voices heard and greater unanimity among those voices given the imposition of dominant narratives even within sub-groups. The result is also a lesser willingness among generalists, and particularly media practitioners, to genuinely engage on policy issues arising from or including identity politics, for fear of being labelled racist/misogynist/homophobic/middle class/transgenderphobic/ableist/fattist/perpetrators of rape culture. They live in fear of fatally missing some critical nuance that would reveal them as inauthentic, or worse.

So, we may no longer be atomised as we were in, say, the 1980s, but we control which communities we now cluster into and control the information we receive. In the smoking remains of the single media space of the twentieth century, an ever-shrinking number of journalists perform rituals mimicking the behaviour of their ancestors, with little of the content the old mass media produced, or waging war on whoever has been identified by their company as this week's target. In politics, the incentives are increasingly structured to discourage complexity, empiricism and nuance, and encourage simplicity, inconsistency and negativity. In discussing complex social issues, we deem experience to be more potent than logic or evidence.

The consequence: informed public debate as a whole of the kind that was, with all its flaws, a feature of the analogue era is becoming difficult to achieve. It has been replaced with a fake environment, a stage backdrop painted to resemble a vast landscape that no longer exists, populated by actors playing roles that once may have held meaning but which are, increasingly, empty and ritualistic. In such an environment, the propagation of Stupid becomes ever easier, because Stupid isn't playing pretend. Stupid is for real.

BK

11

Conspicuous compassion: On consuming Kony

Jason 'Radical' Russell is probably not the only Evangelical Christian father-of-two ever to have had unprotected sex with concrete. He is, however, one of the very few to provide us with a demonstration video of the act. Shot on a San Diego street corner in the days that followed its subject's elevator ride to fame, this film is useful in understanding an emerging kind of Stupid.

Which is to say, compassion has become no more effective but every bit as pleasurable as a sex act with oneself. Compassion, which many people will argue leads us to the light of understanding, increasingly leads us to the darkness of public self-embrace.

And no further.

I appreciate it might seem cruel and unreasonable to declare compassion unproductive, and even unconsciously self-serving. Do understand, however, that this is an observation that itself derives from thinking that could, at a pinch, be seen as compassionate. This argument may be more palatable to you if you believe it is foundationally compassionate. If one believes—and I do—that the billions of people in the world who do not enjoy what could be reasonably called a good life are deserving of better, then one could be said to be compassionate. Of course, there are arguments, and one is made by Immanuel Kant and another by Nietzsche and others still by Peter Singer, that this is not a conclusion to which compassion necessarily draws us. But let's allow ourselves to pretend that it is; if only to agree that a foundational compassion informs this critique of compassion itself.

Compassion could be said to be a fairly atomistic thing. Which is to say, it works fine in the individual mind, but when it attempts to move towards actual social solutions— and its presence is certainly demanded daily as a political tool in news editorials and Facebook feeds which scream 'Why doesn't my government have more compassion?'—it actually slows and even impedes the process. Compassion can even become a bit totalitarian. Yes, I know that is an outrageous claim. But some things that work well when one is alone start to function quite differently when they are applied on a broader scale than 'me'. Compassionate reason is one of these things.

The practise of my individual and ethical reason might lead me to an individually reasonable conclusion that ends up gainsaying all of my ethical and reasonable intent. Say I want to eat the pseudo-cereal quinoa. I want to do this because it is one of the very few protein-rich vegetables in the world and its consumption diminishes my meat and dairy consumption, which in turn supports an industry that is both unsustainable and inhumane. Further, I want to support new and non-corporate growth in a nation like Bolivia because, as a consumer, I am tired of giving my dollar to major agribusiness. So, I buy quinoa for these informed reasons. But, everyone else with my compassionate reason has come to the same conclusion. Within months of the birth of the quinoa craze, the revenue of farmers has soared.

However, consumption in Bolivia of this Incan crop which has been a staple of Bolivian diets falls 34 per cent in 2011, the year I said goodbye to cracked wheat and brown rice. Although foreign aid organisations had worked with Bolivian farmers to make this food-fetish item such a regular feature of my compassionate dining, its nutritional benefits were no longer available to many Bolivians. According to a piece in the *New York Times*, malnutrition among children in quinoa-growing areas had escalated.

Now the sort of tosser, such as myself, who stocks their larder with protein-rich ethics must face another problem. Since news of this disaster brought about by what we'll call instrumental compassion—I'm stealing this from critics of what is called instrumental reason; if you want to learn how this idea of individual reason turned into collective Stupid, go to Heidegger or Horkheimer—the West's ethical cooks withdrew some of their custom. And then, OMG, many Bolivian farmers were sent spiralling into financial chaos.

It was an entirely reasonable decision to buy quinoa, which actually tastes pretty good for a 'super food'. When the decision is individual, it is a good one. When it becomes instrumental and happens on a massive scale, it ends up being pretty shitty. I rather imagine Bolivians make justifiably nasty jokes about me, my cooking and my instrumental compassion.

The quinoa example is a fascinating one that has drawn wide attention. An entire series of good, ethical and compassionate decisions produced a crap result. 'Radical', however, is a far less nuanced matter. His was an entire series of crap decisions that produced both crap and Stupid.

Not to be all I Told You So—after all, I have three kilograms of quinoa in my pantry—but I saw pretty much from the start that this Kony thing was a load of shit. I watched it unfold on Twitter when a prominent self-described humanist said something along the lines of 'This has to be a good thing.' I watched this dude contrast vision of his own happy, healthy white kid with jump-cut horror endured by African children. It was all very 'we are one' and 'why can't we see these poor dark children as important?' You know the deal. One world. All that shit. Set to a sort of empty and hysterical soundtrack that was kind of the depressed relative of the sort of thing you might hear spouted by a 'new age' therapist, this video made me feel like I was being manipulated by an especially bad chiropractor. And just as I suspected that the spine of my charity was about to be snapped by a self-important wellness practitioner, there was KONY, his face in the frame as the centre of all evil.

Seriously. Mate. Are you telling me that by tut–tutting at one dude, we are going to solve all the problems in Africa? And, yes, I know that Africa is a diverse continent that contains more nations than Uganda. But the Stupid who made this video didn't seem to share my basic knowledge of maps. Perhaps it was the great grain controversy of 2011 that had me on high alert. Or perhaps I just don't have enough 'compassion'. But it was pretty plain to me that this was some discount Stupid.

Compassion is a requisite thing in private interactions but it is no longer a useful thing in public discussion. Its everyday personal exercise, of course, is essential and inevitable between adequately social human adults. But the broadly accepted idea that compassion is a necessary and foundational practice in any policy discussion is total pants. Moreover, its public expression has become a total wank.

Before we saw this YouTube video of a guy apparently flogging his log on a California sidewalk outside Sea World, that same guy had just attained nearly 100 million clicks and saturation news coverage in less than a week for his campaign against a warlord. His video was very, very compassionate.

Jason 'Radical' Russell (yes, he really calls himself that) was the guy who gave us one of the world's most apparently effective moments of activism. Appended with the social media hashtag #KONY2012, this awareness-raising campaign was a remarkable moment in the history of, um, awareness-raising campaigns. The object was, according to its chief architect, to 'Make Kony Famous'. Because he was, like, the most evil guy.

Actually, Joseph Kony is the sort of man to whom the descriptor 'total dick' could be effortlessly applied. Or he was. At the time of writing, it is reported that Kony is gravely ill. Strangely, his poor health and subsequent inactivity has not changed all the shit that goes on daily in his home country of Uganda. The fact that he had left Uganda some years before Radical's exercise in 'awareness' does make this harder to measure. But we can say that people are still dying of malaria, AIDS-related illnesses and ethnic and government-endorsed murder. It's a horrible place that produces some horrible people.

But Russell's focus was not on drawing Uganda systematically out of the many large problems it continues to face. Medical, economic and political disaster were not his thing. Instead, he wanted to 'get Kony' by means of an emotional video and related merchandise sales. Which would go on to fund more emotional videos.

Kony, the leader of the Lord's Resistance Army, a strange and violent cult, believes himself to be an instrument of God. Call me an old-fashioned atheist, but I never think that's a good thing. Kony was sort of like a Charles Manson–Jerry Falwell amalgam. Except with even more guns and in a nation already rogered by seventeen kinds of devastation. Worse kinds of hell tend to produce more cartoonish devils and Kony, known to recruit children into his militia and said to endorse rape, was a pretty colourful demon.

A Radical angel came to vanquish him. And the world watched on, for a day at least, in rapturous approval. 'Let's make Kony famous,' said Radical. Within hours, he really was.

Russell had himself become very, very famous in a very short time for his work in highlighting the atrocities committed by this loony thug. To say that Russell's immensely popular promotional video was politically naive is bit like saying the early work of Britney Spears was lyrically simple. Which is to say, oops, not only had Joseph Kony fled Uganda several years before Radical dived in to save the children, but, oops, the International Criminal Court had indicted him for war crimes in 2005, the United States had decried his army as a terrorist organisation in 2001 and the Ugandan government, itself known to soak in the odd luxurious bloodbath filled with the limbs of dismembered children, had declared him a wanted man. (Russell was working with the approval of the Ugandan government. Perhaps, like most of the people who saw and were moved by his YouTube video, he hadn't bothered to type 'Uganda State Sanctioned Death Abduction Horror Show' into Google.)

But some really strange Stupid began to unfold when Radical—a man who is far better suited to making Christian musicals than he is instructing the world in political action—released his video. I have never seen a more 'shared' item on social media. Normally sane people of my actual real-life acquaintance seemed compelled to offer up their endorsement for a video that was as artless as it was politically naive. I don't know if we can say this is instrumental compassion; it was just too Stupid and crap for such a careful account. Maybe it was false consensus. Maybe people just like to see evil personified. Or maybe there are just more fans of amateur Christian musical theatre than I had previously thought.

Maybe it was more a case of what is called pluralistic ignorance; that thing where people might privately disapprove of something—and again this video was so bad I don't know how they couldn't smell its central cheese—but are too afraid to say it in public. I have begun to suspect that there is a real terror of being seen as less than compassionate. In a time that produces complex problems that exceed even quite considered individual ethics such as that which fuelled the quinoa craze, I think there is a romantic return to 'feeling'.

NGOs and charitable organisations are plainly aware that this need to be seen as compassionate fuels an awful lot of giving. Recently, I was asked by a young man in a shopping centre for a donation to an organisation that funds diversionary activities for teenagers with cancer. I actually don't mind the organisation and I understand that diversion is an effective way to deal with pain. But I was shocked by the strong compassion-producing visual technique he employed, which was to appear as though he was a cancer patient. The chap was wearing a printed bandana of the sort we broadly associate with chemotherapy patients.

My immediate thought on seeing him was: 'You shouldn't be in a shopping centre with such compromised immunity.' My next thought was entirely compassionate and I gave him some money.

I was troubled for several days after the exchange. I just couldn't believe that they would compromise the health of a young oncology patient. Also, I'd had a bit of a cold and I was concerned that he would catch it. So I called them to ask about their policy (I know this isn't how a normal human behaves, but I am a writer and therefore perversely entitled to make these sorts of queries). They told me not to worry as these paid employees were, in fact, perfectly healthy. They were just wearing the bandanas 'in solidarity'.

In solidarity with whom and by whose explicit permission? I was actually pretty appalled. I imagine if I had cancer to the degree it would require an immune-compromising toxic treatment such as chemo or radiotherapy, I would not want anyone representing me in fucking cancer drag. What is this? Leukaemia cosplay? What makes it okay to do near-death fancy dress and what the fuck is happening to my actual compassion when it is induced so often by imposters?

What happens is one of two things. You either get so fucking angry about the demands on your emotion and the road to Stupid, you write a book about it. Or, you accept the totalitarian view that public compassion is not only useful but compulsory. And then you buy a ribbon, change your Facebook picture for 'awareness' and accept that everything in the repertoire of compassionate protest is just dandy because it 'shows I care'.

Now, I did this in the case of Bolivian farmers and my participation in instrumental compassion showed me that maybe It Doesn't All Start With Me. It was a useful lesson that it is entire systems and not small, atomised practice that need revision. This was very difficult to predict while making high-end salads. But it is not so difficult to see when one is buying an awareness ribbon.

Think about the famous pink ribbon. October is annually awash with the optimism of pink. But more lately, it is full with the impatience of some breast cancer survivors it purports to assist. Some current and former patients are exasperated with the use of pink as a disingenuous marketing tool, notably the glorious Barbara Ehrenreich, whose book *Smile or Die: How positive thinking fooled America and the world* tears happy-clappy pinkwashing a new rectum. Other survivors have become convinced that pink month is less about awareness than it is obfuscation; many critique what they regard as bad medical information. Growing medical opinion has it that mammograms, which pink month encourages, are a poor diagnostic tool.

But even if they're not, pink month doesn't encourage women to get them. One 2013 study released in the *Journal of Marketing Research* set out to examine the pink campaign's effectiveness. Researcher Stefano Puntoni unexpectedly found that the pink brand made women perceive their risk of breast cancer as lower and tended to dissuade them from donating to breast cancer charities. While it is almost certainly true that the month affords comfort to many breast cancer survivors, it is also almost certainly untrue that it does much more than that. October is a month in which some women get to feel individually good.

I expressed these views on a news site and was privately contacted by a friend whom I had last seen at the funeral for a lovely young woman whose life had been claimed by breast cancer. She was very angry with me and mentioned that her dead friend loved pink month and that I needed to practise greater compassion. Of course, I used the foundational compassion argument I did at the beginning of this chapter; to wit, I care about solutions and will therefore proceed only from that single moment of concern and not be distracted by my emotions, if possible, en route to that solution. She didn't buy it.

Even very bright people buy the idea of compassion as an essential force. When the impressive leader and soldier Nelson Mandela died in 2013, he was eulogised by quite respectable writers as a man who had shown both 'forgiveness' and 'compassion'. This was surprising to me as I, as a young anti-Apartheid activist, had first come to know of this man—then classified as a terrorist by many liberal democracies, including my own—as a leader of armed resistance. Of course, he went on to become a politically astute negotiator and then a president who never quite lost his fondness for buying guns; perhaps everyone but me has forgotten the South African Arms Deal. But there was this great Oprahfication of his legacy that rewrote his life as one that was lived not in battle but in compassion. This keen politician and military mastermind is somehow the only dude in history that has shown us how LOVE can change the law. It wasn't the threat of an unwinnable war that turned South Africa into a (still terribly uneven and violent) democracy. It was a big, cuddly compassionate black teddy bear with guns made out of candy.

Ugh. What a horrible way to remember such an effective individual.

But we ascribe to much-loved leaders those qualities we most value and one of those, right now, is compassion. As quinoa demonstrates before it is artfully thrown through a beet and goat-cheese salad, effective action is difficult. And, yes, people want to feel like they're doing something. And compassion is something. So let's do this.

Let's Show We Care.

Let's Show We Care about being seen to care.

Okay, that's a bit mean. I do understand the despair and have suffered the contradiction carried along in instrumental compassion many times. I don't know what to do about the state of the world, so I choose just to document it and mock it into the possibility of change. This, I think, may be a slightly more effective technique than wearing a ribbon or lighting a candle. But I don't doubt that anyone cares less than me; they may care more. I do doubt the effectiveness of the caring, however. And I do see that there is a certain pleasure taken in the act of care itself.

I'm not the only one with this opinion. Of course, grumpy old Nietzsche said that compassion is the self-indulgent 'multiplication of human suffering'; he's basically calling compassion misery porn. In *The Antichrist* he said of compassion: 'It wants to give birth to its god and see all mankind at his feet.' I think that's maybe a bit harsh, especially coming from a man who was so moved by compassion towards the end of his life that he famously threw himself upon a suffering horse and cried uncontrollably. I know compassion is real. I also know that it needs to be subjugated to reason. Individual will can lead us to a quinoa crisis.

Perhaps we should look at someone with a better rep than Nietzsche. In 2014, a former migration officer who had seen first-hand the rationalised horror of an Australian offshore detention camp for refugees became a 'whistleblower'. In an interview, she explained the horror and protest she had seen within the centre. This came days after the death of Kurdish Iranian detainee Reza Berati.

The day before migration officer Liz Thompson's television interview, candles had been lit in Berati's honour. Of course, when this unusually courageous, and disarmingly eloquent, person spoke of the place where he had died, she became a hero to the many people troubled by conditions on Manus Island. She was asked to speak at another protest and initially agreed. Then she refused. She had been troubled by the lighting of candles for Berati. She was troubled by the widespread practice of individual compassion. On the blog Crossborder Operational Matters, she wrote, 'I am grateful for the support I have received and acknowledge that people are expressing solidarity for a variety of admirable reasons, [but] there is something deeply discomforting about the adulation and the focus on me.'

Thompson was quite Nietzschean in her impatience with those who had been so eager to show their compassion. '"Not in our name" is a self-referential slogan, it speaks about us, not about those behind the wire.' She suggested: 'If you want to close the camps, think about what you can do where you are that will be effective.' She was very clear that lighting a candle and crying for a man who had died was not effective action.

Of course, such critiques are always met with the question: 'Well what *can* we do, then?' The answer is: use your fucking noggin. Outrun the Stupid and instead of instrumental compassion, try instrumental thinking. Compassion will not close Manus Island, itself a deterrent 'solution' said to be derived from compassion. Compassionate conservatives regularly argue that their wish to stop unauthorised maritime arrivals by dangerous vessels has its origin in care. And there is no argument I can think of to 'prove' that they might not, actually, be motivated by compassion.

Compassion does not lead us to the best and most considered solutions. It can lead us to buy ribbons, light candles and open detention centres.

Compassion becomes the kind of Stupid which supplants the act of giving with Facebook sharing.

This is the kind of Stupid where one is led to ethical ends not by ethical thinking but by something more like ethical shopping.

This is the kind of Stupid that empties us of the urge to do social good by turning social good into social capital. You give because you expect to get.

We've spoken before about how the transactional nature of the market tends to govern our everyday exchange, such as it might be in the trade of 'raising awareness' with a ribbon and receiving plaudits for your visible compassion. It is perhaps worth remembering that 'giving' was not always enacted with the hope of a return.

Charity, let it be plainly said, is not the worst product of Christian thought. There are far worse things to do than good-doing, and benevolence has been a subject for some truly great theologians. (I can hear the atheists sniggering up the back and I remind them once more: for more than a millennium, theology was the only game in town. If you wanted to think about ethics, the nature of reality or even mathematics *and* keep most of your limbs, you had to do this within the margins of Mother Church. Please let me mention Christian thinkers or I will turn this car around and confiscate your Flying Spaghetti Monster T-shirt.) The theologian Thomas Aquinas thought charity the 'most excellent of the virtues' (Summa: 1265). And recounted St Augustine on the quality as one 'which, when our affections are perfectly ordered, unites us to God' and to others. So, you could say that there is an implied reward here, but it is one that is a bit better than Facebook likes. Charity unites us to our neighbours by means of God. It connects us to humanity.

And I don't think Russell's Kony video did that at all. This late-capitalist Christian had a very different view of charity. Here, charity was something that could keep funding his Stupid organisation to make more Stupid and misleading videos. Although, the SeaWorld video is perhaps less misleading. Here, a naked white man appears to be taking tap-and-kick instruction from an unseen panel of reality TV dance sadists. If you have not viewed the film, briefly imagine what RuPaul's *Drag Race* might look like if shot on a sunny day at the mouth of hell. This YouTube moment is at once cruel and well-choreographed; Russell—whom we would later learn had been suffering the 'dehydration' diagnosed in the newly famous by imaginary doctors—may have temporarily lost the use of his mind but not of his jazz hands.

To naturally unpleasant persons such as me, the emergence of this peculiar pornography made absolute sense. There could be no postscript more appropriate to Russell's KONY2012 campaign than one that had its star apparently spending himself at a major intersection. One can hate the sexual and military enslavement of African children as much as the next guy. This doesn't mean one cannot be equally troubled by a man who seemed less eager to end injustice than he did to audition for the next season of *Glee*. The campaign had begun and ended in self-embrace.

Of course, this is not for a moment to say that Russell or any of the persons behind the clicks on his YouTube offering did not care for the fortunes of Ugandan orphans. It is, however, to suggest that by 2012, charity had become very non-Aquinas. These days, even Christians out to save African babies from sex slavery would rather spend time with Oprah than with God. Russell would get his time with Oprah, by the way. He talked of his 'struggle'. As people from nice countries often do. Because feelings are important! After all they can change the world.

They have. The primacy of feelings has made our world extraordinarily Stupid. Feelings are fine in private and sometimes inevitable in public, but it seems to me they have become the raison d'être of protest. Some things in the world need changing. Not for our own comfort. Just because they're wrong.

HR

Conclusion—Final words: Towards a taxonomy of Stupid, and other wankery

We warned at the start that we'd be offering no solutions to Stupid. To make up for that, or, more correctly, deflect attention from that, we're going to offer a biographical note. We've only been friends for about two years, which is a bit odd as we went to the same university at the same time and sat in the same philosophy lectures. In that long-ago world, we drank at the same bar and liked the same dreary no-wave music. Later, much later, after at least one other career each, we would work for the same media outlet and develop the same intolerance for what we saw as craven thinking and express the same unpopular absolutism where free speech is concerned. We even got pissed off at the same people and annoyed everyone with the same antisocial willingness to tell everyone, including each other, that they were very wrong. The genesis of this book was, accordingly, a shared loathing of the sloppy thinking, shameless bullshitting and ignorant, amnesiac drivel that passes for so many contributions to rational debate, a feeling we were up to our necks in a tide of Stupid that showed no sign of ebbing, and that it was time Someone Fucking Did Something.

But in truth, as much as we might like to paint ourselves as the curmudgeonly heroes of a War on Stupid, shaped by our intellectual upbringings to have no choice but to take up arms against a sea of cretins, we're more correctly just two more, and rather minor, names in a long and—we think—honourable tradition stretching back two millennia and more. For the history of Stupid is a long one. And in tracing the tangled, matted, strands of human idiocy that unite the greatest of philosophers and the shrillest of pop stars, that connect the mightiest of historical institutions with the most venal individuals and link our forebears to ourselves despite thousands of years of learning, we've seen how the fight against it has been a long one as well.

In many ways, it has been a successful fight: our explorations of the annals of Stupid suggest that things used to be a whole lot Stupider. Many of the most blatantly offensive forms of Stupid are now in retreat, at least in the lands of #firstworldproblems and their contiguous zones. Women are officially no longer second-class citizens, we don't persecute and kill gay or transgender people as a matter of policy, we seek to acknowledge the impacts of imperialism on indigenous people and their prior relationship with the land if we now live on it. We live longer, healthier, wealthier lives than ever before, we place some basic restrictions on how much people can exploit one another (well, other than in the US), and many of the forms of discrimination and harassment that anyone other than an adult white male once endured as a matter of course in Western society are now illegal or considered entirely beyond the pale.

Compared to the 1960s, let alone Enlightenment Europe or the world of the Reformation, Stupid is mostly in retreat.

And yet, Stupid remains, always capable of surging back. It keeps on causing *bad things* to happen, it continues to cost lives, health, liberties, economic opportunity. People still die as a consequence of Stupid—their own, or someone else's, and not just that of ordinary citizens, but of people who should know better, like their parents, or people who are paid, at least notionally, to be Not Stupid. You could take inspiration from one particular sub-branch of Stupid—dodgy economic modelling—and model the cost of Stupid to our economies, loading in everything from bad policy choices to people dying unnecessarily to lower economic growth, but it's more than that. Stupid is pervasive—undermining our rights as citizens, infuriating us when we encounter it in the media or from some officious jobsworth, corrupting our capacity to sensibly debate public issues, alienating us from one another. It's like the background radiation of society, always there, inescapable, the distant but permanent echo of some Big Bang of Idiocy.

You might have noticed a certain philosophical basis for this book: Stupid matters because it has consequences, bad consequences, and they flow even when people seek to do good. Few of the people in this book were or are genuinely and completely evil, but the damage inflicted by the well-intentioned or the ignorant can be just as profound as that caused by actual malice. We're thus professedly consequentialists—although if you tried to pin us down on exactly which type of consequentialism we each adhered to we might have to sneak a quick glance at the Wikipedia entry to be sure. We think that, so long as we're going to live together in societies, we should aim to maximise the positive consequences of the way we interact individually, socially, economically and politically, and minimise the negative consequences.

Of course, that sounds dead easy, but the trick is *seeing* those consequences clearly, a trick that proves beyond a surprising number of otherwise intelligent people—indeed, proves beyond all of us at some point or other. Who has such a cold, dead eye and such a forensic gaze that self-interest or ignorance or haste or emotion has never clouded their judgement? Not bloody *us*, that we can guarantee.

So, conscious that, as Jesus may well have said, the Stupid will always be with us, with us as individuals, as groups and as societies, we must always be on guard against it, must always be examining *consequences*, not merely intentions. And the first step in that process is to understand that Stupid is always driven by the same things, whether it's in the medieval church or a Facebook group about chemtrails. The same core motivations for Stupid exist in human society now that have always existed in it. The first is obvious:

Commercial incentives

Upton Sinclair said it best: 'It is difficult to get a man to understand something, when his salary depends on his not understanding it.' From defence companies that benefit from hyping the threats they claim their products protect against to fossil fuel industries funding propaganda against climate science, from the medicalising for profit of innate human states to academics making a living peddling nanny-state solutions, the connection between Stupid and money is a strong one and has long been so.

Historical digression: one of the most successful rent-seekers in history was the London printing oligopoly, the

Stationers' Company, which long, and successfully, argued for strict censorship of printed material by the Tudor and Stuart regimes of England. That system of censorship also enabled the Stationers' Company to enforce exclusive copyright and block competition for its members from the middle of the sixteenth to the end of the seventeenth centuries—in the same way that the copyright cartel of the movie and music industries now support aggressive internet censorship and anti-privacy laws to support their oligopoly. The Stationers argued that unfettered printing was a 'dangerous innovation', like a 'field overpestered with too much stock', and that the 'public good of the state' was linked to the 'private prosperity of the Stationers' Company'; what England needed was not printing but 'well-ordered printing'.

The Stationers may not have been history's first rent-seekers—religions have long understood the benefit of good relations with secular powers—but they are a splendid model for so many who have come after them. It is true that no industry lobbyist, academic or peak body would now dream of so bluntly associating the national interest with private interests; former General Motors executive Charles Wilson spent years living down his famous quote that 'what was good for our country was good for General Motors, and vice versa'. Instead, there would be modelling produced to demonstrate the additional jobs, or higher economic growth, or lower social costs of measures that just so happened to benefit those urging the measures. But their matter-of-fact insistence that censorship was good for printing and good for England prefigures so much of the casual Stupid to which private interests and governments have subjected us for so long. When money talks, it does so in fluent Stupid.

Of similar long duration is the connection between Stupid and money's close relative . . .

Preservation of power

As with money, power provides a strong incentive for Stupid. For millennia, it motivated institutional religions to insist they alone provided the path to salvation; individuals seeking alternatives were discouraged, then tortured, then killed, within an intellectual framework based on the need to support institutional authority rather than philosophical coherence.

The state—a relative newcomer in political philosophy, having been around less than 500 years (a length of time we don't cavalierly dismiss, but which isn't that long in the history of Stupid)—has long since replaced organised religion as the primary practitioner of Stupid-for-power, particularly but not only through national security laws: in many respects it replicates the intellectual framework of religions, insisting that it alone knows what is best for the safety of citizens, beyond even citizens themselves.

A possible distinction between Stupid produced for commercial purposes and that intended to support positions of power—usually state power—is that lobbyists and economists working for commercial interests often know perfectly well that their case is nonsense, but they are paid to argue it, and thus bring a certain professional commitment—'Hello, Sam' 'Hello, Ralph'—to delivering Stupid. But members of state institutions are much more likely to *believe* the Stupid they utter, having convinced themselves that they are a critical bulwark against the threats they relentlessly hype. This explains why national security officials eventually come to see virtually everything outside themselves as a security threat—why the National Security Agency described anyone using internet cryptography (which is anyone who does online banking or shopping, for starters) as 'adversaries'; why the head of the Australian Security and Intelligence Organisation complained that the internet allowed 'individuals to propagate and absorb unfettered ideas . . . literally, in their lounge rooms.'

The terror of unfettered ideas roaming the nation's lounge rooms (lounge rooms, by god, where you'd assume families were safe!) thanks to the internet aside, not all Stupid is self-interested. Stupid can also advance when we are . . .

Lacking the weapons to combat Stupid

It requires basic skills to combat Stupid, and sometimes new forms of Stupid, or new delivery mechanisms for it, demand new skills. The arrival of printing was not merely immensely disruptive to existing Stupid-based models of commerce and power in the middle of the last millennium, but disruptive to existing analytical techniques as well.

Here, for once, the frequent comparison of the impacts of printing and the internet is justified—just as the internet introduced us both to vast amounts of easily accessible information and vast amounts of complete garbage (sometimes the same thing), so too did printing usher in access both to the great works of Western and Arab philosophy and science and to huge amounts of rubbish. However, as Richard Abel details in his excellent *Gutenberg Revolution: A History of Print Culture*, Western scholars lacked the tools to know the difference between fictions like alchemy, astrology, magic, much of Aristotelian 'science' or ancient mysticism and more rigorously empirical content. That is, they lacked the tools to identify Stupid.

Identifying Stupid took the work of new thinkers, like Paracelsus in medicine and Bruno in cosmology (burned to death by the Catholics for his troubles), to start the process of falsifying much of the material suddenly far more widely available in Europe. Intellectually, the world owes such figures an enormous debt. For those of us worried about Stupid, they are remarkable, unsung heroes, pioneers who, to borrow an imperialist metaphor, ventured into a New World of Stupid and began trying to tame it in a way that none of us can begin to imagine. The whole idea of falsification, in a way, had to be invented by them, in the same way that a primitive kind of peer review was being invented. Before printing, there was intellectual debate, of course, but the scholastic tradition of the high Middle Ages was much more intensively an *oral* culture than that which followed, and not merely because of the dearth of books: the acts of both reading and writing were strongly oral in nature, particularly at those newfangled 'universities' that began spreading across Europe after the turn of the millennium.

Moreover, in the scholastic tradition, much analysis of new ideas was really about preservation of positions of power—for example, focused on assessing their complementarity with the Church's power (meaning, among other things, scholars backed by a strong monastic order or secular ruler had more freedom than those who weren't). But after printing, the size of the audience for new ideas massively increased, and, as we discussed earlier, ideas could actually be transmitted with relative accuracy rather than relying on monks acting as imperfect human photocopiers. Responses to new ideas could be circulated to a large number of readers within a (in historical terms) reasonably short time frame. The wisdom of crowds might be an overhyped phenomenon (for which evidence, Read The Comments), but it bore out in humanism and the beginnings of science as Western minds began acquiring the basics of bullshit detection.

Since then, the West has had 600 years to develop a whole framework of critical analysis, aided by the professionalisation of science and universal education in the twentieth century. Unlike our fifteenth-century ancestors, we don't have the excuse of lacking the tools to combat Stupid. The land has been tamed; the log cabins have given way to luxury apartments; we have a vast array of anti-Stupid tools, but we keep finding reasons not to use them.

Now, true, there are aspects of internet-derived Stupid that make combating it more difficult. The internet is a far more rapid delivery mechanism of Stupid than printing ever was. Online, a lie can circumnavigate the world several thousand times and flog you a wrist band while the truth is still looking up Wikipedia. And true, things can 'go viral', in that term beloved of marketing types, spreading instantly in a raging storm of retweets and likes, although books often 'went viral' back in the day too—it's not so long since *The Secret* shifted tens of millions of units to the intellectually feeble, emotionally crippled and financially desperate via *Oprah*.

The internet *does* demand certain skills more than others compared to print: we no longer need to remember as much, as long as we can recall how to reach important information (in the same way, though to a lesser degree, that writing and later printing ended the centrality of memory in oral culture), but we need to be more sceptical because 'authority' is easier to fake online, whether it's a Photoshopped picture, an invented quote or the life that facts can take on once unchained from their context and source and left free to float about, unfettered, in our lounge rooms.

The internet also strengthens another key motivation for Stupid . . .

Tribality and groupthink

. . . because it strengthens connectedness and enables us to link up with the communities with which we most identify. A sense of tribality drives the 'piling-on' effect of social media, in which online groups come to resemble pitchfork-wielding hordes or lynch mobs pursuing someone deemed to have egregiously offended the group. Criticising online witch-hunts is de rigueur these days; it's forgotten that they frequently happen to those entirely deserving of such a dire fate, but it can also overtake those guilty of, at worst, clumsy expression, with careers and job prospects ruined for some type of –ism more perceived than real.

But that such behaviour is confined to online rather than the real world in the West is one identifiable area of Stupid where history demonstrates significant improvement. Whether it was Christians slaughtering Jews in medieval Europe, or burning witches in early modern England, or lynching African Americans in the US or murdering gays in Australia, the long tradition of tribal violence in the West has receded, and people are alive who otherwise wouldn't be because of it.

Even so, a related component of tribality continues to feature strongly in public debate, something we spent some time on in our Introduction . . .

Ad hominem

In the immortal words of *The Onion*, stereotypes save time—a principle almost all of us, no matter how intellectually rigorous, have employed at some point, in particular in dismissing the argument of someone because of who they are or whom they represent, rather than properly engaging with it.

It's worth going through this slowly because it takes us somewhere close to the final point we want to make. The process of rigorous engagement with the substance of what your interlocutor actually says—or 'listening' as scientists call it—can be difficult. Most of us link our arguments to our egos: to admit that someone else's argument, one that we have been aggressively challenging, has merit is a wounding blow to our pride; to acknowledge our errors is akin to gouging out our own eyes—especially when it relates to what we do for a living. When our interlocutor is someone whom we dislike or whose motives we suspect, our dismissiveness is redoubled. Admitting they are right is a Gethsemanean agony and you'd rather—to hopelessly mix up the metaphor—lop off an ear than do it.

So, yes, unfortunately, rigour can be profoundly annoying. Worse, just because someone *is* biased doesn't mean their arguments can be automatically dismissed. The industry lobbyist touting modelling, the fossil fuel-funded think tank getting press coverage for its new 'research', the be-costumed cleric decrying some social innovation, all indeed *would say that*, but merely pointing that out doesn't necessarily negate the requirement to demonstrate the dearth of evidence, the failure of logic, in their case.

This is not an error that is confined to the intellectual hoi polloi—all of us can do it. In early 2014, eminent Princeton historian Sean Wilentz insisted that true liberals (of which, as a close friend of the Clintons, Wilentz is a kind of *éminence grease*) shouldn't support journalist Glenn Greenwald, publisher Julian Assange and whistleblower Edward Snowden in their efforts to bring transparency to the national security state because each had, at some point, expressed libertarian views. That is, anything they say should be immediately dismissed because they fail to meet some Wilentz-designed test of How to Spot an East Coast Liberal.*

From this point of view, the quality of public debate, alas, has not been helped by the rise of by-lines in news reportage and commentary. Historically, journalists and commentators either used pseudonyms or, with the rise of newspapers, were anonymous—newspapers reported the news and analysed it with a kind of voice-of-God perspective that these days is reserved for editorials, which newspaper editors still like to think should be handed down carved in stone from the nearest mountain. But over the course of the twentieth century by-lines became ubiquitous, more quickly in some newspapers than others, and for different reasons in different countries (by-lined journalism, for example, is easier for governments and corporations to target for retribution). The result is more epistemologically sound journalism—it is clearly one person's, or several people's, view of events rather than an account purporting to complete objectivity. By-lines allow a reader to understand, at least in part, where the information or analysis or comment is coming from.

But it has also driven the rise of celebrity journalism and means journalists and commentators are easier to pigeonhole,

---

* Of course, applying that logic to Wilentz himself, no progressive should heed anything *he* has to say because his *Rise of American Democracy* is not far short of propaganda for the genocidal slave-owner Andrew Jackson (Daniel Walker Howe's *What Hath God Wrought* is far superior, in any case).

given readers can rapidly become familiar with their work even if they don't regularly read them. In that environment, *ad hominem* analysis of media content becomes routine.

However, the problem of *ad hominem* thinking points us towards the nearest thing you'll get to a lesson from this book.

Where to from here, or, Fuck off, you're on your own

Having devoted considerable length to tracing the intellectual roots from which the great flowering weed of Stupid has grown over thousands of years, it's natural to ask what can be done to fight Stupid, what measures will arrest its progress where it's still on the march, to expedite its reversal in those places where it is in retreat, to draw a line in the sand, to take a final stand, and say, 'This far, and no further'?

Alas, we've got nothing. There are no magic solutions to Stupid, other than the accounts we've provided in this book. It is a fight that has already taken millennia. For over 2500 years, people in Western societies have been wrestling with Stupid, locked in Mortal Kombat with it, trying to establish intellectually rigorous frameworks for knowledge, grappling with the most basic questions of epistemology and phenomenology, developing tools for thinking logically and assessing evidence. In the West, we've been able to access the best thinkers from other cultures: the rich tradition of Arab scholarship and philosophy offset the intellectual doldrums that persisted in the West until after the Carolingian Renaissance; we've absorbed Jewish philosophy and thought even as we launched pogroms against Jews; the explorations of a more confident early modern Europe brought contact with the remarkable cultures of India and the Far East and their rich intellectual histories; imperialism, for all its genocidal and exploitative heritage, eventually permitted the filtering back of unique indigenous perspectives and thought to the West.

All of that, and yet we still click on Nigerian scam emails, fail to vaccinate our kids and read celebrity news.

Combating Stupid has been the task of some of history's greatest minds: the Greek philosophers who first gave serious thought to the gap between what we thought we knew, and the world itself—if, for that matter, there *was* a world itself. And then it took over twenty centuries before the European descendants of those first philosophers began wondering not just whether there was a world itself, but about the language we were using to describe the world, and the extent to which epistemology was also about language and, never mind the world, what did using a *word* like 'world' actually mean?

Others shared the burden: Greek and Roman philosophers who first gave thought to how exactly societies should be governed; the Catholic monks in western Europe who slowly lost their eyesight and endured haemorrhoid hell transcribing key patristic works; the Orthodox Church in the eastern Roman Empire that kept safe some of Western philosophy's most important books all the way until the fifteenth century; the scholars of the first renaissances in the eighth and twelfth centuries (as Woody Allen might say, the early, funny renaissances) and their descendants in the fifteenth century in art, science and politics; the first humanists, who began treating the Bible as a work of literature to be investigated in its historical context; the first Reformists who puzzled over why institutional religion differed so markedly from the prescriptions of the Gospel; the early advocates for natural rights like Spinoza and Locke; the people put to death for believing in the wrong religious nuance, or in no religion at all; the

English parliamentarians who fought their own monarch and correctly charged him with levying war on his own people, and their children who resisted that monarch's son and sent him packing as well.

The Enlightenments were a culmination of all of these traditions and more besides. It needs to be repeated that Enlightenments were almost entirely elite phenomena of middle- and upper-class western Europeans, and mainly men. But the emphasis on reason, and the inevitable consequences of its application, at the heart of the Enlightenment projects was what was important, rather than the composition of its advocates.

Many more conservative Enlightenment figures—most notably Voltaire—wouldn't accept those inevitable consequences. Voltaire's target was, above all, the Catholic Church, rather than fundamental political reform. For more radical *philosophes*—most prominently Diderot—anti-clericalism eventually became just one of many facets of their work, because the consistent and full application of reason and the emphasis on individual choice led on to other targets—the repression of women; the exploitation of colonies; the power of aristocrats or any system of government that wasn't democratic.

The radical *philosophes* weren't always consistent—for example, they were often disgustingly anti-Semitic—but they went much further on the journey that Reason took them than their more conservative opponents and colleagues. That's the crucial lesson from the Enlightenments: accepting where Reason takes you, rather than allowing money or power or the source of an idea to derail that journey. And the long list of men and women who have embarked on that journey, to which we're just two minor names on the most recent page, is as close as you're going to get to a solution to Stupid. The nineteenth-century philosopher, scientist, semiotician, mathematician and more Charles Sanders Peirce wrote:

> Different minds may set out with the most antagonistic views, but the progress of investigation carries them by a force outside of themselves to one and the same conclusion. This activity of thought by which we are carried, not where we wish, but to a foreordained goal, is like the operation of destiny. No modification of the point of view taken, no selection of other facts for study, no natural bent of mind even, can enable a man to escape the predestinate opinion. This great law is embodied in the conception of truth and reality. The opinion which is fated to be ultimately agreed to by all who investigate, is what we mean by the truth, and the object represented in this opinion is the real. That is the way I would explain reality.

Peirce is also known as the father of Pragmatism, a much-misunderstood approach to philosophy that rejected the radical scepticism of much of Western philosophy, especially the Cartesian tradition, in favour of a more practical approach to knowledge and truth. It emphasised reason as an instrument for dealing with perceived reality and solving its problems.

Pragmatists like Peirce, William James (brother of Henry) and John Dewey rejected the Cartesian idea that everything must be doubted and knowledge painstakingly built up using only perfectly verifiable blocks (the first of which, for Descartes, was his own existence). Pragmatists instead suggested that doubt is only relevant when it has a real-world significance, and that an understanding of reality can be developed using scientific method and utility (thus, the misinterpretation that

Pragmatism is about believing whatever serves your purposes). This approach is a fallibilist one, accepting that our understanding of what is true may change, but what works for now will serve until that point.

And in particular, in contrast to the individualist approach of radical sceptics, who won't accept that anyone other than themselves even exists until rigorously established, Pragmatists (especially Peirce and Dewey) emphasised the collaborative, community aspect of the search for truth. 'The very origin of the conception of reality shows that this conception essentially involves the notion of a *community*,' Peirce said. For Dewey, the concept of shared inquiry was fundamental, and informed his groundbreaking work on education reform in the US. For Pragmatists, the search for truth was an exchange of views within an intellectual community, perhaps using different techniques and operating from different perspectives, but sharing a respect for scientific method and what could be demonstrated to be consistent with reality.

Pragmatism has had mixed fortunes since the late nineteenth century, but re-emerged via the likes of Richard Rorty nearly a century later. Even if Pragmatism doesn't float your particular epistemological boat, there is much to like about its rejection of radical scepticism and, by implication, other dismissals of external truths: for the Pragmatist, there is truth, and it can exist both within and outside the text, and the search for it is a collaborative one. It's not that sexy a philosophy, really: it lacks the relativism that so entrances first-year philosophy students delighted to discover that nothing is real or true, it has none of the Gallic panache of deconstruction, the Left Bank cool of existentialism or the high Teutonic rigour of classical German philosophy; it's just the product of some rather doughty New

England and New York part-time philosophers, focused on the practicality of establishing working solutions to problems.

But it carries within it the reason why Stupid still plagues us, and how we can continue to fight it like so many generations of grumps, curmudgeons and annoying sceptics before us. In societies in which old forms of Stupid live on, while new ones are being constantly created, it can serve as both a methodological approach and maybe even a rallying cry: that we be carried not where we wish, but to a goal foreordained by the rigour of our thought.

Appendix—Top ten Stupids

Top ten enemies of Stupid

1. Moveable type

(circa 1040)

As the western world was instructed by means of the 2008 Olympic Games Opening Ceremony, it was not Gutenberg that first gave the world mechanised printing in 1450, but an eleventh-century guy called Bi Sheng. China and not Europe first reproduced ideas on paper.

Whenever and by whomever literacy and literature is distributed, though, the results remains the same: freaking awesome.

Sure, the printing press and now the internet disseminates unspeakable idiocy. But it also makes possible the synthesis of thought that can change the world—even, sometimes, for the better.

True and broad engagement with ideas written down with great care is something we can, perhaps, refuse to see as anything other than a universal good. And you can't say that often.

2. Aristotle
(384–322 BCE)
Just thirty-one of the guy's some two hundred written treatises survive, but these were sufficient to carry his influence through the millennia. And to really give his snotty teacher, Plato, the shits right through the ages.

The granddaddy of formal logic, the great Greek whom Aquinas simply called 'The Philosopher', looked to argument as a foundation. This is a great shift from the Platonic idea that there is a perfect Form that is a blueprint for all reality.

Aristotle dragged thinking into matters of the everyday and did quite a good job of convincing some of us that essential 'good' was a bit of a crock.

3. Doubt
(Classical antiquity–present)
In our age of super-smarm, where negativity is seen not as a force for good but nastiness, it is difficult for us to remember the importance of doubt.

Socrates wasn't particularly positive and neither was Descartes, whose methodical doubt forms an important part of all scientific method and discovery. In fact, anyone who ever eliminated ideas and hypotheses by looking at them and testing them is a doubter, and thank goodness for such grumps at laboratory benches who are the sine qua non of useful innovations from vaccination to genuine justice.

Doubt, let it be said, is quite different from kneejerk scepticism or denialism, which simply reject ideas without examining them. Doubt is a tedious process that brings forth the best of history, whereas denialism is enormous fun and just requires that one sticks one's fingers in one's ears while shrieking 'La la la what is even science.'

4. Immanuel Kant
(1724–1804)

There is so much that is wrong with this bourgeois thinker but even an incorrigible pinko like me has to acknowledge that we owe him a great debt.

Okay. So his preoccupation with the idea of a universal good will is an enormous problem. His idea that individual reason is somehow so peachy-keen it can defeat all unreason, or cannot itself become unreason, is wiggety. The guy's not practical.

But, Kant's failure to engage with social forces that causes some reason to die and some reason to rule notwithstanding, his urge to those who read him to *think* was, and remains, pretty compelling. His instructions for thought may not in themselves be anything approaching workable but his passionate belief that thought must be undertaken is a great moment.

5. Western liberal feminism
(1792–present)

The most annoying thing about the many annoying features of liberalism is its failure to see how it rests on an idea of inequality; even and especially those who advance the idea of a 'meritocracy' are all still banging on about a natural hierarchy.

Feminism, which remains for the most part very liberal, also has this problem, and it comes to us first and most compellingly in the form of Mary Wollstonecraft's *A Vindication of the Rights of Women*.

Like most of her present-day daughters, Wollstonecraft sees the arbitrary social division of labour and of opportunity by means of gender as total pants. And this, despite the fact that it is founded on an idea of 'free' enterprise and has a limited political imagination, was, and remains, a courageous and entirely non-Stupid idea.

Using half-arsed ideas of biology and ancient history to justify social organisation is ridiculous. Gender, or biological sex for that matter, is not a foundational truth. It's just a bit of a shame that liberal feminism could see some forms of inequality as 'unnatural' while letting others persist. Like liberalism.

6. Karl Marx
(1818–1883)
There are those who snigger at this great philosopher for what they perceive as his naiveté, and then there are those who laugh a little more kindly at the impossibility of his project. There are very few, however, who actually bother to read his ideas, now mushed and consigned to the insinkerator of the past.

While it is true that Marx's predictions about revolution may have been a tad wrong, his Hegelian idea of history as conflict may now be more or less useless, and his hope that one day we would not need intellectuals is probably impossible, this is no effing excuse not to read him.

Whether you are inclined to Left thinking or not, the first volume of *Capital* is an extraordinary document which shows us how, as foretold in *The German Ideology*, 'the ideas of the ruling class are in every epoch the ruling ideas' and explains how the material organisation of the world makes Stupid.

7. Marcel Duchamp's *Fountain*
(1917)
At the height of the anti-art movement known as Dada, the French-American brat Marcel Duchamp and his genuinely batty collaborator the 'Baroness' Elsa von Freytag-Loringhoven took a urinal and entered it in an art exhibition. Where it was, in fact, held from view.

They had not made the lavatory and they did not affix their names to it and in this rejection of both the idea of an artist and the fundamental 'truth' of art, they flushed some very dearly held ideas about art and purity down the drain forever.

Even if the idea of art seems to you insubstantial or, at most, a matter of beauty, this radical move was utopian. To interrogate our most fondly held ideas about greatness in a swift and naughty moment was marvellous.

Of course, now some artists continue to tediously examine this idea of meaningless nearly a century later and have turned the idea of a readymade toilet into an affront to something that can be collected. But we shall not forget that the disappearance of pompous ideas down the drain is occasionally possible. Viva true punk.

8. The unconscious mind
(Mid-nineteenth century–1970s)
Marx, Nietzsche and Freud are some of my favourite guys. They are often known respectively as idealistic pinko, Nazi and pervert. This is hardly fair.

One of the things I initially liked and continue to like about each of these authors is their explicit and vitally important understanding that we're not as bright as we like to think we are. Or, more to the point, that our actions and responses are dominated by forces we do not fully understand but think of as natural.

Marx examines 'ideology' as the invisible thing that dominates our action, where Nietzsche calls it the 'will to power'. And Freud, of course, brings us the transformational idea of the 'unconscious'.

These are people who reject the state-of-nature account such as we might read in Rousseau, Hume or Locke, and who continue to influence the way we do things in the west.

The idea that we don't know what we are doing pretty much died with the radicalism of the seventies. I'd like to see it back.

9. Black Power/African American civil rights
(1950s–1970s)
There's a tendency these days to remember Martin Luther King, Jr as a nice guy who just wanted all folks to sit at the same lunch counter after they went to church together. And while it is true that the guy was a Christian minister and is fondly remembered by liberals as a force for polite reason, he happened to be a greater and more radical force than he is usually remembered.

When King was assassinated, it was not just his opposition to segregation and the extraordinary forces of racist Stupid that did it. It is worth remembering that he was talking to a group of sanitation workers about their labour rights. The man, just like the great Malcolm X and the Black Power movement which followed these leaders, wanted to change the entire system. It is not just shared swimming pools and the attitudes of tolerance he wanted to transform.

He called for a great change in thinking and rejected namby-pamby strategies for social change. In his 'Letter from Birmingham Jail', he cried out for opposition to the white moderate, which he saw as more invidious than the Ku Klux Klan.

It is not just the will to justice that informs African American civil rights and international Black Power leaders; it is the intelligence of this moment from which we can all learn.

10. Love
(1975)

Courtly. Christian. Romantic. Like just about any other human endeavour, love has its history formed in society and ideas. It has been as unnatural and without essence as any other damn thing, and as a contemporary notion it bolsters some pretty crappy practices, such as marriage, normative sexuality and terrible films.

But, in his 1975 work *Born to Run* and in more or less every recording since, Bruce Springsteen describes the powerful victory of violent love that can exist, just in instants, outside the alienation and the ultra-rationalisation of the everyday.

'Together we can break this trap,' he says to Wendy, and talks of that strange exclusion that chooses love for one person over the rest of the world; it's a feeling that can overcome the broken cars and closing factories of New Jersey and temporarily infuse us with a hope that has nothing to do with the world and all its upward mobility, but is a force of sheer passion.

It is the possibility of this passion for the other, even if it is short-lived, that can deliver us momentarily from the world or New Jersey or whatever disappointments or aspirations otherwise inform us.

While it is probably true that love for the other is some kind of terrible by-product of early childhood, it is also true that it has a logic that precedes most forms of everyday reason. The insanity and the exclusion of love has nothing to do with empathy or morality. In fact, that it delivers us temporarily from these everyday principles into a state that might not be natural, but is certainly as liberated as we're ever going to get, is probably quite useful.

The insanity of affection is not Stupid.

Top Ten Friends of Stupid

1. John Locke
(1632–1704)
There can be no doubt that this Oxford physician and philosopher had a brain at least so big and shiny as a Megachurch—or a shopping mall, if you prefer your references secular. But it is Locke's clever-ness in conflating humanism with material wealth that makes him so useful to Stupid. This guy made property ownership seem like a moral imperative and America seem like a great idea, and it is his compelling view on the loveliness of greed that continues to make it so difficult for us to think beyond liberalism and building enormous blocks of luxury apartments, as though stainless steel European appli-ances are somehow an ethical birthright.

2. Oprah Winfrey
(1954–)
Like so many of history's influential Stupids, Oprah herself is clearly not thick. What she does, though, in so effectively popularising the You Can Do It If You Try view of individual achievement, is blind

us all to social structures and replace them with arse-hat affirmations about bending the universe to our will. She has popularised that shitty book *The Secret,* the tough-love inanity of Dr Phil and that unmitigated twit Eckhart Tolle, who bangs on about something called 'the emotional paidbody', which holds that we are each responsible for our poor fortune. However nice and liberal Oprah might seem, she has done her very best to promote the idea that it is only laziness and a lack of personal empowerment that makes some lives worse than others. In this world view, global poverty is all the fault of starving people themselves. Do some yoga and you'll be right. Fuck off.

3. Richard Dawkins
(1941–)
He who was formerly one of the more effective science communicators of the twentieth century has turned from a guy who can force even idiots like me to truly understand evolution theory into a dangerous shit. By positing science and the idea of pure logic as a panacea for all the world's ills, he has become as fanatical and perilously simple as the new politics of anti-science he seeks to undo. Let us hope he returns to the important work of explaining difficult ideas of good science to a broad audience and away from the humanist pseudo-philosophy of screaming 'god isn't even real!'

4. *Star Wars Episode 1: The Phantom Menace*
(1999)
There is a good deal to loathe about Lucas' clumsy prequel, not least of which is Jar Jar Binks, who is less a being with a character arc than an expensive merchandise puppet. But the real problem here is midi-chlorians.

For decades, the pleasant Buddhism-lite of the Star Wars franchise caused kids and grown-up kids to consider harmless ideas like being a decent person. A Jedi was someone who devoted themselves consciously to good. Like the worst of evolutionary biology or 'state of nature' accounts of How We Really Are, midi-chlorians reduced the Jedi to health and the Sith to a sickness.

As Aristotle said, we are, by nature, social. Any account of our essence in biology is foolish and easy and as Stupid as that turd, Jar Jar.

When Yoda says to Luke 'Do. Or do not. There is no try,' he is speaking as a pre-midi-chlorian Jedi. Post-midi-chlorian, he might as well say 'Don't bother trying because the midi-chlorians have already decided your fate.'

5. Milton Friedman
(1912–2006)
Adviser to US Presidents, leader of the Chicago School and almost without doubt the most influential post-war economist, Milty is what you get when take the moral insanity of Ayn Rand, combine it with the naiveté of Adam 'the market is just awesome' Smith and give it to General Pinochet for a bit of experimental fun.

Friedman was a libertarian and believed, apparently, in freedom for all peoples; he was an occasional advocate for same-sex marriage and believed in the state's retreat from personal affairs. But it is perhaps this belief that creating the conditions for great wealth for the few is not only natural but has no impact on curtailing everyday freedoms of the many that makes his Stupid so stinky.

6. Rupert Murdoch
(1931–)
While it is absolutely true that there are media conglomerates just as pig-bonkingly dull as News Corp and magnates so effectively unpleasant, there is perhaps no force so effective in turning journalism from a profession that occasionally told us something like the truth into a reeking toilet of ideology as Rupe.

Throughout the western world, Murdoch continues to oversee the overproduction of the very worst in churnalism that plays to our simplest fears and the spread of half-ideas that exist for no reason more honourable than the bolstering of his business interests.

We can only suppose that he has never been made aware of the unprecedented good of his product, *The Simpsons*.

7. The American Psychiatric Association
(1884–present)
Once, religion slaughtered those it considered to be possessed by demons. Then, thanks to the great humanity of the Enlightenment, medical science whacked these people in institutions. They were not often murdered, just deadened and hidden.

Then, many more of us became the liberal prisoners of the new idea of 'mental health'.

Thanks to the *Diagnostic and Statistical Manual of Mental Disorders* (DSM), the blockbuster publication of the APA, we are now all largely off our heads. The idea of disorders, which are treated by a one-size-fits-most program of drugs, has taken what some of us see as normal reactions to life, and demonised them softly.

Self-loathing, deep sadness and the apparently widespread urge to just give up are not viewed as responses to a complex world but, despite a complete absence of biological markers, as biology. Basically, midi-chlorians.

That antidepressant medication might make some of us feel a bit more like tolerating the world and behaving to its requirements is not evidence that the depression the APA says one in four of us experiences is medically real. It just shows us that drugs can change our mood.

The APA has helped to make real sadness the fault of biology. The wide acceptance of this deeply antisocial thinking is a new and happy kind of prison.

8. Anti-intellectualism
(Forever–present)
The fear of book-learnin' has a long history, and even precedes

widespread literacy. In 1642, Puritan minister John Cotton, who made America his home, said 'The more learned and witty you bee, the more fit to act for Satan you bee.'

It is certainly true that certain religious fundamentalists continue this idea that thinking is no substitute for being thick as shit, but it is also true that anti-intellectual takes new forms equally as Stupid although not as overt as those ideas of creationists.

The Right these days is marvellous at taking science and making it into a matter of opinion rather than a rigorous system of doubt. But just as some tits bang on and on about climate science, which overwhelmingly tells us that Something Needs To Be Done to reverse terrible outcomes, others talk about 'feelings' as being more important than thinking.

Opposition to rational thought informs progressive politics these days just as much as it does conservatives. 'Lived experience' and emotional storytelling is now seen as a foundation for Meaningful Social Change on all sides.

When we take a feeling or an unexamined urge and use it as the foundation for action, we are pooping on the most decent innovations of history. Pure rationalism and absolute objectivity may be impossible. But this is no good reason to give up on it. To cry and then use one's tears as the foundation for the future gives us nothing but soggy ideas.

9. *MasterChef*
(2009–present)

Reality television can be held largely responsible for the oversupply of meaning. In an era where we can call an appetiser 'clever', 'ironic' or 'witty', as the judges on *MasterChef* so very often do, there can be no real hope for the survival of meaning.

To things that obviously do not matter, such as food or video games or advertisements, we afford a great deal of attention. To the things that might truly impact our lives, such as economic policy or international relations or medical practice, we claim ignorance.

To molecular gastronomy we afford great importance and allow complexity where there is none. We become prisoners of meaninglessness. To the real scandals of our age we give less passion and thought.

We praise the meaningless and debate the inconsequential. We see significance where there is only pastry.

10. History
(circa 3500 BCE–present)
FFS, it is about time we stop seeing history as a linear progression. This is both the single great fault of Marxism and the truest filth of liberal humanism. If we keep believing that things change in a way that moves towards either the improvement or the dwindling of the species, we are stuck in a rut that does not allow for truly ingenious thoughts of a future that is different.

It is certainly true that we can look at ourselves and our institutions and our political past as a guide to what we have become. But to see history as an inevitable force instead of a bunch of stuff that can be broken is the worst kind of intellectual pessimism.

HR

Top ten friends of Stupid

Meletus and the citizens of Athens
Establishing a template that would be used for millennia to come by paternalists, Socrates was charged by prosecutor Meletus with corrupting the youth of Athens and failing to worship the city's gods, found guilty and executed. It's unlikely Socrates was the first to be convicted of heresy and leading the kids astray, but he was and remains the most high-profile victim of the classic accusations of those who would dictate how others live. While the philosopher ignored several opportunities to escape, suggesting he was relaxed about his fate, his execution also demonstrated the use of persecution and killing

as official responses to both political and religious scepticism. And apparently hemlock tastes like mouse, whatever mouse tastes like.

Sigismund of Hungary and the Catholic Church

This was a bit like the Iraq War of the fifteenth century, only it went for even longer. Anxious to put an end to a religious split in Bohemia and settle an ongoing schism within the Catholic Church, King Sigismund of Hungary invited the leader of the widespread but heretical Wycliffite movement, Jan Huss, to a council in Constance in 1414, with a promise of safe conduct. Once in Constance, Huss was imprisoned and burnt at the stake by Sigismund, on the basis that promises to a heretic weren't considered binding. Five separate Crusades were launched by the Church against Huss's followers in ensuing decades, and all were repelled by the Hussites. By 1436, when moderate Hussites negotiated a peace with surrounding powers and the Church that preserved their beliefs, Bohemia was completely destroyed and tens of thousands had been killed.

Henry VIII

Out of the millions of examples of censorship throughout history, Henry VIII's decision to try to protect Christianity in England by banning the reading of the Bible in 1543 has never been bettered—except, possibly, when a Kansas community banned *Charlotte's Web* because it featured the blasphemy of talking animals. It was extraordinary not merely for its bizarrely contradictory logic, but because Bluff King Hal himself had sponsored the translation of the Bible into English to help spread the Gospel just a few years before.

Rousseau

Rousseau could make this list for his misogyny alone, but he seals the deal with his passionate—literally—assault on reason as a corruption of humankind's natural, Edenic state. Rousseau's misogyny wasn't the standard loathing of women that characterised his age—even his readers criticised his views on women—but a more complicated, more modern affair: he portrayed women as essentially a different species, fundamentally, biologically incapable of participating in contemporary society, needing to be confined to the domestic sphere. Rousseau's extraordinarily eccentric view of human history—primitive man wasn't merely irrational but solitary, he believed—was a prelude to his elevation of instinct and emotion over reason, which not merely paved the way for Romanticism (which is bad enough) but for every anti-intellectual ever since. Although, in his defence, he got a bum rap for 'the noble savage', which wasn't his creation—he merely thought 'savages' had a good thing going compared to the civilised world.

Sir Francis Galton and Karl Pearson

Eminent mathematicians and key figures in the development of classical statistical methods, Sir Francis Galton and his protégé Karl Pearson were also the leading eugenicists of their age. While Galton laid much of the groundwork for theories of racial superiority before his death in 1911, Pearson advocated race war, argued against assistance for people 'from poor stock' and opposed Jewish immigration as Jews were 'inferior physically and mentally to the native population' of Britain. Before depriving the world of the benefit of his genetic superiority by dying in 1936, Pearson was unsurprisingly a professed admirer of the Nazis, having done much to establish, promote and give the aura of intellectual legitimacy to the idea of race war and racial inferiority.

Andrew Wakefield

Whether Wakefield's manufacturing of a link between autism and measles vaccination slides over into outright evil rather than merely profoundly, despicably Stupid is debatable; certainly his actions were dishonest and have been alleged to have been motivated by expectations of financial gain from the vaccination scare he unleashed. But his actions gave a figleaf of credibility to the conspiracy theories, froth-mouthed rantings and self-obsessed idiocy of millions of anti-vaxers throughout the world, resulting in the deaths of who knows how many children, and the illness and often permanent injury to many, many more.

Reality TV
The carefully scripted nature of reality TV shows of all genres, from the now hoary elimination-based shows to talent shows to the cooking shows that now infest much of the Australian TV schedule, is well known. These are dirt-cheap dramas scripted and cut together by program makers and TV networks. But in foregoing the services of creative talents that are normally required for drama production, producers rely on the same limited number of narratives and stock characters over and over, rather than risk the danger of actual story-telling artistry. While few shows in the genre are outright misogynist and infantilising of women as the various versions of *The Bachelor*, that merely typifies the extent to which the entire genre relies for its narratives on stereotyping women and minorities under the guise of offering a glimpse of the real world. Watching reality TV doesn't merely make you stupid—something even its biggest fans would admit—but it makes you Stupid.

George W. Bush, Dick Cheney and Tony Blair
9/11 had exactly the result intended by Osama Bin Laden: a furious America lashed out at whatever Muslim country it could plausibly attack. Saddam Hussein, a secular, oil-rich dictator opposed by al-Qaeda, was the lucky victim. The result was, literally, history's costliest mistake, with a $4 trillion war, hundreds of thousands of dead Iraqis, thousands of dead US and American troops, the fragmentation of Iraq, the empowerment of Iran and the creation of a terrorist group so brutal they were regarded as extreme even by al Qaeda. Poor Rupert Murdoch didn't even get the $20-a-barrel oil price he predicted would result. And now Western politicians want to do it all again.

Todd Akin

Don't be misled by Missouri Republican congressman Todd Akin's notoriety as the man who, in 2012, said women's bodies can prevent pregnancy in the event of 'legitimate rape'. Akin is the complete package of denialism, the highest evolutionary stage (sorry, Intelligent Design stage) of conservative irrationality, the political pin-up boy of postmodern politics, who claimed in 2008 that women who aren't pregnant have abortions (reminiscent of Sarah Silverman's complaint that she wanted an abortion but was having trouble getting pregnant), that the arrival of spring was a demonstration of 'good' climate change that shouldn't be stopped and that there was no science in evolution. Akin even linked autism to vaccination and home-schooled his children—not a guarantee of Stupid but a useful indicator. So perfect a summation of all that is wrong with the modern GOP is Akin that the Democrats actually ran ads for him to ensure he won his party primary in the lead-up to the 2012 election. In mid-2014, Akin launched a book, *Firing Back: Taking on the party bosses and media elite to protect our faith and freedom*, and claimed his 'legitimate rape' comment was merely an 'abbreviation'.

Top ten enemies of Stupid

Charlemagne

While famed for such laudable traits as incessant warfare and demanding conversion to Christianity by conquered communities on pain of death, the aptly named Charlemagne has a strong case for being the one indispensable figure of Western history. His unification of western Europe, his wide-ranging administrative and religious reforms, and the revival of learning and scholarship he actively encouraged under Alcuin of York (despite himself being unable to write and not learning to read until adulthood) had a major impact on the course of western European history. The renaissance of the late eighth and early ninth centuries that he sparked, if short-lived, was crucial in providing a link between classical scholarship and later centuries, preserving most of the key classical texts that eventually made it through to the Europe of the more economically and politically stable second millennium. Without Charlemagne, the Dark Ages would have stayed dark in the West; there would have been no future renaissances, and possibly no modern Europe as we understand it. Which you may or may not think would be a bad thing.

Paracelsus
Nearly forgotten centuries later, Paracelsus, who lived in the first half of the sixteenth century, is a key figure in the development of modern scientific method. He rejected scholasticism and reliance on ancient texts for science and medicine, preferring observation and experiment. This sounds like a statement of the obvious, but it was considered near-heretical at the time (he was often compared to Luther, and had his works banned). He was also a chemist and botanist, as well as an occultist, demonstrating the hazy nature of early modern science, but his work was critical in allowing the Western mind to adopt a more rational, sceptical outlook in response to the torrent of works released by the printing press.

The sturdy beggar of Amsterdam
Early modern Europe was obsessed with unemployment, or what they called 'sturdy beggars', because unemployment was thought to be a moral failing rather than an economic outcome. 'Sturdy beggars', as opposed to run-of-the-mill beggars who had some legitimate disability, were able-bodied and capable of working, but, it was believed, refused to. The solution to unemployment, some thought, was to force them to work—a concept that survived into the nineteenth century 'poor house' and, indeed graces our society still

via contemporary 'work for the dole' schemes. The good burghers of sixteenth century Amsterdam developed an early mechanism for curing sturdy beggars of their idleness: a room set at water level that would fill up and drown the occupant unless he pumped furiously to empty the water out. This treatment, however, was peremptorily ended after one sturdy beggar, perhaps less sturdy than he or she appeared, or keen to demonstrate a point of principle, simply refused to pump and allowed him or herself to be drowned. The story may be apocryphal, like much else in early modern Europe, but the perhaps fictional beggar deserves memorialising for treating a facile elite economic philosophy with such contempt, even at the cost of their life.

Spinoza

Now primarily known by philosophy students and then not many of them, Spinoza's writings were profoundly influential on most of the key figures of the Enlightenment, even if, like Voltaire, they were hostile to his conclusions. His theology and his demonstration of the importance of religious freedom and free speech, as much as his monism and determinism, were critical in paving the way not merely for the Enlightenment but for much of subsequent Western philosophy. He also refused offers of honours and university positions, preferring to remain a lens grinder who also wrote philosophy. Sadly, this modesty was particularly costly to Western thought, since he is said to have died of silicosis from glass dust.

The Glorious Revolution

More correctly, the Glorious Invasion—in late 1688, William of Orange successfully conquered England (Scotland and Ireland took quite some time longer), displacing the Catholic James II, who had alienated the British ruling class with not merely his religion but his growing French-style authoritarianism and policy of religious toleration. The British elite understood the lessons of the Civil War fifty years earlier and resolved not to let an intra-elite conflict turn into an open struggle that would allow non-elite forces the opportunity to seize power, as Cromwell and the New Model Army had in the 1640s. Instead, the Protestant Dutch ruler William was accepted as Britain's legitimate monarch. The road to a genuinely constitutional monarchy stretched well into the eighteenth century for what would shortly be the United Kingdom, but the exceptionalism of English parliamentary rule was made permanent by the ousting of a would-be Catholic absolutist.

Paul-Henri Thiry, Baron d'Holbach

A key French Enlightenment figure, translator, *bon vivant* and atheist, D'Holbach kept an extraordinarily diverse Paris salon that was a key centre for both *philosophes* and mainstream cultural figures. He also wrote (perhaps with Diderot) *System of Nature*, a rigorous advocacy of materialism and probably the single most reviled book of the entire Enlightenment, drawing a furious reaction from both the Catholic Church (which demanded its suppression) and moderate *philosophes* like Voltaire. His later works developed the case for a rational, constitutional government aimed at maximising the community welfare, anticipating utilitarianism.

The suffragettes

As a democracy, Great Britain was hopeless in the nineteenth century—the franchise had been *reduced*, and significantly so, since the seventeenth century, until the Reform Acts began extending the franchise once again to a significant portion of the male population. But the sheer unadulterated Stupid of not enfranchising half the electorate on the grounds that they possessed uteruses remained fixed in place until after the Great War. It galled large numbers of women, many of whom weren't content with 'constitutional' forms of campaigning: many, especially after 1912, adopted more radical, disruptive tactics, civil disobedience, self-defence and militant protest. Enduring first abuse, then imprisonment, then in many cases torture via forced feeding, the suffragettes provided a remarkable contrast between the ineffable idiocy of the British establishment and aggressive, effective street-level direct action.

John Maynard Keynes

Keynes would have had a sufficient claim to fame merely for *The Economic Consequences of the Peace*, which accurately anticipated how the Allies' treatment of Germany after the Great War guaranteed another conflict, or his work on probability in the 1920s, or for regularly infuriating fellow Bloomsbury Set member Lytton Strachey. But his revolutionary opposition to austerity economics and advocacy and theoretical justification for fiscal stimulus, along with the Bretton Woods system he helped found after World War II, paved the way for the long post-war boom of the West. Countries with politicians intelligent enough to remember the lessons of Keynesianism in 2008—like Australia—benefited in the wake of the financial crisis, while European countries that embraced Depression-style austerity got exactly what they paid for—an extended economic slump that has ruined the lives of millions. Seldom has one man brought so much economic benefit to so many human beings across the planet. And to this day, the Right continues to attack Keynes for his homosexuality and claim that it shaped his economic theories.

Chelsea Manning and Edward Snowden

The two most important whistleblowers in Western thought have reshaped recent history by revealing the true nature of Anglophone governments and, in particular, the US government. Taking advantage of the transition of information from a substance measured in grams per square metre to one composed purely of zeroes and ones, each released vast troves of information exposing war crimes, hypocrisy, illegality and global surveillance. The system of power they revealed is one operated by corporations, tame politicians, soldiers and bureaucrats for their own advantage, not that of the populations they ostensibly serve. Manning was tortured and jailed for her actions; Snowden has been vilified and chased into hiding for his; both are true heroes in an age seemingly devoid of them.

Snark

Much vilified as a symptom of the profound cynicism in the internet age, snark is in fact the antibody produced by a healthy, intelligent mind in response to the presence of Stupid. Matching the egregiousness of the idiocy that induces it, snark is offensive, wilfully transgressive and anti-social, and delightful both to produce and to consume, unless it is directed at oneself or something one values. Snark is a refusal to suspend disbelief; in fact, snark puts wheels on disbelief, sticks an engine in it and tries to run over whoever is demanding it be suspended. Like actual antibodies, on which this mess of metaphors is based, snark can become unhealthily surfeit to requirements and start attacking whatever is producing it, but on the whole we are far healthier for its presence than without it, no matter how many complaints of butthurt get aired, no matter how often the wambulance is called, no matter who theatrically takes umbrage at it.

BK

Recommended reading

Introduction—We don't know what we are doing

In the introduction we talk a little about the great bourgeois liberal humanist Immanuel Kant. Any study of ethics must include a long initial date with Kant, whose *Critique of Pure Reason* (1781) and *Grounding for the Metaphysics of Morals* (1785) are arguably some of the Enlightenment's most enlightened moments. It is easy for the new student of philosophy to be seduced by the thinker's attempts to devise a universal way to make good decisions. It might not surprise you to learn that Kant's 'categorical imperative' instrument of universal ethics never quite fixed everything. Actually, it's quite flawed. But his attempts to beat the everyday reader into a philosopher are so beautiful, it is enough to make you again believe in the possibility that we can all be reasonable. Or, at least try to be.

I was very influenced by:

*   Max Horkheimer and Theodor W. Adorno, *Dialectic of Enlightenment* (1972, Herder and Herder, New York)
*   Herbert Marcuse, *One-Dimensional Man* (1964, Beacon Press, Boston)

and also Slavoj Žižek, *The Parallax View* (2006, MIT Press, Cambridge, Mass.), which is a book that has given me a good deal of comfort. Not only does Žižek help to fill in the gaps in a less-than-classical education and let me know what might be meant by 'Aristotelian', or remind me what might be meant by the Hegelian dialectic view of history, he does so with a strategic passion for popular culture that keeps trashy people like myself reading.

1. 'I'm worth it': L'Oréal and the fade-resistant rise of liberal individualism

In this chapter where we discuss the emerging idea of the modern individual, our primary text is John Locke, *Two Treatises of Government* (1680–1690). Chapters Five and Nineteen of the Second Treatise will give you a good overview of not only what Locke had to say about the individual responsibility to accumulate property, but will show you how good he was in argument.

Here, we also look at Magna Carta, written by a bunch of Medieval barons and King John in 1215, the US Declaration of Independence written by some dudes and John Locke's *An Essay Concerning Human Understanding* (1689). For more on the moral justification of wealth, look into Adam Smith's lesser-known *The Theory of Moral Sentiments* (1759). There's also obviously some Marx here, especially *The German Ideology* (translated in 1932) and Jacob Burckhardt, *The Civilization of the Renaissance in Italy* (1860).

There is a bit of hidden Nietzsche here; it inheres in the idea that morality is largely relative to the time in which it exists. See *The Genealogy of Morals* (1887).

2. Suffer the little children: Enlightenment and denialism

In recent years, denialism has attracted increasing scientific study and media commentary, though many of the themes in its research are decades old. Michael Specter's *Denialism: How irrational thinking hinders scientific progress, harms the planet, and threatens our lives*, 2009

(Penguin Press, New York), for example, explains the US context. But much good work on the sociological and intellectual context of denialism is readily available online: *New Scientist*, for example, now has an entire section of its website devoted to the intellectual processes and methods of denialism: www.newscientist.com/special/living-in-denial.

The Reformation is one of the most examined and contested fields of historiography that has seen entire schools of historical thought rise and fall. Traditional Protestant historiography of a corrupt Catholic church and pat, determinist accounts of rising middle classes and the development of capitalism (thanks both to the Whig and Marxist schools for those) have yielded in recent decades to more nuanced accounts of important factors like popular piety and the role of urban political elites. Bear in mind, too, Anglophone historiography tends to focus on the English Reformation, which starts with Lollardy rather than Henry VIII and then segues into the lead-up to the Civil War in the seventeenth century; for some scholars, it doesn't quite end until the Glorious Revolution in 1688. But the more important, and certainly far bloodier, events in Germany, Switzerland and France (not to mention eastern Europe) have received more attention from European historians, often in German and French. Diarmaid MacCulloch's *The Reformation*, 2005 (Penguin Books, New York) is a recent, well-regarded introduction that will serve the lay reader. Jacques Barzun in *From Dawn to Decadence: 500 years of Western cultural life*, 2001 (HarperCollins, London) has a thoughtful section on the cultural impact of Luther.

The Enlightenment has similarly been a playground for determinists. The crucial Enlightenment study for our purposes is Jonathan Israel, *A Revolution of the Mind: Radical Enlightenment and the intellectual origins of modern democracy*, 2010 (Princeton University Press, Princeton). The work of J.G.A. Pocock, *Barbarism and Religion*, volumes 1 and 2, 1999 (Cambridge University Press, Cambridge) is more for specialists who know their érudits from their *philosophes*, but lays out the variety of different Enlightenments of the eighteenth century. Robert Wuthnow's *Communities of Discourse: Ideology and social structure in the Reformation, the Enlightenment, and European socialism*, 1989 (Harvard University Press, Cambridge, Mass.) discusses common socio-economic factors in the Reformation, the Enlightenment and nineteenth-century socialism and provides a useful guide to each.

A brisk and readable guide to the western philosophical tradition, by the way, is Anthony Kenny (ed), *Oxford Illustrated History of Western Philosophy*, 1994 (Oxford University Press, Oxford, New York); the concept of nothingness is elegantly demonstrated by how much the illustrations add to the work. It's okay to skip the more complicated bits.

A key intellectual–political history of the US is Richard Hofstadter, *Anti-Intellectualism in American Life*, 1963 (Knopf, New York)—a book that plainly was strongly influenced by the Eisenhower years, but is still fresh. Three works complement Hofstadter: H.W. Brands' *The First American: The life and times of Benjamin Franklin*, 2000 (Doubleday, New York) is a life of Benjamin Franklin that also works as a history of colonial and revolutionary America, including the arrival of Methodism. Two standard but excellent textbooks take the story of the infant republic forward to the mid-nineteenth century: Gordon S. Wood, *Empire of Liberty: A history of the early republic, 1789-1815*, 2009 and Daniel Walker Howe, *What Hath God Wrought: The transformation of America, 1815-1848*, 2007 (both Oxford University Press, New York).

The essential, and least inaccessible, McLuhan cultural history text is Marshall McLuhan, *The Gutenberg Galaxy: The making of typographic man*, 1962 (University of Toronto Press, Toronto), but Douglas Coupland, *Marshall McLuhan: You Know Nothing Of My Work!*, 2011 (Atlas, New York) offers a far more reader-friendly tour of both McLuhan's key messages and why they're still critical—as well as explaining why McLuhan's remarkable brain worked like it did.

More useful is the unheralded but quite outstanding Richard Abel, *The Gutenberg Revolution: A history of print culture*, 2011 (Transaction Publishers, New Brunswick, NJ), which explains the asteroid-like impact of printing and how it changed European thinking and scholarship.

3. Look who's talking: Why uttering our 'identity' makes us Stupid Babies

This chapter is a look at the populist space currently obsessed as it is with 'personal stories' and the idea of a person as a narrative. I'm very much drawing on things like Oprah here and thinking less about classical texts, although there is some digression on ethics, and I again point you to Kant the deontologist and his ethical foes, the utilitarians. See Jeremy Bentham, *An Introduction to the Principles of Morals and Legislation* (1823) and John Stuart Mill, *Utilitarianism* (1863).

Notable contemporary utilitarians are Sam Harris, who gives me the absolute shits so I shan't bother further publicising his ranting atheism, and Peter Singer, whose preference utilitarianism, also known as consequentialism, gives us *Practical Ethics* (1979, Cambridge University Press, Cambridge, New York), which is a must-read, even if you, as I do, find yourself disagreeing with many of its moral claims. Singer is one of those guys, like Kant, you have to engage with in order to dismiss. He's really important.

I also mention an autobiography that I think does serve an important purpose which is that penned by Malcolm X with Alex Haley (*The Autobiography of Malcolm X.*, 1965, Grove Press, New York). Anyone interested in the radical good sense of true anti-racism should probably read that.

4. 'Nudge them all—God will know his own': Soft, hard and extreme paternalism

Australia is fortunate enough to be served by two excellent statistical institutions, the Australian Bureau of Statistics and the Australian

Institute of Health and Welfare, both of which have websites with easily accessible time-series data on Australian health outcomes (www. abs.gov.au and www.aihw.gov.au). The ABS also has crime and social data as well as, of course, extensive economic data.

Excellent background on the London gin craze can be found in Paul Langford's textbook on eighteenth-century England, *A Polite and Commercial People: England 1727–1783*, 1989 (Clarendon Press, Oxford).

The comprehensive work on falling crime rates in the West is Steven Pinker, *The Better Angels of Our Nature: Why violence has declined*, 2011 (Viking, New York).

5. The inflexible Safe Space: The injurious yoga class of the mind

In this chapter I am, again, virtually reference-free and more absorbed with the character of popular 'safe' discourse than anything written in proper books without meditation exercises and pictures of goddesses in them.

6. National stupidity: How the War on Terror is killing and impoverishing us

The work of John Mueller and Mark G. Stewart demolishing the myths of homeland security began with the 2011 article 'Balancing the risks, benefits, and costs of homeland security' (www.hsaj. org/?article=7.1.16)—read that if you can't get their book.

Former senior US government financial officer Linda Bilmes has the best readily accessible guide to where US government spending on the Iraq War went: 'Who Profited from the Iraq War?', 2012: www. epsusa.org/publications/newsletter/2012/mar2012/bilmes.html.

Entr'acte—*From Dallas with Love to Moonfaker*: The lost films of Stanley Kubrick

Like denialism, conspiracy theories have attracted growing analysis by social scientists in recent years—and clearly there are significant links between the two. However, Richard Hofstadter's *The Paranoid Style in American Politics* (first a 1964 essay, then the title of an essay collection published in 1965 by Knopf, New York) is the seminal work on the ways in which paranoia and conspiracy theory has played a key role in US politics, particularly US conservative politics, since colonial times.

Apropos of not much, the work to read on Kubrick is Michael Herr's remarkable August 1999 article 'Kubrick' in *Vanity Fair* (later expanded into a short book by the same name; 2001, Grove Press, New York). The only thing missing from Herr's posthumous tribute is the famous but perhaps apocryphal anecdote about Kubrick's obsessive perfectionism: to determine where he would shoot the (ill-fated) *Napoleon*, Kubrick assembled the researchers who had been investigating locations around Europe at his estate, where they would each explain the merits of the locations they had investigated. To make the process completely balanced, each would have two minutes to make their pitch, at which point a bell would be rung. However, Kubrick insisted on selecting the bell himself and, unhappy at the available selection, demanded a catalogue of bells he could pick from before, ultimately, demanding a full list of bell manufacturers. He later abandoned the whole idea.

The 2012 documentary *Room 237* documents the Kubrick-faked-the-moon-landing conspiracy in all its hilarious detail, among many other lurid claims about the flawed masterpiece that is *The Shining*.

7. Reason and unreason: How we've all gone Stupid-mad in an age of absolute sanity

In this chapter I make up for my lack of references in Chapter 5 with the following:

* Michel Foucault, *Madness and Civilization*, 1965 (Pantheon Books, New York)
* Aristotle, *Problems*, c. 300 BCE–c. 600 CE
* American Psychiatric Association, *Diagnostic and Statistical Manual of Mental Disorders: DSM-5*, Fifth edition, 2013 (American Psychiatric Association, Arlington, VA)

- Sigmund Freud, *Civilization and its Discontents*, 1930
- David Healy, *Let Them Eat Prozac: The unhealthy relationship between the pharmaceutical industry and depression*, 2004 (New York University Press, New York, London)
- Allan V. Horwitz and Jerome C. Wakefield, *The Loss of Sadness: How psychiatry transformed normal sorrow into depressive disorder*, 2007 (Oxford University Press, Oxford, New York).

I would also say that Michel Foucault, *Discipline and Punish: The birth of the prison* (1997, Allen Lane, London) was quite important. Because even though this is about technologies for controlling criminals instead of the 'mentally unwell', it is a *lot* easier to read than his stuff on psychiatry. His view of ideas and how their development can be traced through our social institutions is bracing. Foucault was a radically 'unnatural' thinker and he continues to make my head hurt.

8. Political arithmetic, or, Slack hacks lack facts when flacks stack the stats

There's only one book that provides a proper history of statistics and their political significance: Alain Desrosières, *The Politics of Large Numbers: A history of statistical reasoning*, 1998 (originally published in French; an English translation was published by Harvard University Press, Cambridge, Mass.) although readers are advised to familiarise themselves with the basics of statistical methods before opening it.

9. Postmodern nausea: Derrida, vomit and the rise of relativity

This chapter is a postmodern soup featuring:
- Jacques Derrida, *Of Grammatology*, 1976 (Johns Hopkins University Press, Baltimore)
- Virginia Woolf, *Orlando*, 1928
- Herman Melville, *Moby Dick*, 1851
- Plato, *The Republic*, c. 380 BCE

- William Shakespeare and George Peele, *Titus Andronicus*, c. 1590
- Jean Baudrillard, *Simulacra and Simulation*, 1994 (University of Michigan Press, Ann Arbor)
- Fredric Jameson, *Postmodernism, or, The cultural logic of late capitalism*, 1991 (Duke University Press, Durham).

10. Hyperreality, authenticity and the fucking up of public debate

Much of the history of pre-twentieth-century media is available in works previously cited: Langford on England; Brands (Franklin was one of colonial America's most successful printers and writers), Wood and Walker Howe for the US (the last in fact ends with the first successful use of the telegraph in the US, the dawn of the new electric media). Tim Wu, *The Master Switch: The rise and fall of information empires*, 2010 (Alfred A. Knopf, New York), is a brilliant account of the development of US media and its regulation since the telegraph that has many parallels with Australia in the immense power of incumbents. Johnny Ryan's *A History of the Internet and the Digital Future*, 2010 (Reaktion, London) recounts, in terms accessible to lay readers, the development of the internet.

Sideshow: Dumbing down democracy, 2012 (Scribe Publications, Brunswick, Vic.), by former senior Labor figure Lindsay Tanner, is an imperfect but honest account of some of the deeply unhealthy feedback loops between politicians and media practitioners in Australian public life in the last decade. At the time of writing, a number of books from veterans of the Rudd–Gillard years were being published.

11. Conspicuous compassion: On consuming Kony

This chapter gives us:
- Barbara Ehrenreich, *Smile or Die: How positive thinking fooled America and the world*, 2009 (London, Granta)

- Friedrich Nietzsche, *The Antichrist*, 1895
- Thomas Aquinas, Summa Theologica, c. 1270

But I was very influenced by Marcuse and Adorno also, listed above.

Conclusion—Final words: Towards a taxonomy of Stupid, and other wankery

On William James, the book to skim is Jacques Barzun *From Dawn to Decadence: 500 years of Western cultural life*, 2001 (HarperCollins, London).

Acknowledgements

Thanks to all of those in the Arts faculty at Sydney University 1986–1993 who taught me to think critically; most especially the late Iain Cameron and Alastair MacLachlan, without whom . . . *BK*

Thanks to Beth Cole, Dr Gary Foley, Dr Shakira Hussein and Erik Jensen for their kindness in discussing ideas. To Sam Quigley for similar generosity and efforts in amending my poor punctuation. Thanks to dear Kylie Miller for allowing me to use her wonderful yoga story. To Carlene Colahan for her stubborn ability to research ridiculous facts and to Annelise Magee for providing the feminine leisurewear in which I wrote this book. Particular thanks to Bernard Keane and to the very great force of publishing Jane Palfreyman, to whom I have been accumulating a debt of gratitude for some time.

Finally FUCK YEAH to my friend Nadine von Cohen. *HR*